Henry Fielding:

by

G. M. Godden

The Echo Library 2006

Published by

The Echo Library

Echo Library
131 High St.
Teddington
Middlesex TW11 8HH

www.echo-library.com

Please report serious faults in the text to complaints@echo-library.com

ISBN 1-40681-061-4

HENRY FIELDING

A MEMOIR
INCLUDING NEWLY DISCOVERED LETTERS
AND RECORDS
BY

G. M. GODDEN

"I am a man myself, and my heart is interested in whatever can befall the rest of mankind."
JOSEPH ANDREWS.

PREFACE

New material alone could justify any attempt to supplement the *Fielding* of Mr Austin Dobson. Such material has now come to light, and together with reliable facts collected by previous biographers, forms the subject matter of the present volume. As these pages are concerned with Fielding the man, and not only with Fielding the most original if not the greatest of English novelists, literary criticism has been avoided; but all incidents, disclosed by hitherto unpublished documents, or found hidden in the columns of contemporary newspapers, which add to our knowledge of Fielding's personality, have been given.

The new material includes records of Fielding's childhood; documents concerning his estate in Dorsetshire; the date and place, hitherto undiscovered, of that central event in his life, the death of his beloved wife, whose memorial was to be the imperishable figure of "Sophia Western"; letters, now first published, adding to our knowledge of his energies in social and legislative reform, and of the circumstances of his life; many extracts from the columns of the daily press of the period; notices, hitherto overlooked, from his contemporaries; and details from the unexplored archives of the Middlesex Records concerning his strenuous work as a London magistrate. The few letters by Fielding already known to exist have been doubled in number; and a reason for the extraordinary rarity of these letters has been found in the unfortunate destruction, many years ago, of much of his correspondence. The charm of the one intimate letter that we possess from the pen of the 'Father of the English Novel,' that written to his brother John, during the voyage to Lisbon, enhances regret at the loss of these letters.

Among the contemporary prints now first reproduced that entitled the *Conjurors* is of special interest, as being the only sketch of Fielding, drawn during his lifetime, known to exist. Rough as it is, the characteristic figure of the man, as described by his contemporaries and drawn from memory in Hogarth's familiar plate, is perfectly apparent. The same characteristics may be distinguished in a small figure of the novelist introduced into the still earlier political cartoon, entitled the *Funeral of Faction.*

Such in brief are the reasons for the existence of this volume. It remains to express my warmest acknowledgment of Mr Austin Dobson's unfailing counsel and assistance. My thanks are also due to Mr Ernest Fielding for permission to reproduce the miniature which appears as the frontispiece; to Mr Aubrey Court, of the House of Lords; to Mr E. S. W. Hart, for his help throughout the necessary researches among the Middlesex Records; to Mrs Deane of Gillingham; and to Mr Frederick Shum of Bath. And I am indebted to Mr Sidney Colvin, Keeper of the Department of Prints and Drawings in the British Museum, in regard to almost every one of the thirty-two rare prints and cartoons now reproduced.

G. M. GODDEN.

CONTENTS

HENRY FIELDING

CHAPTER I

YOUTH

"I shall always be so great a pedant as to call a man of no learning a man of no education."—*Amelia.*

Henry Fielding was born at Sharpham Park, near Glastonbury, on the 22nd of April 1707. His birth-room, a room known as the Harlequin Chamber, looked out over the roof of a building which once was the private chapel of the abbots of Glastonbury; for Sharpham Park possessed no mean history. Built in the sixteenth century by that distinguished prelate, scholar, and courtier Abbot Richard Beere, the house had boasted its chapel, hall, parlour, chambers, storehouses and offices; its fishponds and orchards; and a park in which might be kept some four hundred head of deer. It was in this fair demesne that the aged, pious, and benevolent Abbot Whiting, Abbot Richard's successor, was seized by the king's commissioners, and summarily hung, drawn, and quartered on the top of the neighbouring Tor Hill. Sharpham thereupon "devolved" upon the crown; but the old house remained, standing in peaceful seclusion where the pleasant slope of Polden Hill overlooks the Somersetshire moors, till the birth of the 'father of the English Novel' brought a lasting distinction to the domestic buildings of Abbot Beere. In the accompanying print, published in 1826, the little window of the Harlequin Chamber may be seen, above the low roofs of the abbots' chapel.

That Henry Fielding should have been born among buildings raised by Benedictine hands is not incongruous; for no man ever more heartily preached and practised the virtue of open-handed charity; none was more ready to scourge the vices of arrogance, cruelty and avarice; no English novelist has left us brighter pictures of innocence and goodness. And it was surely a happy stroke of that capricious Fortune to whom Fielding so often refers, to allot a Harlequin Chamber for the birth of the author of nineteen comedies; and yet more appropriate to the robust genius of the Comic Epic was the accident that placed on the wall, beneath the window of his birth-room, a jovial jest in stone. For here some sixteenth-century humorist had displayed the arms of Abbot Beere in the form of a convivial rebus or riddle—to wit, a cross and two beer flagons.

Soon after the Civil Wars, Sharpham passed into the hands of the 'respectable family' of Gould. By the Goulds the house was considerably enlarged; and, at the beginning of the eighteenth century, was in the possession of a distinguished member of the family, Sir Henry Gould, Knight, and Judge of the King's Bench. Sir Henry had but two children, a son Davidge Gould, and a daughter Sarah. This only daughter married a well-born young soldier, the Hon. Edmund Fielding; a marriage which, according to family assertions, was without the consent of her parents and "contrary to their good likeing." [1] And it was in the old home of the Somersetshire Goulds that the eldest son of this marriage, Henry Fielding, was born.

Thus on the side of his mother, Sarah Gould, Fielding belonged to just that class of well-established country squires whom later he was to immortalise in the beautiful and benevolent figure of Squire Allworthy, and in the boisterous, brutal, honest Western. And the description of Squire Allworthy's "venerable" house, with its air of grandeur "that struck you with awe," its position on the sheltered slope of a hill enjoying "a most charming prospect of the valley beneath," its surroundings of a wild and beautiful park, well-watered meadows fed with sheep, the ivy-grown ruins of an old abbey, and far-off hills and sea, preserves, doubtless, the features of the ancient and stately domain owned by the novelist's grandfather.

If it was to the 'respectable' Goulds that Fielding owed many of his rural and administrative characteristics, such as that practical zeal and ability which made him so excellent a magistrate, it is in the family of his father that we find indications of those especial qualities of vigour, of courage, of the generous and tolerant outlook of the well-born man of the world, that characterise Henry Fielding. And it is also in these Fielding ancestors that something of the reputed wildness of their brilliant kinsman may be detected.

For in her wilful choice of Edmund Fielding for a husband, Sir Henry Gould's only daughter brought, assuredly, a disturbing element into the quiet Somersetshire home. The young man was of distinguished birth, even if he was not, as once asserted, of the blood royal of the Hapsburgs. [2] His ancestor, Sir John Fielding, had received a knighthood for bravery in the French wars of the fourteenth century. A Sir Everard Fielding led a Lancastrian army during the Wars of the Roses. Sir William, created Earl of Denbigh, fell fighting for the king in the Civil Wars, where, says Clarendon, "he engaged with singular courage in all enterprises of danger"; a phrase which recalls the description of Henry Fielding "that difficulties only roused him to struggle through them with a peculiar spirit and magnanimity." Lord Denbigh fell, covered with wounds, when fighting as a volunteer in Prince Rupert's troop; while his eldest son, Basil, then a mere youth, fought as hotly for the Parliament. Lord Denbigh's second son, who like his father was a devoted loyalist, received a peerage, being created Earl of Desmond; and two of his sons figure in a wild and tragic story preserved by Pepys. "In our street," says the Diarist, writing in 1667, "at the Three Tuns Tavern I find a great hubbub; and what was it but two brothers had fallen out and one killed the other. And who s'd. they be but the two Fieldings; one whereof, Bazill, was page to my Lady Sandwich; and he hath killed the other, himself being very drunk, and so is sent to Newgate." It was a brother of these unhappy youths, John Fielding, a royal chaplain and Canon of Salisbury, who by his marriage with a Somersetshire lady, became father of Edmund Fielding.

Such was Henry Fielding's ancestry, and it cannot be too much insisted on that, throughout all the vicissitudes of his life, he was ever a man of breeding, no less than a man of wit. "His manners were so gentlemanly," said his friend Mrs Hussey, "that even with the lower classes with which he frequently condescended to chat, such as Sir Roger de Coverley's old friends, the Vauxhall watermen, they seldom outstepped the limits of propriety." And a similar recognition comes from the hand of a great, and not too friendly, critic. To "the very last days of his life," wrote Thackeray, "he retained a grandeur of air, and although worn down by disease his aspect and presence imposed respect on the people around him."

This Denbigh ancestry recalls a pleasant example of Fielding's wit, preserved in a story told by his son, and recorded in the pages of that voluminous eighteenth-century anecdotist, John Nichols. "Henry Fielding," says Nichols, "being once in company with the Earl of Denbigh, and the conversation's turning on Fielding's being of the Denbigh family, the Earl asked the reason why they spelt their names differently; the Earl's family doing it with the E first (Feilding), and Mr Henry Fielding with the I first (Fielding). 'I cannot tell, my Lord,' answered Harry, 'except it be that my branch of the family were the first that knew how to spell.'"

In accordance with the fighting traditions of his race, Edmund Fielding went into the army; his name appearing as an ensign in the 1st Foot Guards. Also, as became a Fielding, he distinguished himself, we are told, in the "Wars against France with much Bravery and Reputation"; and it was probably owing to active service abroad that the birth of his eldest son took place in his wife's old Somersetshire home. The date fits in well enough with the campaigns of Ramilies, Oudennarde and Malplaquet. Soon after Henry's birth, however, his father had doubtless left the Low Countries, for, about 1709, he appears as purchasing the colonelcy of an Irish Regiment. This regiment was ordered, in 1710, to Spain; but before that year the colonel and his wife and son had a separate home provided for them, by the care of Sir Henry Gould. At what precise date is uncertain, but some time before 1710, Sir Henry had purchased an estate at East Stour in Dorsetshire, consisting of farms and lands of the value of £4750, intending to settle some or the whole of the same on his daughter and her children. And already, according to a statement by the colonel, the old judge had placed his son-in-law in possession of some or all of this purchase, sending him oxen to plough his ground, and promising him a "Dairye of Cows." Sir Henry moreover had, said his son-in-law, declared his intention "to spend the vacant Remainder of his life," sometimes with his daughter, her husband, and children at Stour, and sometimes with his son Davidge, presumably at Sharpham. But in March, 1710, Sir Henry's death frustrated his planned retirement in the Vale of Stour; although three years later, in 1713, his intentions regarding a Dorsetshire home for his daughter were carried out by the conveyance to her [3] and her children of the Stour estate, for her sole enjoyment. The legal documents are careful to recite that the rents and profits should be paid to Mrs Fielding or her children, and her receipt given, and that the said Edmund "should have nothing to do nor intermeddle therewith."

In this settlement of the East Stour farms, to the greater part of which Henry Fielding, then six years old, would be joint heir with his sisters, Colonel Fielding himself seems to have had to pay no less than £1750, receiving therefor "a portion of the said lands." So by 1713 both Edmund Fielding and his wife were settled, as no inconsiderable landowners, among the pleasant meadows of Stour; and there for the next five years Henry's early childhood was passed. Indeed, Mrs Fielding must have been at Stour when her eldest son was but three years old, for the baptism of a daughter, Sarah, appears in the Stour registers in November 1710. This entry is followed by the baptism of Anne in 1713, of Beatrice in 1714, of Edmund in 1716, and by the death of Anne in the last-named year, Henry being then nine years old.

According to Arthur Murphy, Fielding's earliest and too often inaccurate biographer, the boy received "the first rudiments of his education at home, under the care of the Revd. Mr Oliver." Mr Oliver was the curate of Motcombe, a neighbouring village; and we have the authority of Murphy and of Hutchins, the historian of Dorset, for finding 'a very humorous and striking portrait' of this pedagogue in the Rev. Mr Trulliber, the pig-breeding parson of *Joseph Andrews*. If this be so, Harry Fielding's first tutor at Stour was of a figure eminently calculated to foster the comic genius of his pupil. "He" (Trulliber), wrote that pupil, some thirty years later, "was indeed one of the largest Men you should see, and could have acted the part of Sir *John Falstaff* without stuffing. Add to this, that the Rotundity of his Belly was considerably increased by the shortness of his Stature, his shadow ascending very near as far in height when he lay on his Back, as when he stood on his Legs. His Voice was loud and hoarse, and his Accents extremely broad; to complete the whole he had a Stateliness in his Gait when he walked, not unlike that of a Goose, only he stalked slower." It appears that the widow of the Motcombe curate denied the alleged portrait; but the house where Mr Oliver lived, "seemed to accord with Fielding's description ... and an old woman who remembered him observed that 'he dearly loved a bit of good victuals, and a drop of drink.'" Bearing in mind the great novelist's own earnest declaration that he painted "not men but manners," we may fairly assume that his Dorsetshire tutor belonged to that class of coarse farmer-parson so justly satirised in the person of Trulliber. According to another sketch of Fielding's life, his early education was also directed by the rector of Stour Provost, "his Parson Adams." [4]

While Harry Fielding was thus learning his first rudiments, his father, the colonel, seems to have been engaged in less useful pursuits in London. The nature of these pursuits appears from a *Bill of Complaint*, which by a happy chance has been preserved, between "Edmund Fielding of East Stour, Dorsetshire," and one Robert Midford, pretending to be a captain of the army. In this *Bill* [5] the said Edmund declares that in 1716, being then resident in London, he often frequented Princes Coffee-house in the Parish of St James. At Princes he found his company sought by the reputed Captain Robert Midford, who "prevailed upon him to play a game called 'Faro' for a small matter of diversion, but by degrees drew him on to play for larger sums, and by secret and fraudulent means obtained very large sums, in particular notes and bonds for £500." Further, the colonel entered into a bond of £200 to one Mrs Barbara Midford, "sister or pretended sister of the said Robert"; and so finally was threatened with outlawry by 'Captain' Midford for, presumably, payment of these debts. How Colonel Edmund finally escaped from the clutches of these rogues does not appear; but it is clear enough that his Dorsetshire meadows were a safer place than Princes Coffee-house for a gentleman who could lose £500 at faro to a masquerading army captain. Also Sir Henry Gould's wisdom becomes apparent, in bequeathing his daughter an inheritance with which her husband was to have "nothing to doe."

In 1718, two years after Colonel Fielding's experience at Princes, Mrs Fielding died, leaving six young children to her husband's care, two sons and four daughters, Henry, the eldest being but eleven years old. Her death is recorded in the East Stour registers as follows:—"Sarah, Wife of the Hon. Edmund Fielding Esqre. and daughter of Sir Henry Gould Kt. April 18 1718."

About this time (the dates vary between 1716 and 1719) Edmund Fielding was appointed Colonel of the Invalids, an appointment which he appears to have held until his death. And within two years of the death of his first wife, Colonel Fielding must have married again, for in 1720 we find him and his then wife, *Anne*, selling some 153 acres with messuages, barns and gardens, in East and West Stour, to one Awnsham Churchill, Esquire. What relation, if any, this land had to the property of the colonel's late wife and her children does not appear.

Some time in 1719, the year after his mother's death, or early in 1720, Henry was sent to Eton, as appears from his father's statement, made in February 1721, that his eldest son "who is now upwards of thirteen yeares old is and for more than a yeare last past hath been maintained ... at Eaton schoole, the yearely expence whereof costs ... upwards of £60." And the boy must have been well away from the atmosphere of his home, in these first years after his mother's death, if the allegations of his grandmother, old Lady Gould, may be believed.

These hitherto unknown records of Henry Fielding's boyhood are to be found in the proceedings of a Chancery suit begun by Lady Gould, on behalf of her six grandchildren, Henry, Edmund, [6] Katherine, Ursula, Sarah and Beatrice, three years after the death of their mother—namely, on the 10th of February 1721, and instituted in the name of Henry Fielding as complainant. Lady Gould opens her grandchildren's case with a comprehensive indictment of her son-in-law. After reciting that her daughter Sarah had married Edmund Fielding "without the consent of her Father or Mother and contrary to their good likeing," Lady Gould mentions her husband's bequest to their daughter, Sarah Fielding, of £3000 in trust to be laid out in the purchase of lands for the benefit of her and her children "with direction that the said Edmund Fielding should have nothing to do nor intermeddle therewith." And how Sir Henry did in his lifetime purchase "Eastover" estate for his daughter, but died before the trust was completed; and that in 1713 his trustees, Edmund Fielding consenting, settled the said estate upon trust for Sarah Fielding and her children after her, the rents and profits to be paid for her, and acknowledged by her receipt "without her Husband." And that if Sarah Fielding died intestate the estate be divided among her children. The bill then shows that Sarah Fielding did die intestate; and that then Henry and his sisters and brother "being all Infants of tender years and uncapable of managing their own affairs and to take Care thereof, well hoped that ... their Trustees would have taken Care to receive the Rents of the said premises," and have applied the same for their maintenance and education. One of these trustees, we may note, was Henry Fielding's uncle, Davidge Gould. This reasonable hope of the six "Infants" was however, according to their grandmother, wholly disappointed. For their uncle Davidge and his co-trustee, one William Day, allowed Edmund Fielding to receive the rents, nay "entered into a Combination and Confederacy to and with the said Edmund Fielding," refusing to intermeddle with the said trust, whereby the children were in great danger of losing their means of maintenance and education. And this was by no means all. Lady Gould proceeds to point out that her son-in-law had, since his wife's death, "intermarried with one ... Rapha ... Widow an Italian a Person of the Roman Catholick Profession who has severall children of her own and one who kept an eating House in London, and not at all fitt to have the care of [the complainants'] Education and has now two daughters in a Monastery beyond Sea." It is not difficult to conceive the attitude of Lady Gould of Sharpham Park to an Italian widow who kept an eating-house; but worse yet, in the view of those 'No Popery' days, was to follow. "Not only so," says her ladyship, "the said Edmund Fielding ... threatens to take your [complainants] from school into his own custody altho' [their] said Grandmother has taken a House in the City of New Sarum with an intent to have [her granddaughters] under her Inspection and where ... Katherine, Ursula and Sarah are now at school"; and "the said Mr Fielding doth give out in speeches that he will do with [the complainants] what he thinks fitt, and has openly commended the Manner of Education of young persons in Monasteryes."

This comprehensive indictment against Colonel Fielding received a prompt counter, the "Severall Answere of Edmund Fielding Esqre ... to the Bill of Complaint of Henry Fielding, Katherine Fielding, Ursula Fielding, Sarah Fielding, and Beatrice Fielding, Infants, by Dame Sarah Gould, their Grandmother and next Friend," being dated February 23 1721, but thirteen days after Lady Gould had opened her attack. Out of "a dutiful Regard to the said Lady Gould his Mother-in-Law," Colonel Fielding declares himself unwilling to "Controvert anything with her further than of necessity." But he submits that, in the matter of his marriage, he was "afterwards well approved of and received" by Sir Henry Gould and his family; that he was also so happy as to be in favour with Lady Gould "till he marryed with his now wife"; which he believes "has Occasioned some Jealosye and Displeasure in the Lady Gould, tho' without Just Grounds." Edmund Fielding then draws a pastoral picture of himself in occupation of the East Stour estate, placed there by his father-in-law; of his oxen and dairy; and of the judge's intention of spending half the remainder of his days with his son-in-law on this Dorsetshire farm. He admits his share in the trust settlement after Sir Henry's death; and points out that his brother-in-law, Davidge Gould, made him pay heavily on a portion of the estate. And he believes that, as his wife died intestate, all his children are "Intituled to the said Estate in Equall proportions."

Then follows the colonel's main defence. His eldest son Henry not being yet fourteen years of age, he has, ever since the death of his wife, continued in possession of the premises, taking the rents and profits thereof, which amount to about £150; and he positively declares that he has expended more annually on the maintenance and education of the said complainants, ever since the death of their mother, than the clear income of the said estate amounts to, and that he shall continue to take "a Tender and affectionate care of all his said Children." Further, he professes himself a "protestant of the Communion of the Church of England," and asserts that he shall and will breed his said children Protestants of that communion. He protests that his second wife is not an Italian; nor did she keep an eating-house. He suggests that Lady Gould took her house at Salisbury "as well with an Intent to convenience herselfe by liveing in a Towne" as for the inspection of his children. He "denyeth that he ever Comended the Manner of Education of young persons in monasterys if it be meant in Respect of Religion." Finally, he says that he has spent much money on improving the estate; that the income from the estate is hardly sufficient to maintain his children according to their station in the world since he is "nearly related to many Noble Familys"; and he "veryly believes in his conscience he can better provide for his said Children by reason of his relation to and Interest in the said noble Familys than their said Grandmother (who is now in an advanced age, being seventy yeares old or thereabouts)."

Here, it is plain, was a very pretty family quarrel. No man likes his mother-in-law to say that he has married the keeper of an Italian eating-house, especially if the fact is correct; or that he is perverting his young children's trust money. Neither was Lady Gould likely to be pacified by her son-in-law's remark that she was now "in an advanced age"; while his suggestion that his "noble" family would be of far more advantage to his children than that of the respectable Goulds would have the added sting of undeniable truth.

The next extant move in the fray bears date five months later, July 18 1721, and includes a petition by 'Dame Sarah Gould' that the children be not removed from the places where they then were until the case be heard; and Lady Gould adds that if the children's persons or estates be "under ye management or power of ye said Mr Fielding and his now wife ye Estate would not be managed to ye best advantage and their Education would not be taken care of and there would be a great hazard that ye children might be perverted to ye Romish Religion." Then follows an order in Chancery, under the same date, "that ye eldest son of ye Defend't. Fielding ... be continued at Eaton School where he now is and that ye rest of ye children be continued where they now are."

The next document merely records the inclusion of Henry's five-year-old brother Edmund among the plaintiffs. And this is followed by a brief Chancery order of November 30 1721, that "ye, plaintiff Henry Fielding who is not [*sic*] at Eaton Schoole be at liberty to go to ye said Dame Sarah Gould, his Grandmother and next friend during ye usual time of recess from School at Xmas."

After these Christmas holidays spent by Henry Fielding with Lady Gould, doubtless at her house in Salisbury, the Chancery records pass on to the April following, 1722, when the boy's uncle and trustee Davidge Gould makes a statement "sworn at Sharpham Park," which concludes that the witness hears and believes that Edmund Fielding "has already three children by his present wife who is reputed to be of the Romish church." In this same month comes another order from the court that Henry be at liberty to leave Eton for the Whitsun holidays 1722, and to go to Lady Gould's house. In May Edmund Fielding appears as "of the Parish of Saint James, in the County of Middlesex," and also as his children's "next Friend and Guardian." But two days later the long suit is concluded by the decision of the court, and here Colonel Fielding is, as heretofore, defendant, Lady Gould being the children's "next friend."

The case came before the Lord Chancellor on the 28th of May 1722, and was "debated in the presence of learned Counsels." The trust was upheld, and Edmund Fielding was required to deliver possession of the estate, rendering account of the rents and profits thereof since the death of his first wife; but he was to have "any and what" allowance for improvements, and for the children's maintenance and education. And it was further ordered that the children then at school continue at such schools till further order, and that "upon any breaking up at ye usuall times they do go and reside with ye Lady Gould their Grandmother that they may not be under the influence of ye Defendant Fielding's Wife, who appeared to be a papist." [7]

So Lady Gould, for all her seventy years, won her case at every point. And Colonel Edmund Fielding did not only lose the guardianship of his six children, and the administration of their estate. For there was, we learn, in court, during the hearing, one Mrs Cottington, the plaintiffs aunt, "alleadging that there was a debt of £700 due from ye Defendant Fielding to her"; which debt she offered should be applied for the benefit of her nephews and nieces. Whereupon the court ordered that if Mrs Cottington proved the same, a Master in Chancery should purchase therewith lands to be settled for the "Infants" in like manner as the trust estate.

It may be only a coincidence, but £700 is the sum specifically mentioned in the proceedings brought by Colonel Fielding in October 1722, five months after the loss of his Chancery suit, against the cardsharper, Robert Midford, who was then apparently threatening him with outlawry for the recovery of the gambling debt begun, as we have seen, at Princes' Coffee-house six years before. Had the colonel borrowed the £700 from Mrs Cottington, with intent to discharge those debts; and, on being brought to law by her (on her nephews' and nieces' behalf) for that debt, did it occur to him to escape from the clutches of the psuedo

"Captain" Midford by pleading, as he now does in this Bill of 1722, that he "was tricked," and also "that gaming is illegal"? The latter plea has something of unconscious humour in the mouth of a gentleman who had lately lost £500 at faro. With this last echo of the coffee-house of St James's, and of the colonel's financial difficulties, that brave soldier, if somewhat reckless gambler, the Hon. Edmund Fielding vanishes from sight, as far as the life of his eldest son is concerned.

At the triumphant conclusion of his grandmother's suit Henry Fielding would be just fifteen years of age, and it is impossible not to wonder what side he took in these spirited family conflicts. No evidence, however, on such points appears in the dry legal documents; and all that we have for guide as to the effect in this impressionable time of his boyhood of the long months of contest, and of his strictly ordered holidays with his grandmother, is the declaration on the one hand that "filial piety ... his nearest relations agree was a shining part of his character," and on the other, the undeniably strong Protestant bias that appears in his writing. Of his aunt, Mrs Cottington, we get one later glimpse, when in 1723 she is made his trustee, in place of his uncle, Davidge Gould, Mrs Cottington being then resident in Salisbury. At the end of the following year, however, in December 1724, Davidge Gould resumes his trusteeship, and with the record of that fact the disclosures yielded by these ancient parchments as to Henry Fielding's stormy boyhood come to an end.

From these records it becomes possible to gain some idea of the surroundings of the great novelist's early youth. Before his mother's death, indeed, when he was a boy of eleven, we already knew him as suffering the rough jurisdiction of his Trulliberian tutor, Parson Oliver of Motcombe village, and perhaps as under the wise and kindly guidance of the good scholar-parson, who was later to win the affection and respect of thousands of readers under the name of "Parson Adams." But now, for the first time, we learn of the disastrous second marriage by which Colonel Fielding, within two years of his first wife's death, placed a lady of at least disputable social standing at the head of his household, and one, moreover, whose Faith roused the bitter religious animosities of that day. What wonder that the old Lady Gould strove fiercely to remove Henry Fielding, and his sisters and young brother, from East Stour, when a Madame Rasa was installed in her daughter's place. And accordingly, as we have seen, even before the conclusion of the suit, Henry was provisionally ordered by the Court of Chancery to spend his holidays with his grandmother. Fielding would then be fourteen years old; and the judge's decision six months later that future holidays should be passed with Lady Gould, away from the influence of the second Mrs Fielding, doubtless severed the lad's connection with his dubious stepmother for the next six years. His home life, then, during the latter part of his Eton schooling would be under Lady Gould's care; and was probably spent at Salisbury.

Of his Eton life, from his entrance at the school, when twelve years old, we know practically nothing. From the absence of his name on the college lists, it may be inferred that he was an Oppidan. It is said that he gave "distinguished proofs of strong and peculiar parts"; and that he left the school with a good reputation as a classical scholar. And it is not surprising to learn that here, as he himself tells us, his vigorous energies made acquaintance with that 'birchen altar' at which most of the best blood in England has been disciplined. "And thou," he cries, "O Learning (for without thy Assistance nothing pure, nothing correct, can Genius produce) do thou guide my Pen. Thee, in thy favourite Fields, where the limpid gently rolling *Thames* washes thy *Etonian* banks, in early Youth I have worshipped. To thee at thy birchen Altar, with true *Spartan* Devotion, I have sacrificed my Blood." [8] That the sacrifice was not made in vain appears from the reputation with which Fielding left Eton of being "uncommonly versed in the Greek authors and an early master of the Latin classics"; and also from the yet better evidence of his own pages. Long after these boyish days we find him, in the words of "The man of the Hill," thus eloquently acknowledging the debt of humanity, and doubtless his own, to those inestimable treasures bequeathed to the world by ancient Greece: "These Authors, though they instructed me in no Science by which Men may promise to themselves to acquire the least Riches, or worldly Power, taught me, however, the Art of despising the highest Acquisitions of both. They elevate the Mind, and steel and harden it against the capricious Invasions of Fortune. They not only instruct in the Knowledge of Wisdom, but confirm Men in her Habits, and demonstrate plainly, that this must be our Guide, if we propose ever to arrive at the greatest worldly Happiness; or to defend ourselves, with any tolerable Security, against the Misery which everywhere surrounds and invests us." [9] And that this was no mere figure of speech appears from that touching picture which Murphy has left us of the brilliant wit, the 'wild' Harry Fielding, when under the pressure of sickness and poverty, quietly reading the *De Consolations* of Cicero. His Plato accompanied him on the last sad voyage to Lisbon; and his library, when catalogued for sale on behalf of his widow and children, contained over one hundred and forty volumes of the Greek and Latin classics.

Thus, supreme student and master as he was of "the vast authentic book of nature," there is abundant proof that Fielding fulfilled his own axiom that a "good share of learning" is necessary to the equipment of a novelist. Let the romance writer's natural parts be what they may, learning, he declared, "must fit them for use, must direct them in it, lastly must contribute part at least of the materials." [10] Looking back on such utterances by the 'father of the English Novel,' written at the full height of his power, it is but natural to wonder if the boy's eager application to Greek and Latin drudgery had in it something of half-conscious preparation for the great part he was destined to play in the history of English literature.

It is clear that Henry Fielding flung his characteristic energies zealously into the acquirement of the classical learning proffered him at Eton; but a fine scholarship, great possession though it be, was not the only gain of his Eton years. Here, says Murphy in his formal eighteenth-century phrasing, young Fielding had "the advantage of being early known to many of the first people in the kingdom, namely Lord Lyttelton, Mr Fox, Mr Pitt, Sir Charles Hanbury Williams, and the late Mr Winnington, etc."

Of these companions at Eton, George Lyttelton, afterwards known as the "good Lord Lyttelton," statesman and orator, stands foremost by virtue of the generous warmth of a friendship continued throughout the novelist's chequered life. To Lyttelton *Tom Jones* was dedicated; it was his generosity, as generously acknowledged, that supplied Fielding, for a time, with the very means of subsistence; and to him was due the appointment, subsequently discharged with so much zealous labour, of Magistrate for Westminster and Middlesex. It is recorded that George Lyttelton's school exercises "were recommended as models to his schoolfellows." Another Eton friend, Thomas Winnington, made some figure in the Whig political world of the day; he was accredited by Horace Walpole with having an inexhaustible good humour, and "infinitely more wit than any man I ever knew." Of the friendship with Sir Charles Hanbury Williams, of which we first hear at Eton, little is known, save the curious episode of the recovery, many years after its author's death, of Fielding's lost play *The Good-Natured Man]*, which had apparently been submitted to Sir Charles, whose celebrity was great as a brilliant political lampoonist. Of the acquaintance with Henry Fox, first Baron Holland, we hear nothing in later life; but the name of the greatest of all these Eton contemporaries, that of the elder Pitt, recurs in after years as one of the party at Radway Grange, in Warwickshire, to whom Fielding, after dinner, read aloud the manuscript of *Tom Jones*. [11] A reference to his fellow-Etonian may be found in one of the introductory chapters of that masterpiece, where Fielding, while again advocating the claims of learning, takes occasion to pay this sonorous tribute to Pitt's oratory: "Nor do I believe that all the imagination, fire, and judgment of Pitt, could have produced those orations that have made the senate of England in these our times a rival in eloquence to Greece and Rome, if he had not been so well read in the writings of Demosthenes and Cicero, as to have transferred their whole spirit into his speeches and, with their spirit, their knowledge too."

However excellent a knowledge of the classics the youthful scholar took away with him from Eton, the rigours of his studies do not appear to have diminished that zest for life with which the very name of Henry Fielding is invested. For the obscurity of these early years is for a moment lifted to disclose the young genius as having already, before he was nineteen, fallen desperately in love with a beautiful heiress in Dorsetshire; and, moreover, as threatening bodily force to accomplish his suit. The story, as indicated in the surviving outlines, might be the draft for a chapter of *Tom Jones*. The scene is Lyme Regis. The chief actors are Harry Fielding, scarce more than a schoolboy; a beautiful heiress, Miss Sarah Andrew; [12] and her uncle, one Mr Andrew Tucker, a timorous and crafty member of the local corporation. The handsome Etonian, who had been for some time resident in the old town, fell madly in love, it seems, with the lady, who is stated to have been his cousin on his mother's side. The views of her guardian were, however, opposed to the young man's suit, Mr Andrew Tucker mercenarily designing to secure the heiress for his own son. Thereupon Harry

Fielding is said to have made a desperate attempt to carry the lady off by force, and that, moreover, "on a Sunday, when she was on her way to Church." Further, the efforts of the impetuous youth would seem to have extended to threatened assaults on the person of his fair cousin's guardian, Mr Tucker; for we find that affrighted worthy flying for protection to the arm of the law, as recorded in the *Register Book* of Lyme Regis, under date of the 14th November 1725:—"... Andrew Tucker, Gent., one of the Corporation, caused Henry Fielding, Gent., and his servant or companion, Joseph Lewis—both now for some time past residing in the borough—to be bound over to keep the peace, as he was in fear of his life or some bodily hurt to be done or to be procured to be done to him by H. Fielding and his man. Mr A. Tucker feared that the man would beat, maim, or kill him." No words could more aptly sum up this delightful story than those of Mr Austin Dobson: "a charming girl, who is also an heiress; a pusillanimous guardian, with ulterior views of his own; a handsome and high-spirited young suitor; a faithful attendant ready to 'beat, maim or kill' on his master's behalf; a frustrated elopement and a compulsory visit to the mayor—all these with the picturesque old town of Lyme for a background, suggest a most appropriate first act to Harry Fielding's biographical tragi-comedy." [13] It is possible that Fielding's own pen supplied the conclusion to this first act. For he tells us, in the preface to the *Miscellanies*, that a version, in burlesque verse, of part of Juvenal's sixth satire was originally sketched out before he was twenty, and that it was "all the Revenge taken by an injured Lover." The story loses none of its zest, moreover, when we remember that Harry Fielding was at this time still a Ward of Chancery.

[1] Chancery Proceedings 1720 sqq. *Fielding* v. *Fielding.* From the records of this Chancery suit, instituted on behalf of Henry Fielding and his brother and sisters, as minors, by their grandmother Lady Gould, are taken the hitherto unpublished facts concerning the novelist's boyhood, contained in this chapter. The original documents are preserved in the Record Office.

[2] See Appendix A.

[3] By means of a legacy of £3000 left by her father for his daughter's sole use, "her husband having nothing to doe with it."

[4] *History and Antiquities of Leicestershire.* J. Nichols. 1810. Vol. iv. Part i. p. 292. Nichols does not state his authority for this statement, and it is not confirmed by local records. See Hutchins' *History of Dorset* for the list of Stour Provost rectors.

[5] Chancery Proceedings, 1722. *Fielding* v. *Midford.* Record Office.

[6] Edmund's name was added in October following.

[7] *Chancery Decrees and Order Books.* Record Office.

[8] Tom Jones, Book xiii. Introduction.

[9] Ibid., Book viii., ch. xiii.

[10] *Tom Jones*, Book ix. Introduction.

[11] See *infra*, chap. xi.

[12] Fifty years ago a portrait of the beautiful heiress, in the character of Sophia Western, was still preserved at the house of Bellairs, near Exeter, then

the property of the Rhodes family. The present ownership of the picture has, so far, eluded inquiry.

[13] *Fielding*, Austin Dobson, p. 202.

CHAPTER II

PLAYHOUSE BARD

"I could not help reflecting how often the greatest abilities lie
wind-bound, as it were, in life; or if they venture out, and
attempt to beat the seas, they struggle in vain against wind and
tide."—*Journal of a Voyage to Lisbon.*

It was but three years after the Lyme Regis episode that Henry Fielding, then
a lad of one and twenty, won attention as a successful writer of comedy. Of this
his first entry into the gay world there are little but generalities to record; but,
inaccurate as Murphy is in some matters of fact, there seems no reason to doubt
the truth of the engaging picture which he draws of the young man's *début* upon
the Town. We read of the gaiety and quickness of his fancy; the wild flow of his
spirits; the brilliancy of his wit; the activity of his mind, eager to know the world.
To the possession of genius allied to the happiest temper, a temper "for the
most part overflowing into wit, mirth, and good-humour," young Fielding added
a handsome face, a magnificent physique (he stood over six feet high), and the
fullest vigour of constitution. "No man," wrote his cousin, Lady Mary Wortley
Montagu, "enjoyed life more than he did." What wonder that he was soon "in
high request with the men of taste and literature," or that report affirms him to
have been no less welcome in ranks of society not at all distinguished by a
literary flavour.

That a youth so gifted, so "formed and disposed for enjoyment," should find
himself his own master, in London, almost presupposes a too liberal indulgence
in the follies that must have so easily beset him. When the great and cold Mr
Secretary Addison, no less than that "very merry Spirit," Dick Steele, and the
splendid Congreve, drank more than was good for them, what chance would
there be for a brilliant, ardent lad of twenty, suddenly plunged into the robust
society of that age? If Fielding, like his elders, indisputably loved good wine, let
us remember that none of the heroes of his three great novels, neither that rural
innocent Joseph Andrews, nor the exuberant youth Tom Jones, nor erring,
repentant Captain Booth are immoderate drinkers. The degradation of drinking
is, in Fielding's pages, accorded to brutalised if honest country squires, and cruel
and corrupt magistrates; and there is little evidence throughout his life to
indicate that the great novelist drank more freely than did the genial heroes of
his pen. As regards Murphy's general assertion that, at this his entrance into life,
young Fielding "launched wildly into a career of dissipation" no other reputable
contemporary evidence is discoverable of the "wildness" popularly attributed to
Fielding. That his youth was headlong and undisciplined is a plausible surmise;
but justice demands that the charge be recognised as a surmise and nothing
more. How keenly, twenty years later, he could appreciate the handicap that such
early indulgences impose on a man's future life may be gathered from a passage

in *Joseph Andrews* which is not without the ring of personal feeling. The speaker is a generous and estimable country gentleman, living in Arcadian retirement with his wife and children. Descended of a good family and born a gentleman, he narrates how his education was acquired at a public school, and extended to a mastery of the Latin, and a tolerable knowledge of the Greek, language. Becoming his own master at sixteen he soon left school, for, he tells his listeners, "being a forward Youth, I was extremely impatient to be in the World: For which I thought my Parts, Knowledge, and Manhood thoroughly qualified me. And to this early Introduction into Life, without a Guide, I impute all my future Misfortunes; for besides the obvious Mischiefs which attend this, there is one which hath not been so generally observed. The first Impression which Mankind receives of you, will be very difficult to eradicate. How unhappy, therefore, must it be to fix your Character in Life, before you can possibly know its Value, or weigh the Consequences of those Actions which are to establish your future Reputation?" [1] That the wise and strenuous Fielding of later years, the energetic student at the Bar, the active and patriotic journalist, the merciless exponent of the hypocrite, the spendthrift, and the sensualist, the creator of the most perfect type of womanhood in English fiction (so said Dr Johnson and Thackeray) should look back sadly on his own years of hot-blooded youth is entirely natural; but even so this passage and the well-known confession placed in the mouth of the supposed writer of the *Journey from this World to the Next*, [2] no more constitute direct evidence than do Murphy's unattested phrases, or the anonymous scurrilities of eighteenth-century pamphleteers.

By birth and education Fielding's natural place was in the costly society of those peers and men of wealth and fashion who courted the brilliant young wit; but fortune had decreed otherwise, and at this his first entrance on the world he found, as he himself said, no choice but to be a hackney writer or a hackney coachman. True, his father allowed him a nominal £200 a year; but this, to quote another of his son's observations, "anybody might pay that would." The fact was that Colonel Fielding's marriage with Madame Rasa had resulted in a large and rapidly increasing family; and this burden, together with "the necessary demands of his station for a genteel and suitable expence," made it impossible for him to spare much for the maintenance of his eldest son. Launched thus on the Town, with every capacity for spending an income the receipt of which was denied to him, the young man flattered himself that he should find resources in his wit and invention; and accordingly he commenced as writer for the stage. His first play, a comedy entitled *Love in Several Masks*, was performed at Drury Lane in February 1728, just before the youthful dramatist had attained his twenty-first year. In his preface to these 'light scenes' he alludes with some pride to this distinction—"I believe I may boast that none ever appeared so early on the stage";—and he proceeds to a generous acknowledgment of the aid received from those dramatic stars of the eighteenth-century, Colley Gibber, Mr Wilks and Mrs Oldfield, all of whom appeared in the cast. Of the two former he says, "I cannot sufficiently acknowledge their civil and kind behaviour previous to its representation"; from which we may conclude, as his biographer Laurence points out, that Harry

Fielding was already familiar with the society of the green-room. To Mrs Oldfield,—that charming actress
"In publick Life, by all who saw Approv'd
In private Life, by all who knew her Lov'd"—

the young man expresses yet warmer acknowledgments. "Lastly," he declares, "I can never express my grateful sense of the good nature of Mrs Oldfield ... nor do I owe less to her excellent judgment, shown in some corrections which I shall for my own sake conceal." The comedy is dedicated, with the graceful diction and elaborate courtesies of the period, to Fielding's cousin, that notable eighteenth-century wit, the Lady Mary Wortley Montagu; and from the dedication we learn that to Lady Mary's approval, on her first perusal, the play owed its existence. What the approval of a great lady of those times meant for the young writer may be measured by the fact that Fielding concludes his dedication by solemnly 'informing the world' that the representation of his comedy was twice honoured with Her Ladyship's presence.

In view of the frequent accusation of coarseness brought against Fielding, we may quote a few lines of the prologue with which he made his literary entry into the world. Here his audience are promised

"Humour, still free from an indecent Flame,
Which, should it raise your Mirth, must raise your Shame:
Indecency's the Bane to Ridicule,
And only charms the Libertine, or Fool:
Nought shall offend the Fair One's Ears to-day,
Which they might blush to hear, or blush to say.
No private Character these Scenes expose,
Our Bard, at Vice, not at the Vicious, throws."

Thus it was with an honourable declaration of war against indecency and libel that the young wit and man of fashion, began his career as "hackney writer." If to modern taste the first promise lacks something of fulfilment, it is but just to remember that to other times belong other manners.

In the play, rustic and philosophic virtue is prettily rewarded by the possession of a beautiful heiress, while certain mercenary fops withdraw in signal discomfiture; and that Fielding, at one and twenty, had already passed judgment on that glittering 'tinsel' tribe, is clear enough from his portrait of the "empty gaudy nameless thing," Lord Formal. Lord Formal appears on the stage with a complexion much agitated by a day of business spent with "three milleners, two perfumers, my bookseller's and a fanshop." In the course of these fatigues he has "rid down two brace of chairmen"; and had raised his colour to "that exorbitancy of Vermeille" that it will hardly be reduced "under a fortnight's course of acids." It is the true spirit of comedy which introduces into this closely perfumed atmosphere the bluff country figure of Sir Positive Trap, with his exordiums on the rustic ladies, and on "the good old English art of clear-starching." Sir Positive hopes "to see the time when a man may carry his daughter to market with the same lawful authority as any other of his cattle"; and causes Lord Formal some moments' perplexity, his lordship being "not perfectly determinate what species of animal to assign him to, unless he be one of those barbarous insects the polite call country squires." In this production of a youth of twenty we may find a foretaste of that keen relish in watching the human comedy, that vigorous scorn of avarice, that infectious laughter at pretentious folly, which accompanied the novelist throughout his life.

To this same year is attributed a poem called the *Masquerade*, which need only be noticed as again emphasising its author's lifelong war against the evils of his time. The *Masquerade* is a satire on the licentious gatherings organised by the notorious Count Heidegger, Master of the Revels to the Court of George II.

Many years later Fielding reprinted [3] two other poetical effusions bearing the date of this his twenty-first year. Of these the first, entitled "A Description of U——n G——(alias *New Hog's Norton*) in *Com-Hants*" identified by Mr Keightley as Upton Grey in Hampshire, is addressed to the fair *Rosalinda,* by her disconsolate *Alexis*. Alexis bewails his exile among

"Unpolish'd Nymphs and more unpolish'd Swains,"

and describes himself as condemned to live in a dwelling half house, half shed, with a garden full of docks and nettles, the fruit-trees bearing only snails—
"Happy for us had Eve's this Garden been
She'd found no Fruit, and therefore known no Sin,"—

the dusty meadows innocent of grass, and the company as innocent of wit. This sketch of rural enjoyments recalls a later utterance in *Jonathan Wild,* concerning the votaries of a country life who, with their trees, "enjoy the air and the sun in common and both vegetate with very little difference between them." With one or two eloquent exceptions there is scarce a page in Fielding's books devoted to any interest other than that of human nature.

The second fragment is a graceful little copy of verse addressed to *Euthalia,* in which we may note, by the way, that the fair Rosalinda's charms are ungallantly made use of as a foil to Euthalia's dazzling perfections. As Fielding found these verses not unworthy of a page in his later *Miscellanies* they are here recalled:

TO EUTHALIA.
WRITTEN IN THE YEAR 1728.

"Burning with Love, tormented with Despair,
Unable to forget or ease his Care;
In vain each practis'd art *Alexis* tries;
In vain to Books, to Wine or Women flies;
Each brings *Euthalia's* Image to his Eyes.
In *Lock's* or *Newton's* Page her Learning glows;
Dryden the Sweetness of her Numbers shews;
In all their various Excellence I find
The various Beauties of her perfect Mind.
How vain in Wine a short Relief I boast!

Each sparkling Glass recalls my charming Toast.
To Women then successless I repair,
Engage the Young, the Witty, and the Fair.
When *Sappho's* Wit each envious Breast alarms,
And *Rosalinda* looks ten thousand Charms;
In vain to them my restless Thoughts would run;
Like fairest Stars, they show the absent Sun."

Love in Several Masks was produced, as we have seen, in February, 1728; and it is a little surprising to find the young dramatist suddenly appearing, four weeks later, as a University student. He was entered at the University of Leyden, as "Litt. Stud," on the 16th of March 1728. The reason of this sudden change from the green-room of Drury Lane to the ancient Dutch university must be purely matter of conjecture, as is the nature of Fielding's undergraduate studies, Murphy having lately been proved to be notably erroneous as to this episode. [4] His name occurs as staying, on his entry at Leyden, at the "Casteel von Antwerpen"; and again, a year later, in the *recensiones* of the University for February 1729, as domiciled with one Jan Oson. As all students were annually registered, the omission of any later entry proves that he left Leyden before 1730; with which meagre facts and his own incidental remark that the comedy of *Don Quixote in England* was "begun at Leyden in the year 1728," our knowledge of the two years of Fielding's university career concludes. In February 1730 he was presumably back in London, that being the date of his next play, the *Temple Beau*, produced by Giffard, the actor, at the new theatre in Goodman's Fields.

The prologue to the *Temple Beau* was written by that man of many parts, James Ralph, the hack writer, party journalist and historian, who was in after years to collaborate with Fielding, both as a theatrical manager and as a journalist. Ralph's opening lines are of interest as bearing on Fielding's antagonism to the harlequinades and variety shows, then threatening the popularity of legitimate drama:

"Humour and Wit, in each politer Age,
Triumphant, rear'd the Trophies of the Stage:
But only Farce, and Shew, will now go down,
And HARLEQUIN'S the Darling of the Town."

Ralph bids his audience turn to the 'infant stage' of Goodman's Fields for matter more worthy their attention; and his promise that there
"The Comick Muse, in Smiles severely gay,
Shall scoff at Vice, and laugh its Crimes away"
must surely have been inspired by the young genius from whom twenty years later came the formal declaration of his endeavour, in *Tom Jones*, "to laugh mankind out of their favourite follies and vices."

The special follies of the *Temple Beau* have, for background, of course, those precincts in which Fielding was later to labour so assiduously as a student, and as a member of the Middle Temple; but where, as the young Templar of the play observes, "dress and the ladies" might also very pleasantly employ a man's time. But except for an oblique hit at duelling, a custom which Fielding was later to attack with curious warmth, this second play seems to yield few passages of biographical interest. Of very different value for our purpose is the third play, which within only two months appeared from a pen stimulated, presumably, by empty pockets. This was the comedy entitled the *Author's Farce*, being the first portion of a medley which included the '*Puppet Show call'd the Pleasures of the Town*; the whole being acted in the Little Theatre in the Haymarket, long since demolished in favour of the present building.

In the person of Harry Luckless, the hero of the *Author's Farce*, it is impossible not to surmise the figure of young Fielding himself; a figure gay and spirited as those of his first comedy, but, by now, well acquainted with the hungers and the straits of a 'hackney writer.' Mr Luckless wears a laced-coat and makes a handsome figure (we remember that Fielding had always the grand air), whereby his landlady, clamouring for her rent, upbraids him for deceiving her: "Cou'd I have guess'd that I had a Poet in my House! Cou'd I have look'd for a Poet under lac'd Clothes!" The poor author offers her the security of his (as yet unacted) play; whereupon Mrs Moneywood (lineal ancestress of Mrs Raddles) pertinently cries out: "I would no more depend on a Benefit-Night of an unacted Play, than I would on a Benefit-Ticket in an undrawn Lottery." Luckless next appeals to what should be his landlady's heart, assuring her that unless she be so kind as to invite him "I am afraid I shall scarce prevail on my Stomach to dine to-day." To which the enraged lady answers: "O never fear that: you will never want a Dinner till you have dined at all the Eating-houses round.—No one shuts their Doors against you the first time; and I scarce think you are so kind, seldom to trouble them a second." And that the good landlady had some grounds for her wrath is but too apparent when she announces: "Well, I'm resolv'd when you are gone away (which I heartily hope will be very soon) I'll hang over my Door in great red Letters, *No Lodging for Poets* ... My Floor is all spoil'd with Ink, my Windows with Verses, and my Door has been almost beat down with Duns.' While the landlady is still fuming, enters our author's man, Jack.

"*Jack*. An't please your Honour, I have been at my Lord's,
and his Lordship thanks you for the Favour you have offer'd of
reading your Play to him; but he has such a prodigious deal of
Business he begs to be excus'd. I have been with Mr *Keyber*
too: he made no Answer at all...."
"*Luckless*. Jack.
"*Jack*. Sir.
"*Luckless*. Fetch my other Hat hither. Carry it to the Pawnbroker's.
"*Jack*. To your Honour's own Pawnbroker.
"*Luckless*. Ay And in thy way home call at the Cook's Shop.
So, one way or other I find, my Head must always provide for my

Belly."

At which moment enters the caustic, generous Witmore, belabouring the profanity, the scurrility, the immodesty, the stupidity of the age with one hand, the while he pays his friend's rent with the other; and who, incidentally, is requested by that irascible genius to kick a worthy publisher down the stairs, on the latter's refusal to give fifty shillings "no, nor fifty farthings" for his play. Once mollified by the settlement of her bill, we have the landlady playing advocate for her hapless lodger in words that sound very like the apologia of Mr Harry Fielding himself: "I have always thought, indeed, Mr *Luckless* had a great deal of Honesty in his Principles; any Man may be unfortunate: but I knew when he had Money I should have it...." And the good woman's reminiscence that while her lodger had money her doors were thundered at every morning between four and five by coachmen and chairmen; and her wish that that pleasant humour'd gentleman were "but a little soberer," finishes, we take it, the portrait of the Fielding of 1730. "Jack call a coach; and d'ye hear, get up behind it and attend me," cries the improvident poet, the moment his generous friend has left him; and so we are sure did young Mr Fielding put himself and his laced coat into a coach, and mount his man behind it, whenever the exigencies of duns and hunger were for a moment abated. And with as gallant a humour as that of his own Luckless did he walk afoot, when those "nine ragged jades the muses" failed to bring him a competency.

Such failure on the part of the Muses was due to no want of wooing on his part. During the six years between Fielding's first appearance as dramatic author in 1728, and his marriage in 1734, there stand no fewer than thirteen plays to his name. Of these none have won any lasting reputation; and to this period of the great novelist's life may doubtless be applied Lady Mary Wortley Montagu's description, when lamenting that her kinsman should have been "forced by necessity to publish without correction, and throw many productions into the world he would have thrown into the fire, if meat could have been got without money, and money without scribbling." Lady Mary's account moreover is reinforced by Murphy's classical periods: "Mr Fielding's case was generally the same with that of the poet described by Juvenal; with a great genius, he must have starved if he had not sold his performance to a favourite actor. *Esurit, intactam Paridi, nisi vendit Agaven.*" A complete list of all these ephemera will be found in the bibliography at the end of this volume; here we need but notice those to which a special interest attaches. Thus, that incomparable comic actress, Kitty Clive, was cast for a part in the *Lottery*, a farce produced in 1731; and three years later Fielding is adapting for her, especially, the *Intriguing Chambermaid*. It was in these two plays, and that of the *Virgin Unmasked*, that the town discovered the true comic genius of Kitty Clive "the best player I ever saw," in Dr Johnson's opinion. For this discovery Fielding takes credit to himself, in the dedication addressed to Mrs Clive, which he prefixed to the *Intriguing Chambermaid*; and in which he finds opportunity to pay a noble tribute to the private life of that inimitable hoyden of the stage. "I cannot help reflecting" he writes, "that the Town hath one great obligation to me, who made the first discovery of your great capacity, and brought you earlier forward on the theatre, than the ignorance of some and the envy of others would have otherwise permitted.... But as great a favorite as you at present are with the audience you would be much more so were they acquainted with your private character ... did they see you, who can charm them on the stage with personating the foolish and vicious characters of your sex, acting in real life the part of the best Wife, the best Daughter, the best Sister, and the best Friend." That this splendid praise was as sincere as it was generous need not be doubted. No breath of slander, even in that slanderous age, seems ever to have dulled the reputation of the queen of comedy, and "better romp than any I ever saw in nature"—to quote Dr Johnson again,—Kitty Clive.

So few of Fielding's letters have been, to our knowledge, preserved, that the following note addressed to Lady Mary Wortley Montagu, and concerning the *Modern Husband*, a comedy produced in 1731 or 1732, must here be given, though containing little beyond the fact that the dramatist of three years' standing seems still to have placed as high a value on his cousin's judgment, as when recording her approval of his first effort for the stage. The play was a piece of admittedly moral purpose, and was dedicated to Sir Robert Walpole. The first line of the autograph is, apparently, missing.

"I hope your Ladyship will honour the Scenes, which I presume to lay before you, with your Perusal. As they are written on a Model I never yet attempted, I am exceedingly anxious least they should find least Mercy from you than my lighter Productions. It will be a slight compensation to the modern Husband, that your Ladyship's censure will defend him from the Possibility of any other Reproof, since your least Approbation will always give me a Pleasure, infinitely superior to the loudest Applauses of a Theatre. For whatever has past your judgment, may, I think without any Imputation of Immodesty, refer Want of Success to Want of Judgment in an Audience. I shall do myself the honour of waiting on your Ladyship at Twickenham next Monday to receive my Sentence, and am, Madam, with the most devoted Respect
"Your Ladyship's
"most Obedient most humble Servant
"Henry Ffielding. [5]
    "London 7'br 4."

In 1731-32 the burlesque entitled the *Tragedy of Tragedies; or the Life and Death of Tom Thumb the Great*, took the Town. The *Tragedy* parodies the absurdities of tragedians; and so far won immortality that in 1855 it was described as still holding the stage. But its chief modern interest lies in the tradition that Swift once observed that he "had not laughed above twice" in his life,—once at the tricks of a merry-andrew, and again when Fielding's Tom Thumb killed the ghost. The design for the frontispiece of the edition of 1731, here reproduced, is from the pencil of Hogarth; and is the first trace of a connexion between

Fielding and the painter who was to be honoured so frequently in his pages. An adaptation from Molière, produced in 1733, under the title of the *Miser*, won from Voltaire the praise of having added to the original "quelques beautes de dialogue particulières a sa [Fielding's] nation." The leading character in the *Miser*, Lovegold, became a stock part, and survived to our own days, having been a favourite with Phelps. In *Don Quixote in England*, produced in 1733 or 34, [6] Fielding reappears in the character of patriotic censor with the design, as appears from the dedication to Lord Chesterfield, of representing "the Calamities brought on a Country by general Corruption." No less than fifteen songs are interspersed in the play, and it is matter for curious conjecture why none of them was chosen for a reprint among the collected verses published ten years later in the *Miscellanies*. Time has almost failed to preserve even the hunting-song beginning finely—

"The dusky Night rides down the Sky,
　And ushers in the Morn;
The Hounds all join in glorious Cry,
　The Huntsman winds his Horn:"

But a happier fate has befallen the fifth song, now familiar as the first verse of the *Roast Beef of Old England*. It is eminently appropriate that the most distinctly national of English novelists should have written:

"*When mighty Rost Beef was the* Englishman's *food,*
It ennobled our Hearts, and enriched our Blood;
Our Soldiers were brave and our Courtiers were good.
　Oh, the Rost Beef of old England,
　And old England's *Rost Beef!*

"*Then,* Britons, *from all nice Dainties refrain,*
Which effeminate Italy, France, *and* Spain;
And mighty Rost Beef shall command on the Main.
　Oh, the Rost Beef, etc."

To this truly prolific period of the young 'hackney writer's' pen belongs an *Epilogue*, hitherto overlooked, written for Charles Johnson's five-act play *Caelia or the Perjur'd Lover*, and spoken by Kitty Clive. The lines, which are hardly worth reprinting, consist of an ironic attack on the laxity of town morals, where "Miss may take great liberties upon her," and each woman is virtuous till she be found out.

An average of two plays a year is a record scarcely conducive to literary excellence; any more than is the empty cupboard, and the frequent recourse to 'your honour's own pawnbroker,' so often and so honourably familiar to struggling genius. "The farces written by Mr Fielding," says Murphy"... were generally the production of two or three mornings, so great was his facility in writing"; and we have seen Lady Mary Wortley Montagu's assertion that much of his work would have been thrown into the fire had not his dinner gone with it. Of the struggles of these early years [7] (struggles never wholly remitted, for, to quote Lady Mary again, Fielding would have wanted money had his hereditary lands been as extensive as his imagination) we get further suggestions in the *Poetical Epistle* addressed to Sir Robert Walpole when the young poet was but twenty-three. The lines go with a gallant spirit, but it is not difficult to detect a savour of grim hardship behind the jests:

"While at the Helm of State you ride,
Our Nation's Envy and its Pride;
While foreign Courts with Wonder gaze,
And curse those Councils which they praise;
Would you not wonder, Sir, to view
Your Bard a greater Man than you?
Which that he, is you cannot doubt,
When you have heard the Sequel out.
.   .   .   .   .
"The Family that dines the latest,
Is in our Street esteem'd the greatest;
But latest Hours must surely fall
Before him who ne'er dines at all.

Your Taste in Architect, you know,
Hath been admir'd by Friend and Foe;
But can your earthly Domes compare
With all my Castles—in the Air?

"We're often taught it doth behove us
To think those greater who're above us;
Another Instance of my Glory,
Who live above you, twice two Story,
And from my Garret can look down
On the whole Street of Arlington." [8]

Not to depend too greatly on Mr Luckless for our picture of Fielding as a playwright, we will conclude it with the well-known passage from Murphy: "When he had contracted to bring on a play, or a farce, it is well known, by many of his friends now living, that he would go home rather late from a tavern, and would the next morning deliver a scene to the players, written upon the papers which had wrapped the tobacco in which he so much delighted." Would that some of those friends had recorded for our delight the wit that, alas! has vanished like the smoke through which it was engendered. What would we not give for the table-talk of Henry Fielding.

[1] *Joseph Andrews*, Book iii. Chap. iii.

[2] *Miscellanies*, ed. 1743, vol. ii. p. 62.

[3] In the *Miscellanies* of 1743.

[4] *Fielding*, Austin Dobson, 1907. App. iv.

[5] What appears to be the original autograph of the above letter is now (1909) in the library of the Boston Athenaeum, having been presented by Mr C. P. Greenough.

[6] *Notitia Dramatica* (British Museum. MSS. Dept.) and Genest give 1734 as the date of Don Quixote; Murphy, edition of 1766, vol. iii p. 249, gives 1733.

[7] For the refutation of Genest's confusion of Timothy Fielding, a strolling player, with Henry Fielding, see Austin Dobson, *Fielding*, pp. 28, 29.

[8] The *Miscellanies*. Edition 1743.

CHAPTER III

MARRIAGE

"What happiness the world affords equal to the possession of such
a woman as Sophia I sincerely own I have never yet discovered."
—*Tom Jones.*

Out of the paint and powder of the green-room, the tobacco clouds of the
tavern, the crowded streets where hungry genius went afoot one day, and rode in
a coach the next—in a word, out of the Town as Harry Fielding knew it—we
step, in the year 1734, into the idyll of his life, his marriage with Charlotte
Cradock. For to Fielding the supreme gift was accorded of passionate devotion
to a woman of whose charm and virtue he himself has raised an enduring
memorial in the lovely portrait of Sophia Western. It is this portrait, explicitly
admitted [1], that affords almost our only authentic knowledge of Charlotte
Cradock, beyond the meagre facts that her home was in Salisbury, and that there
she and her sisters reigned as country belles. For it was not in the gay world of
'Riddoto's, Opera's, and Plays,' nor among the humbler scenes of the great city
in which he delighted to watch the humours of simple folk (the highest life being
in his opinion 'much the dullest'), that Fielding found his wife. Doubtless his six
years about town, as hackney author, with his good birth, his brilliant wit, and
his scanty means, had made him well acquainted with every phase of society,
"from the Minister at his Levee, to the Bailiff at his spunging-house; from the
Duchess at her drum, to the Landlady behind her bar"; but it was in the rural
seclusion of an old cathedral town that he wooed and won the beautiful Miss
Cradock. Indeed it is impossible to conceive of Sophia as for ever domiciled in
streets. The very apostrophe which heralds her first appearance in *Tom Jones* is
fragrant with flower-enamelled meadows, fresh breezes, and the songs of birds
"whose sweetest notes not even Handel can excel"; and it is thus, with his
reader's mind attuned to the appropriate key, that Fielding ushers in his heroine:
"... lo! adorned with all the Charms in which Nature can array her; bedecked
with Beauty, Youth, Sprightliness, Innocence, Modesty, and Tenderness,
breathing Sweetness from her rosy Lips, and darting Brightness from her
sparkling Eyes, the lovely *Sophia* comes." Of middle size, but rather inclining to
tall, with dark hair "curled so gracefully on her neck that few could believe it to
be her own," a forehead rather low, arched eyebrows, and lustrous black eyes, a
mouth that "exactly answered Sir John Suckling's description in those lines

'Her lips were red and one was thin,
Compar'd to that was next her chin.
Some bee had stung it newly,'"

with a dimple in the right cheek, and a complexion rather more of the lily than the rose unless increased by exercise or modesty when no vermilion could equal it—such was the appearance of Sophia, who, most of all "resembled one whose image never can depart from my breast."

Nor was the beautiful frame, Fielding hastens to add, disgraced by an unworthy inhabitant. He lingers on the sweetness of temper which "diffused a glory over her countenance which no regularity of features can give"; on her perfect breeding, "though wanting perhaps a little of that ease in her behaviour which is to be acquired only by habit, and living within what is called the polite circle"; on the "noble, elevated qualities" which outshone even her beauty.

The only facts recorded concerning Miss Cradock are that her home was in Salisbury, or New Sarum as the city was then called, and that she possessed a small fortune. It is said, but on what authority is not stated, that she was one of three beautiful sisters, the belles of the country town; and it is in accordance with this tradition that Fielding should celebrate in some verses "writ when the Author was very young," the beauty and intellectual charm of the Miss Cradocks. When printing these verses many years afterwards, in his *Miscellanies* he describes the poem as originally partly filled in with the 'Names of several young Ladies,' which part he now omits, "the rather, as some Freedoms, tho' gentle ones, were taken with little Foibles in the amiable Sex, whom to affront in Print, is, we conceive, mean in any Man, and scandalous in a Gentleman." Certainly the Miss Cradocks suffered no affront in the lines retained, wherein the young poet affirms that of all the famed nymphs of Sarum, that favoured city,

"Whose Nymphs excel all Beauty's Flowers,
As thy high Steeple doth all Towers"

the 'C——cks' were the best and fairest. Nay, has not great Jove himself apportioned a 'celestial Dower' to these most favoured of maidens,

"To form whose lovely Minds and Faces
I stript half Heaven of its Graces."

From this charming sisterhood Harry Fielding won his bride, but not until four years of waiting had been accomplished. So much may be assumed from the early date of the verses entitled "Advice to the Nymphs of *New S—m*. Written in the Year 1730." Here the newly returned student from Leyden, the successful dramatist from Drury Lane, bids the Salisbury beauties cease their vain endeavours to contend with the matchless charms of his Celia. And here, in a pretty compliment introduced to the great Mr Pope, then at the height of his fame, we are reminded that Celia's lover is already a man of letters, for all his mere three and twenty years. When Celia meets her equal, then, he declares, farthing candles shall eclipse the moon, and "sweet *Pope* be dull."

It is these youthful love-verses, verses as he himself was the first to admit, that were 'indeed Productions of the Heart rather than the Head,' that afford our only record of Fielding's wooing. Thus, he sings his passion for *Celia* in the declaration

"I hate the Town, and all its Ways;
Ridotto's, Opera's, and Plays;
The Ball, the Ring, the Mall, the Court;
Where ever the Beau-Monde resort....
All Coffee-houses, and their Praters;
All Courts of Justice, and Debaters;
All Taverns, and the Sots within 'em;
All Bubbles, and the Rogues that skin 'em,"

in short, the whole world 'cram'd all together,' because all his heart is engrossed for Celia. Again, Cupid is called to account, in that the careless urchin had left Celia's house unguarded from thieves, save for an old fellow "who sat up all Night, with a Gun without any Ammunition." Celia, it seems, had apprehended robbery, and her poet's rest is troubled:

"For how should I Repose enjoy,
While any fears your Breast annoy?
Forbid it Heav'n, that I should be
From any of your Troubles free."

Cupid explains his desertion by ingeniously declaring that a sigh from Celia had blown him away
"*to Harry Fielding's breast,*"
in which lodging the 'wicked Child' wrought unconscionable havoc. Again, Celia wishes to have a "Lilliputian to play with," so she is promptly told that her lover would doff five feet of his tall stature, to meet her pleasure, and

"Then when my Celia walks abroad
I'd be her pocket's little Load:
Or sit astride, to frighten People,
Upon her Hat's new fashion'd Steeple."

Nay, to be prized by Celia, who would not even take the form of her faithful dog Quadrille.

Jove, we may remember, had dowered the lovely Miss Cradocks with minds as fair as their persons; and the excellence of Celia's understanding is again celebrated in a neatly turned verse upon her 'having blamed Mr Gay for his Severity on her Sex.' Had other women known a tenderness like hers, cries the poet, Gay's darts had returned into his own bosom; and last of all should such blame come from her
"in whose accomplish'd Mind
The strongest Satire on thy Sex we find."

The love story that first ran to such pleasant rhymes, in the old cathedral town, was destined to know many a harsh chapter of poverty and sickness; but throughout it all the affection of the lovers remained true; and there is no reason to doubt that, had it been in Harry Fielding's power to achieve it, the promise of perhaps the most charming of his love verses would have been fulfilled:

"Can there on Earth, my *Celia*, be,
A Price I would not pay for thee?
Yes, one dear precious Tear of thine
Should not be shed to make thee mine."

To read Swift's *Journal to Stella* is almost a sacrilege; the little notes that Dick Steele would write to his 'dearest Prue' at all hours of day and night, from tavern and printing office, are scarce less private; no such seals have been broken, no such records preserved, of the love story of Harry Fielding. But to neither Swift nor Steele was it given to raise so perfect and imperishable a memorial of the women loved by them, as that reared by the passionate affection and grief of Fielding for Charlotte Cradock. To this day the beautiful young figure of Sophia Western, all charm and goodness, is alive in his immortal pages. And if, as her friend Lady Bute asserts, Amelia also is Mrs Fielding's portrait, then we know her no less intimately as wife and mother. We watch her brave spirit never failing under the most cruel distresses and conflicts; we play with her children in their little nursery; we hear her pleasant wit with the good parson; we feel her fresh beauty, undimmed in the poor remnants of a wardrobe that has gone, with her trinkets, to the pawnbroker; we see a hundred examples of her courage and tenderness and generosity. There is nothing in Fielding's life that is more to his honour than the brief words in which so competent an observer as Lady Bute summed up his marriage with Charlotte Cradock, "he loved her passionately and she returned his affection."

It was in the little country church of St Mary Charlcombe, a remote village some two miles from Bath, that "Henry Fielding, of ye Parish of St James in Bath, Esq., and Charlotte Cradock of ye same Parish, spinster" were married, on the 28th of November 1734. [2] Fifty years later the village was described as containing only nine houses, the church, well fitted for the flock, being but eighteen feet wide. The old Somerset historian, Collinson, tells us how the hamlet stood on rising ground, in a deep retired valley, surrounded by noble hills, and with a little stream winding through the vale.

In the January following Fielding and his wife were presumably back in town; for in this month he produced, at Drury Lane, the brisk little farce called *An Old Man taught Wisdom*, a title afterwards changed to the *Virgin Unmasked*. It is probable that this farce was especially written to suit Kitty Clive in her excelling character of hoyden; and to it, as we have seen, together with two of its predecessors, is assigned the credit of having first given that superb comic actress an opportunity of revealing her powers. Mrs Clive here played the part of Miss Lucy, a forward young lady who after skittishly interviewing a number of suitors proposed by her father, finally runs away with Thomas the footman. The little piece is said to have achieved success; but scarce had it been staged when "the prolific Mr Fielding," as a newspaper of the day styles him, brought out a five-act comedy, named the *Universal Gallant: or The different Husbands*, which wholly failed to please the audience, and indeed ran but for three nights.

The dedication of this play is dated from "Buckingham Street, Feb. 12," and assuming Buckingham Street, Strand, to be the district meant, it is probable that the newly married 'poet' and his wife were then living with Mrs Fielding's relatives; for although the rate-books for Buckingham Street fail to show the name of Fielding, they do show that a Mr Thomas Cradock was then a householder in the street. In an *Advertisement*, prefixed to the published copies of this ill-fated comedy, the disappointed author deprecates the hasty voice of the pit in words that suggest the anxiety of a man now responsible for a happiness dearer than his own. "I have heard," he writes, "that there are some young Gentlemen about this Town who make a Jest of damning Plays—but did they seriously consider the Cruelty they are guilty of by such a Practice, I believe it would prevent them"; the more, that if the author be "so unfortunate to depend on the success of his Labours for his Bread, he must be an inhuman Creature indeed, who would out of sport and wantonness prevent a Man from getting a Livelihood in an honest and inoffensive Way, and make a jest of starving him and his Family." There is other evidence that young men about town were wont to amuse themselves by damning plays 'when George was King.' In the *Prologue* to this same condemned play, spoken by the actor Quin, and said to have been written after the disastrous first night's performance, a more elaborate indictment is laid against the audiences of the day. The *Critick*, it seems, is grown so captious that if a poet seeks new characters he is denounced for dealing in monsters; if they are known and common, then he is a plagiarist; if his scenes are serious they are voted dull; if humorous they are 'low' (a true Fielding touch). And not only the critic but also the brainless beau stands, as we have seen, ready to make sport of the poor author. For such as these

"'Tis not the Poet's wit affords the Jest,
But who can Cat-call, Hiss, or Whistle best."

In previous years the brilliant Leyden student might have merely derided his enemies; to the Fielding of February 1735, struggling to support himself and his beautiful country bride, this 'cruel usage' of his 'poor Play' assumed a graver aspect:

"Can then another's Anguish give you Joy?
Or is it such a Triumph to destroy?
We, like the fabled Frogs, consider thus,
This may be Sport to you, but it is Death to us."

This note of personal protest recalls an indisputably reminiscent observation in *Amelia*, to the effect that although the kindness of a faithful and beloved wife compensates most of the evils of life, it "rather serves to aggravate the misfortune of distressed circumstances, from the consideration of the share which she is to bear in them." We all know how bravely Amelia bore that share; how cheerfully she would cook the supper; how firmly she confronted disaster.

To realise how deeply Fielding felt the pain of such struggles when falling upon "the best, the worthiest and the noblest of women" we need but turn again to his own pages. If, cries Amelia's husband, when his distresses overwhelm him, "if I was to suffer alone, I think I could bear them with some philosophy"; and again "this was the first time I had ever felt that distress which arises from the want of money; a distress very dreadful indeed in the married state for what can be more miserable than to see anything necessary to the preservation of the beloved creature and not be able to supply it?"

To supply for his Celia much less than the necessities of life Harry Fielding would undoubtedly have stripped his coat, and his shirt with it, off his back; but, at the end of this same month of February, fortune made the young couple sudden amends for the anxieties that seem to have surrounded them. This turn of the wheel is reflected with curious accuracy by an anonymous satirist of 1735:

"F—g, who *Yesterday* appear'd so rough,
Clad in coarse Frize, and plaister'd down with *Snuff*,
See how his *Instant* gaudy *Trappings* shine;
What *Play-house* Bard was ever seen so fine!
But this, not from his *Humour* glows, you'll say
But mere *Necessity*;—for last Night lay
In pawn the Velvet which he wears to Day." [3]

This relief, for a time at least, from the pressing anxieties of a 'play-house bard,' befell by the death of Charlotte Fielding's mother, Mrs Elizabeth Cradock of Salisbury, who died in February, but a week or two after the execution of a will wholly in favour of that 'dearly beloved' daughter. As the details of Mrs Fielding's inheritance have not hitherto been known, some portions of her mother's will may be quoted. "... I Elizabeth Cradock of Salisbury in the County of Wilts ... do make this my last will and testament ... Item I give to my daughter Catherine one shilling and all the rest and residue of my ready money plate jewels and estate whatsoever and wheresoever after my debts and funeral charges are fully paid and satisfied I give devize and bequeath the same unto my dearly beloved daughter Charlott Ffeilding wife of Henry Ffeilding of East Stour in the County of Dorset Esqre." Mrs Cradock proceeds to revoke all former wills; and appoints her said daughter "Charlott Ffeilding" as her sole executrix. The will is dated February 8 1734, old style, viz. 1735; and was proved in London on the 25th of the same month, 'Charlott Ffeilding,' as sole executrix, being duly sworn to administer. The provision of one shilling for another, and apparently *not* dearly beloved, daughter, Catherine, recalls the wicked sister in *Amelia* who "had some way or other disobliged her mother, a little before the old lady died," and who consequently was deprived of that inheritance which relieved Amelia and her husband from the direst straits.

As no plays are credited to Fielding's name for the ensuing months of 1735, it is a reasonable inference that the young Salisbury heiress, whose experience of London had, doubtless, included a pretty close acquaintance with the hardships of struggling genius, employed some of her inheritance to enable her husband to return to the home of his boyhood, on the "pleasant Banks of sweetly-winding Stour." There is no record of how the Stour estate, settled on Henry Fielding and his brother and sisters, was apportioned; but an engraving published in 1813 shows the old stone "farmhouse," which Fielding occupied, the kitchen of which then still remained as it was in the novelist's time, when it served as a parlour. Behind the house stood a famous locust tree; and close by was the village church served at this time, as the parish registers show, by the Rev. William Young, the original of the immortal Parson Adams of *Joseph Andrews*. [4] From a subsequent deed of sale we know that the estate consisted of at least three gardens, three orchards, eighty acres of meadow, one hundred and forty acres of pasture, ten acres of wood, two dove-houses, and "common of pasture for all manner of cattle." To the stone farmhouse, and to these orchards and meadows, commons and pastures, Fielding brought his wife, probably in this year of 1735; and memories of their sojourn at Stour surely inspired those references in *Amelia* to the country life of 'love, health, and tranquillity,' a life resembling a calm sea which "must appear dull in description; for who can describe the pleasures which the morning air gives to one in perfect health; the flow of spirits which springs up from exercise; the delights which parents feel from the prattle and innocent follies of their children; the joy with which the tender smile of a wife inspires a husband; or lastly the cheerful solid comfort which a fond couple enjoy in each others' conversation.—All these pleasures, and every other of which our situation was capable we tasted in the highest degree."

That a man endowed with Fielding's intense joy in living—he was "so formed for happiness," wrote his cousin Lady Mary, "it is a pity he was not immortal"—should eagerly taste all the pleasures of life as a country gentleman, and that in 'the highest degree,' is entirely consonant with his character. At the very end of his life, when dying of a complication of diseases, his happy social spirit was still unbroken; for we find him even then writing of his inability to enjoy an agreeable hour "without the assistance of a companion which has always appeared to me necessary to such enjoyment." [5] Nor would the generous temper, which was ever ready to share his most needed guinea with a friend scarce poorer than himself, be infected with niggardliness by the happy enjoyment of that position to which he was by birth entitled. The well-known account therefore, given by Murphy, of the East Stour episode is exactly what we might have expected of Harry Fielding in the part of country gentleman: "To that place [*i.e.* his estate of East Stour]," says Murphy, "he retired with his wife, on whom he doated, with a resolution to bid adieu to all the follies and intemperances to which he had addicted himself in the career of a town life. But unfortunately a kind of family pride here gained an ascendant over him, and he began immediately to vie in splendour with the neighbouring country 'squires. With an estate not much above two hundred pounds a year, and his wife's fortune, which did not exceed fifteen hundred pounds, he encumbered himself with a large retinue of servants, all clad in costly yellow liveries. For their master's honour, these people could not descend so low as to be careful of their apparel, but in a month or two were unfit to be seen; the 'squire's dignity required that they should be new-equipped; and his chief pleasure consisting in society and convivial mirth, hospitality threw open his doors, and, in less than three years, entertainments, hounds, and horses, entirely devoured a little patrimony...." This account is prefaced by gross inaccuracies of fact, inexplicable in a biographer writing but ten years after the death of his subject; but, as Mr Austin Dobson says, "there can be little doubt that the rafters of the old farm by the Stour, with the great locust tree at the back, which is figured in Hutchins's *History of Dorset*, rang often to hunting choruses, and that not seldom the 'dusky Night rode down the Sky' over the prostrate forms of Harry Fielding's guests." Petty-minded moralists like Murphy have gravely admonished the great novelist's memory for not having safely bestowed his estate in the consols of the period; they forget that a spirit of small economy is generally the compensation awarded to the poor average of humanity. The genius of Fielding knew how to enjoy splendidly, and to give lavishly.

[1] *Tom Jones.* Book xiii. Introduction.

[2] See the registers of St Mary Charlcombe. As Sarah Fielding, the novelist's sister, was buried in the entrance to the chancel of this church, it would appear that some connection existed between Charlcombe and the Fielding family.

[3] *Seasonable Reproof—a Satire in the manner of Horace*, 1735.

[4] The entry in the East Stour Registers is "W'm. Young, Curate 1731-1740."

[5] *Voyage to Lisbon.*

CHAPTER IV

POLITICAL PLAYS

"Whoever attempteth to introduce corruption into any community,
doth much the same thing, and ought to be treated in much the
same manner with him who poisoneth a fountain."
—Dedication of the *Historical Register.*

A prolonged retirement into Dorsetshire, however pleasant were the banks
of Stour with a beautiful young wife, and a sufficient estate, could scarce be
expected of Fielding's restless genius. He was now thirty-five; his splendid
physique was as yet unimpaired by the gout that was so soon to attack him; his
powers were still hardly revealed; and, as far as we can discover, he was, at the
moment, under no pressure for money. Still, the hunting choruses of the Squire
Westerns of Dorsetshire can hardly have long sufficed for one whom Lyttelton
declared to have had "more wit than any man I ever knew"; and the social and
political conditions of the country were increasingly calculated to inflame into
practical activity that "enthusiasm for righteousness," which Mr Gosse has so
well detected in Fielding. [1] The distracted state of the London stage, divided by
the factions of players and managers, afforded moreover an excellent
opportunity for a dramatist of some means to essay an independent venture.
And accordingly, at the beginning of 1736, we find the Harry Fielding of the
green-room and the poet's garret, the Henry Fielding Esqre of East Stour,
suddenly throwing the full force of his energies into political life, as the manager
of, and writer for, a theatre with indisputable political aims. For the next eight
years of his short life Fielding was largely occupied in the lively turmoil of
eighteenth-century politics; and here, first by means of the stage, and later as
journalist, he played a part which has perhaps been somewhat unduly
overshadowed by the surpassing achievements of his genius as father of the
English novel. But if we would perceive the full figure of the man this time of
boisterous political warfare is of no mean account. In the dedication of his first
party play, the amazingly successful *Pasquin*, Fielding subscribes himself as "the
most devoted Servant of the public"; and no more appropriate keyword could
be found for the energies which he threw into those envenomed political
struggles of 1736-41.

At the date of his first plunge into these struggles England stood sorely in
need of a pen as biting, as witty and as fearless, as that of Henry Fielding. For
over ten years the country had been ruled by one of those "peace at any price"
Ministers who have at times so successfully inflamed the baser commercial
instincts of Englishmen. Sir Robert Walpole, the reputed organiser of an
unrivalled system of bribery and corruption, the Minister of whom a recent
apologist frankly declares that to young members of Parliament who spoke of
public virtue and patriotism he would reply "you will soon come off that and

grow wiser," the autocrat enamoured of power who could brook no colleague within measurable distance, the man of coarse habits and illiterate tastes, above all the man who induced his countrymen to place money before honour, and whose administration even an admirer describes as one of unparalleled stagnation—such a man must have roused intense antagonism in Fielding's generous and ardent nature. For, from the days of his first boyish satires to the last energetic acts of his life as a London magistrate, for Fielding to see an abuse was to set about reforming it. To his just sense of the true worth of money, the wholesale corruption of English political life accredited to Walpole, the poisoning, to adopt his own simile, of the body politic, must have seemed the vilest national crime. There could never have been the least sympathy between the mercenary and apathetic methods of Walpole and the open-hearted genius of Fielding. And, added to such fundamental opposition of character, the influence of Fielding's old school friend, George Lyttelton, would, at this juncture especially, draw him into the active ranks of the Opposition.

Lyttelton was then rising into celebrity as a ready parliamentary speaker; a celebrity as yet not wholly eclipsed by the youthful oratory of William Pitt, the young cornet of the horse, who also had lately taken his seat on the Opposition benches. It was the burning patriotism, the lofty character and the towering genius of Pitt, the fluency and personal integrity of Lyttelton, that led the younger members of the Opposition in the House of Commons; while in the Lords another friend from whom Fielding was to receive "princely benefactions," the young Duke of Bedford, a man of "inflexible honesty and goodwill to his country," attacked Walpole's alleged corrupt practices in the election of Scottish peers. With leaders such as William Pitt and Lyttelton on the one hand, and the corrupt figure of Walpole on the other, there is no wonder that Fielding flung all his generous force into the effort to free England from so degrading a domination. Accordingly, in 1736, when the young Pitt's impassioned eloquence was soon to alarm the *Great Man*—"we must muzzle that terrible Cornet of the Horse," Sir Robert said—and when fierce and riotous hostility to the government had broken out in the country over an attempted Excise Bill, Fielding appears as a frankly political manager of the "New Theatre" in the Haymarket. This small theatre stood precisely adjoining the present Palladian structure, as may be seen from a print of 1820, showing the demolition of the old building and the adjacent façade of the modern "Haymarket." According to Tom Davies, who, as an actor in Fielding's company and as an author of some pretensions should be reliable, Fielding was a managing partner of this "New Theatre," in company with James Ralph, "about the year 1735." [2] And apparently early in 1736 [3] his political, theatrical, and social satire of *Pasquin* appeared on the little stage, and immediately captured the town.

In *Pasquin* a perfectly outspoken attack on Walpole's corrupt methods is united with a comprehensive onslaught on abuses in the stage, law, divinity, physic, society, and on the odes of Colley Cibber, sufficient one might suppose to satisfy even Fielding's zeal. In an exuberant newspaper advertisement of the 5th of March Mr Pasquin is announced as intending to "lay about him with great impartiality," and throughout the play Fielding's splendid figure may be felt, swinging his satiric club with a boisterous enjoyment. The immediate success achieved by the piece was certainly not due to any great dramatic excellence; and that so loosely knit a medley as *PASQUIN, a Dramatic Satire on the Times: Being the Rehearsal of Two Plays, viz. A Comedy call'd THE ELECTION and a Tragedy, call'd The Life and Death of COMMON-SENSE* should have achieved almost as long a run as the *Beggars Opera*, shows that the public heartily sympathised with the satirist. *Pasquin* begins with the rehearsal of a comedy, called *The Election*, consisting of a series of broadly humorous scenes in which the open and diverse bribery at elections, the equally open immorality of fashionable town life, the connivance of country dames, and the inanity of the beau monde, are satirised. The country Mayor, the Ministerial candidates and the Opposition squire drink, bribe and are bribed with complete impartiality. A scene devoted to the political young lady of the day affords opportunity for a hit at the sickly and effeminate Lord 'Fanny' Hervey, that politician whom Pope described as a "mere white curd of Asse's milk," and of whom Lady Mary Wortley Montagu observed that "the world consisted of men, women, and Herveys." Pope had stigmatised Hervey as *Lord Fanny*, and Fielding obviously plays on the nickname by references to the value attached by certain young ladies to their fans. "Faith," says his comic author, "this incident of the fan struck me so strongly that I was once going to call this comedy by the name of the Fan." The comedy ends with the successful cooking of the election returns by Mr Mayor in favour of the Ministerial candidates, for which "return" he is promised a "very good turn very soon"; and by the precipitate marriage of one of the said candidates to the Mayor's daughter "to strengthen his interest with the returning officer."

Having settled the business of the corrupt and corrupting Ministry in his comedy, Mr Pasquin proceeds to exhibit the rehearsal of his tragedy, *The Life and Death of Common Sense*. Here the satirist, leaving politics, applies his cudgel mainly to the prevailing taste for pantomime, a form of entertainment introduced it was said some thirty years previously by one Weaver, a country dancing master, and already lashed by Sir Richard Steele in his couplet:
"Weaver, corrupter of the present age,
Who first taught silent sins upon the stage."

That the Covent Garden manager, John Rich, [4] could engage four French dancers, and a German with two dogs, taught to dance the *Louvre* and the *Minuet*, at ten pounds a night, and clear thereby "above 20 good houses," while the Othello of Booth and the Wildair of Wilkes were neglected, was sufficient to rouse the indignation alike of moralists, dramatists and playgoers. Fielding in turn took the matter up with all his natural warmth; and in *Pasquin* he represents the kingdom of the Queen of Common Sense as invaded by a vast army of "singers, fidlers, tumblers, and ropedancers," who moreover fix their standard in Covent Garden, the headquarters of Rich.

Not content with assailing this public folly, the 'Tragedy' of *Pasquin* strikes a higher note by ranging among the foes of Common Sense three unworthy professors of Law, Medicine, and Religion; callings, as Fielding is careful to point out,

"in themselves designed
To shower the greatest blessings on Mankind."

Queen Common Sense seemingly receives her deathblow; but her ghost finally rises victorious, and so justifies the author's contention that his "is almost the only play where she has got the better lately." The vigour with which Mr Pasquin here 'laid about him,' in such matters as the legal abuses relating to imprisonment for debt, may be inferred from the following passage. Queen Common Sense is speaking to the representative of *bad* Law, and tells him she has heard that men

"unable to discharge their debts
At a short warning, being sued for them,
Have, with both power and will their debts to pay,
Lain all their lives in prison, for their costs.
Law. That may perhaps be some poor person's case
Too mean to entertain your royal ear.
Q.C.S. My Lord, while I am Queen I shall not think One man too mean, or poor, to be redress'd."

So too, the great genius of Fielding, when in long after years harnessed to the drudgery of a London magistrate, held no porter's brawl or beggar's quarrel too mean "to be redress'd."

The immediate success of *Pasquin* attests, as we have said, the readiness of London audiences in 1736 to applaud an honest and humorous presentation of wicked Ministers, corrupt clergy, lawyers, and doctors, inane Laureates, and degrading public entertainments. Mrs Delany, gathering London news for Dean Swift, writes on April 22, "When I went out of Town last Autumn, the reigning madness was Farinelli; I find it now turned on *Pasquin*, a dramatic satire on the times. It has had almost as long a run as the Beggar's Opera; but in my opinion not with equal merit, though it has humour." [5] We are told how the piece drew numerous enthusiastic audiences "from *Grosvenor, Cavendish, Hanover,* and all the other fashionable Squares, as also from *Pall Mall* and the *Inns of Court*" And on the 26th of May a benefit performance for the author was announced as the "60th. Day." The vogue of the satire even demanded a key, as may be seen in an advertisement in the *London Daily Post* for May 17: *This Day is published, Price Four-Pence. A Key to Pasquin, address'd to Henry Fielding Esqre.*

Mr Pasquin's own advertisements for his little theatre are not without the zest with which our beef-eating ancestors attacked politics, social abuses and one another. The announcement for March 5, ran as follows:—

"*By the* Great Mogul's *Company of* English
Comedians, Newly Imported. At the New Theatre in the
Haymarket, this Day, March 5, will be presented

PASQUIN,
A Dramatick SATYR on the times.

Being a Rehearsal of two PLAYS, viz. a Comedy call'd The
ELECTION; and a Tragedy, call'd The Life and Death of COMMON
SENSE....

N.B.—Mr Pasquin intending to lay about him with great
Impartiality, hopes the Town will all attend, and very civilly
give their Neighbours what the find belongs to 'em.

N.B.—The Cloaths are old, but the Jokes entirely new...."

In the following month the Opposition was busy over the marriage of their
chief supporter, the Prince of Wales; and Mr Pasquin duly chronicles the event
in his advertisements of the 28th of April, observing that his company "by
reason of the Royal Wedding expecting no Company but themselves, are obliged
to defer Playing till tomorrow." A few days later, on the 12th of May, Sir Robert
Walpole celebrated the royal marriage by a grand evening entertainment given at
his house in St James Park; and on the same night 'Pasquin' had the audacity to
advertise a special performance, in the following terms (the "country party," it
should be understood, was a usual name for Walpole's opponents):—
"For the Benefit of Miss Burgess, who has so zealously espoused the
Country Interest.... Miss Burgess hopes all Patriots and Lovers of their Country
will appear in her favour and give all encouragement to one who has so early
distinguished herself on the side of Liberty." In Pasquin's *Election* scenes, this
lady played the part of Miss Stitch, a political damsel, opposed to Walpole's
candidate. Next day appeared an ironic counter-advertisement of a performance
for "the Benefit of Miss Jones (the Mayor's daughter who hath so furiously
espoused the Court [*i.e.* Walpole's] Interest....) N.B.—Miss Jones does not doubt
that all true loyal People will give her all Encouragement in their Power, as she
has engaged in so unpopular a Side and even given away her FAN (which very
few young ladies would) for the service of the Country: she hopes the Courtiers
will not let her be out of pocket by the Bargain." Here, again, is doubtless a hit at
Lord 'Fanny' Hervey; as well as a plain hint that those who espoused Walpole's
cause might expect ample payment for their trouble.
Is there any wonder that a wrathful and uneasy Minister, not yet
overthrown, shortly took stringent measures against the 'liberty' of the stage;
measures by which a political stage censorship was formally established, and the
topical gaiety of our theatre, and the pungency of our theatrical announcements,
henceforth immeasurably dulled.

A few further points of minor interest remain to be noted concerning that popular and scathing personage Mr Pasquin. By May the company styled themselves "Pasquin's Company of Comedians"; a fresh indication of the credit attaching to the performance. In the previous month a contributor to *The Grub Street Journal* tells "Dear Grub" that he has seen Pope applauding the piece; and, although the statement was promptly denied, a rare print by Hogarth lends some colour to a very likely story; for the great Mr Pope, the terror of his enemies, the autocrat of literature, was warmly on the side of the Opposition. Hogarth depicts the stage of Fielding's theatre, and thereon a scene in the fifth act of *Pasquin*, in which the foes of Queen Common Sense are for the moment triumphant. The side boxes are well filled; and in one of them Mr Pope's deformed figure, apparently, turns away, declaring: "There is no whitewashing this stuff." The curious may find another plate by Hogarth in which Pope *is* busy whitewashing Lord Burlington; but the drift of the remark for the Opposition drama of *Pasquin* seems obscure. The gains that accrued to Fielding from the success of *Pasquin* are indicated by another rare print, that entitled the *Judgement of the Queen o' Common Sense. Addressed to Henry Fielding Esqre.* Here, again, it is *Pasquin's* satire on the prevailing furore for pantomime that is chiefly illustrated; as Common Sense gives to Rich, the harlequin, a halter, while to Fielding she accords an overflowing purse. Supporting Fielding are a long lean Shakespeare, and two figures, possibly the distinguished players Kitty Clive and Quin; on the opposite side, behind Harlequin, are figures representing the bad clergy, lawyers, and doctors satirised in the *Tragedy*; and the whole is balanced by the emergence of the ghost in Hamlet, from a trap door in the foreground. Doggerel verses, at the foot of the print, celebrate the arrival of a bard, "from ye Great Mogul," bringing with him *Wit, Humour, and Satyr*, and receiving the Queen's "honest favour," in "show'rs of gold."

Under those golden showers, and with the applause of 'all the fashionable Squares' ringing in his ears, we may leave Mr Pasquin. Fielding's first venture as political dramatist and theatrical manager had proved brilliantly successful; his little theatre, like his own Tom Thumb, had assailed a dozen giant abuses, an all-powerful Minister among them, and the town had applauded the courage and wit of the performance. In the following season, those same boards were to witness the author of *Pasquin* "laying about him" with an even greater political audacity.

Content, doubtless, with the success of *Pasquin*, Fielding does not seem to have launched any further political attacks during the remaining months of 1736. A newspaper advertisement of June announces the intention of the 'Great Mogul's Company of Comedians' to continue "playing twice a week during the summer season," and *Pasquin* remained occasionally in the bills as late as the 2nd of July. The public were advised that "This is much the coolest House in Town"; and audiences must have been drawn even in August, for in that month one small and presumably party play was performed, the *New Comi-Tragical Interlude call'd the Deposing and Death of Queen Gin.* This little piece consisted of only two scenes, and was probably a skit on a Bill "against spirituous liquors" which Walpole had supported earlier in the year. The measure met with violent opposition, including petitions from the Liverpool and Bristol merchants; and in view of Sir Robert's own notorious excesses with the bottle a temperance Bill from his hands may well have roused Fielding's ironic laughter. The authorship of the satire is unknown; but the moral appears to have been unexceptionable, as *Queen Gin*, in the final scene, "drinks a great quantity of liquor and at last dies."

Fielding clearly began his second year at the 'little theatre' with some social or political exhortation, as the following bill appears for January:—"By a Company of Comedians, At the New Theatre in the Haymarket, this Day, January 26, will be presented a Dramatick Satire on the Times (never performed before) call'd The Mirrour." By February "the Original Company who perform'd *Pasquin*" are notified on the bills; and on the 2nd of March a performance is announced of a *Dramatick Tale of the King and the Miller of Mansfield*, presumably the same *Miller of Mansfield* openly declared by one of Walpole's "hired scribblers" to be aimed at the overthrow of the Ministry. [6] All such preliminary skirmishes, however, served but to introduce the grand attack of the *Historical Register for the Year 1736*, the first performance of which may be assigned to the end of March 1737. [7]

In the *Register* we have the most complete display of Fielding's vigour as a fighting politician. Here, to recur to Mr Pasquin's characteristic phrase, he "lays about him" with a gusto and honest frankness quite lost among our own tepid conventions. But however hard the hitting, however boisterous the broad humour, however biting the irony, it is noteworthy that in this his chief political satire, written moreover for a yet unregulated stage, Fielding never stoops to the shameless personalities of his day. The fashion of the eighteenth-century permitted even the great and classical genius of Pope to hurl lines at the persons of his opponents that, to modern ears, scarcely bear quotation. Fielding, as we know, constantly asserted his intention of throwing not at the vicious but at vice; and accordingly, even in this party play, flung openly in the face of the Minister, there is but one reference (and that only a fling at his "lack of any the least taste in polite literature") to the notorious personal failings of Sir Robert. It is against the Minister, and not the man, that the hot-blooded Opposition dramatist directs his humour and his irony. Fielding's manly and generous nature here permitted no virulent personalities to blacken his pages. [8]

The irony of the *Register* is chiefly reserved for the *Dedication to the Public*, designed for the reader at leisure; though here Walpole is indicated broadly enough, first in the figure of an ass hung out on a signpost, and again as "Old Nick," for "who but the devil could act such a part." Here the attacks of the Ministerial papers are parried by ironic explanations that "The Register is a ministerial pamphlet calculated to infuse into the minds of the people a great opinion of their ministry," explanations full of admirable fencing and excellent hits. And in these dedicatory pages Fielding utters a sonorous warning to his countrymen concerning the insidious policy that was undermining their very constitution: "... Here is the danger, here is the rock on which our constitution must, if it ever does split. The liberties of a people have been subdued by conquests of valour and force, and have been betrayed by the subtle and dexterous arts of refined policy, but these are rare instances; for geniuses of this kind are not the growth of every age, whereas if a general corruption be once introduced, and those, who should be the guardians and bulwarks of our liberty, once find or think they find an interest in giving it up, no great capacity will be required to destroy it. On the contrary the meanest, lowest, dirtiest fellow, if such an one should ever have the assurance in future ages to mimick power, and browbeat his betters, will be as able as Machiavel himself could have been, to root out the liberties of the bravest people." From the solemnities of the *Dedication* we come to the "humming deal of satire," and the boisterous action, of the play itself. As in the case of *Pasquin* the form of the drama is that of a rehearsal, a form which affords excellent opportunities for such explanatory asides as that addressed to the critic who complains of the attempt to review a year's events in a single play: "Sir," says the author, "if I comprise the whole actions of a year in half an hour, will you blame me, or those who have done so little in that time?" The long years of Walpole's power were admittedly "years without parallel in our history, for political stagnation." Scene one discovers five 'blundering blockheads' of politicians, in counsel with one silent "little gentleman yonder in the chair;" who knows all and says nothing, and whose politics lie so deep that "nothing but an inspir'd understanding can come at 'em." The blockheads, however, have capacity enough to snatch hastily at the money lying on their council table. Walpole's jealousy of power, it may be remembered, had driven almost every man of ability out of his ministry. Then comes a vivacious parody on the fashionable auctions of the day. Lots comprising "a most curious remnant of Political Honesty," a "delicate piece of Patriotism," and a "very clear Conscience which has been worn by a judge and a bishop" and on which no dirt will stick, go for little or nothing, while Lot 8, "a very considerable quantity of Interest at Court," excites brisk bidding, and is finally knocked down for one thousand pounds. From the excellent fooling of the auction, the action suddenly changes to combined satire on the Ministry and on the two Cibbers, father and son. The Ministry are ingeniously implied to have been damn'd by the public; to give places with no attention to the capacity of the recipient; and to laugh at the dupes by whose money they live. A like weakness for putting blockheads in office and for giving places to rogues, and a like contempt of the public, is allegorically conveyed in the third act, in which 'Apollo' casts the parts for a performance among sundry unworthy actors, and declares that the people may grumble 'as much as they please, as long as we get their money.' "There sir," cries the author to the critic of the rehearsal, "is the sentiment of a great man." The *Great Man* was a phrase, to use Pope's words, "by common use appropriated to the first minister"—that is, to Walpole. In the next scene the effrontery of the piece culminates in a ballet where the Prime Minister appears, leading a chorus of false patriots, who, to use Fielding's own words, are set in the 'odious and contemptible light' of a set of "cunning self-interested fellows who for a little paltry bribe would give up the liberties and properties of their country." These worthy patriots are of four types, the noisy, the cautious, the self-interested (he whose shop is his country) and the indolent ("who acts as I have seen a prudent man in company, fall asleep at the beginning of a fray and never wake 'till the end o't"). To them enters Quidam, unblushingly announced in the play bill as "Quidam, Anglice a Certain Person," in other words Walpole himself. Quidam pours gold into the pockets of the four patriots, drinks with them, and then, when the 'bottle is out' (a too frequent occurrence at Sir Robert's table) takes up his fiddle, strikes up a tune and dances off, the patriots dancing after him. But even this is not all. "Sir," says the author, "every one of these patriots have a hole in their pockets as Mr Quidam the fiddler there knows; so that he intends to make them dance 'till all the money is fall'n through, which he will pick up again and so not lose one halfpenny by his generosity...." We may suppose that the final scene lost nothing in breadth by the acting of Quidam; and it is not surprising that the immediate result was the subjugation not, alas! of the Ministry, but of the liberty of the stage. Walpole's fall was delayed for three years; the destruction of the political stage was accomplished in three months.

It is difficult to imagine that any party, in those days of comparatively arbitrary power, would venture a public satire so unveiled and so menacing as that of the *Register*, unless supported by some confidence in the immediate fall of their opponents. Without such confidence the political tactics of such an onslaught would be simple foolhardiness. Signs of these false hopes are not wanting in the slight, but equally bold, satire on the sycophants represented as composing Walpole's *levée*, which was shortly added to the *Register*. This little sketch, in which a protest concerning the damning, early in the year, of Fielding's ballad farce *Eurydice* is combined with the political satire, was advertised as follows:—

"EURYDICE HISS'D: or, a Word to the Wise, giving an Account of
the Rise, Progress, Greatness, and Downfal of Mr Pillage, ... with
the dreadful Consequence and Catastrophe of the whole." [9]

We have the authority of Tom Davies, at this time a member of Fielding's company, for the statement that "Fielding in his *Eurydice Hiss'd* had brought on the Minister [Walpole] in a *levée* scene" [10]; and as Pillage is the "very great man" who holds the *levée* in the fragment, the above allusion to an expected downfall of Walpole's Ministry seems obvious. Passages of similar import to the advertisement occur in the piece itself. Thus the play is declared to convey a "beautiful image of the instability of human greatness"; and the spectacle is promised of the 'author of a mighty farce' at the pinnacle of human greatness and adored by a crowd of dependants, become by a sudden turn of fortune, scorned, "deserted and abandon'd."

The single scene of the play opens when Pillage is at the zenith of his power; a stage direction orders that "The Lèvee enters, and range themselves to a ridiculous tune"; a partition of places ensues under the allegory of the business arrangements of a theatrical manager; and the author explains that by this *levée* scene he hopes that persons greater than author-managers may learn to despise sycophants. Close on the heels of the *levée* comes the catastrophe. Not one honest man, Pillage sadly admits, is on his side; as his 'shallow plot' opens out the first applause changes to hisses; his farce is damn'd; and he himself is left consoling the solitude of his downfall by getting exceedingly drunk on a third bottle.

The figure of a fallen Minister boozing away his own intolerable reflections, was not calculated to pacify that notoriously hard drinker, Sir Robert, already soundly pilloried in the *Register*, and severely indited by *Pasquin*. By the end of April the *Register* had reached its thirty-first performance, a good run at that date; and according to an advertisement in the *Craftsman* the satire was still being played on the 7th of May. In little more than four weeks, and after the alleged perpetration of a treasonable and profane farce called *The Golden Rump*, a Bill for stifling the liberty of the stage under a censorship was introduced, had passed through both Houses, and received the royal assent. Well might Lord Chesterfield exclaim in the brilliant speech which, in Smollet's words, "will ever endear his character to all the friends of genius and literature, to all those who are warmed with zeal for the liberties of their country," that the Bill was not only "of a very extraordinary nature, but has been brought in at a very extraordinary season and pushed with very extraordinary despatch." Concerning the nature of the measure Chesterfield had no doubt. He saw its tendency towards restraining the "liberty of the Press which will be a long stride towards the destruction of Liberty itself"; he pointed out that a Minister who has merited the esteem of the people will neither fear the wit nor feel the satire of the theatre; he denounced the subjugation of the stage under "an arbitrary Court license" which would convert it into a canal for conveying the vices and follies of "great men and Courtiers" through the whole kingdom; he protested against the Bill as an encroachment not only on liberty but also on property, for "Wit, my Lords, is a sort of property; it is the property of those that have it, and too often the only property that they have to depend on."

As a manager of the intrepid little theatre in the Haymarket, as well as the author of the most successful of the offending plays, the Licensing Act fell with double weight on Fielding. "When I speak against the Bill," cried Chesterfield, "I must think I plead the cause of Wit, I plead the cause of Humour, I plead the cause of the British Stage, and of every gentleman of taste in the Kingdom." Looking back over two centuries, we honour Chesterfield in that, unknown to himself, he also pleaded the cause of the greatest of English humourists. But appeals on behalf of genius and freedom were thrown away upon Walpole; the Act received the royal assent on June 21 1737; and, in the honourable company of Wit, Humour, and Taste, Fielding was forced to retire from the theatre, on the boards of which he had for two years so vigorously assailed Ministerial corruption and autocracy.

[1] *Works of Henry Fielding*, Edited by Edmund Gosse. Introduction, p. xxi.

[2] *Life of Garrick*. T. Davies. 1780, vol. i. p. 223.

[3] *Notitia Dramatica*, MSS. Dept. British Museum, speaks of *Pasquin* as performed for the fortieth time on April 21, 1736: and quotes an advertisement of the play for March 5. There seems to be no record of the actual first night.

[4] Rich appears to have been the manager at Covent Garden from 1733 to 1761.

[5] *Autobiography of Mrs Delany*. 1861. Vol I. p. 554.

[6] See Fielding's ironic reference to such "iniquitous surmises" in the Dedication to the *Historical Register*.

[7] The earliest newspaper reference, so far available, is that of the *Daily Journal* for April 6 1737, which speaks of April 11 as the ninth day of the *Register*.

[8] In the succeeding Epilogue of *Eurydice Hiss'd* it must be admitted that Sir Robert's love of the bottle is broadly satirised.

[9] *Daily Advertiser*, April 29. 1737.

[10] *Life of Garrick*, T. Davies, vol. ii. p. 206.

CHAPTER V

HOMESPUN DRAMA

"Virtue distrest in humble state support."
Prologue to *Fatal Curiosity*.

The Licensing Act of June 1737 thus brought Henry Fielding's career as political dramatist to a hasty conclusion; a conclusion quite unforeseen by the luckless author, as appears from his *Dedication* to the *Historical Register*, published almost at the moment when the Act became law: "The very great indulgence you have shown my performances at the little theatre these two last years," he says, addressing his public, "have encouraged me to the proposal of a subscription for carrying on that theatre, for beautifying and enlarging it, and procuring a better company of actors."

Before finally losing sight of the stage on which *Pasquin* and the *Register* had scored such signal success, we may notice some minor incidents of these two years of Fielding's administration. His company does not seem to have included either Macklin, Quin, or Kitty Clive; but that distinguished actress Mrs Pritchard, the central figure of Hogarth's charming group called "The Green Room, Drury Lane," is said to have made her first appearance on his boards, [1] and his players also included that man of many parts Tom Davies. Davies was a student of Edinburgh University; an actor at Drury Lane and elsewhere; a bookseller of whom the elder D'Israeli said 'all his publications were of the best kind'; the writer of various works including a *Life of Garrick*; and a particular friend of Dr Johnson. In the first year of Fielding's management in the Haymarket, Davies was cast for a principal part in George Lillo's tragedy *Fatal Curiosity*; and it is to his pen that we owe the only known contemporary reference to the active part taken by Fielding himself in the affairs of his theatre.

Lillo, a jeweller of Moorfields, had captured the town, a few years previously, by his tragedy of common life, *George Barnwell*; and among the dramatists selected by Fielding for representation on his stage the most interesting is undoubtedly this pioneer of the coming revolution in English literature. For, incredible as it may seem, until that first performance of *Barnwell*, no writer, to quote Tom Davies' own words "had ventured to descend so low as to introduce the character of a merchant or his apprentice into a tragedy." Certain "witty and facetious persons who call themselves the town," continues Davies, brought to the first night copies of the old ballad on which the jeweller's play was based, meaning to mock the new tragedy with the old song; but so forcible and pathetic were Lillo's scenes that these merry gentlemen were obliged "to throw away their ballads, and take out their handkerchiefs." More tears, we learn, were shed over this 'homespun drama' than at all the imitations of ancient fables by learned moderns. To Fielding this revolution, from the buskin'd heroics of the Alexanders and Clelias to the living and natural pathos of the tragedy of a poor London apprentice, must have appealed with extraordinary force; for it is the especial glory of his own genius that, throwing aside all the traditions of his age, and 'adventuring on one of the most original expeditions that ever a writer undertook,' [2] he was to discover a new world for English fiction, the world of simple human nature. That expedition must have been already forming in his mind when, night after night, in the hottest part of the year, *George Barnwell* was playing to crowded houses, and convincing the astonished audiences of 1731 that even so low a creature as a London apprentice was possessed of passions extremely like their own. Some ten years later, when Fielding revealed the first true sign of his own surpassing genius in the *History of the Adventures of Joseph Andrews*, he chose for his hero a country footman. The worthy City jeweller was, in his own limited measure, the forerunner, on the stage, of that new era in English literature created by honest Andrews and Parson Adams, Partridge and Mrs Slipslop, Fanny and Sergeant Atkinson, Towwouse and Mrs Miller, to name but a few of Fielding's immortal portraits, drawn from the 'vast authentic book of Nature.'

It is no wonder then, to return to Tom Davies, that a play by Lillo was announced on the bills of Fielding's theatre within a few months of the opening of his management. On May 27, 1736, the following advertisement appeared:

"Guilt its Own Punishment. Never Acted before. By Pasquin's
Company of Comedians. Being a True Story in Common Life and the
Incidents extremely affecting." By the Author of George Barnwell.

Davies' part in the play was a chief one, that of young Wilmot, and the story of the performance may be given in his own words. "Mr Fielding, who had a just sense of our author's merit, and who had often in his humourous pieces laughed at those ridiculous and absurd criticks who could not possibly understand the merit of Barnwell, because the subject was low, treated Lillo with great politeness and friendship. He took upon himself the management of the play and the instruction of the actors. It was during the rehearsal of the *Fatal Curiosity* that I had an opportunity to see and to converse with Mr Lillo. Plain and simple as he was in his address, his manner of conversing was modest affable and engaging. When invited to give his opinion how a particular sentiment should be uttered by the actor he expresst himself in the gentlest and most obliging terms, and conveyed instruction and conviction with good nature and good manners.... Fielding was not content merely to revise the 'Fatal Curiosity,' and to instruct the actors how to do justice to their parts. He warmly recommended the play to his friends and to the public. Besides all this he presented the author with a well written prologue."

This *Prologue*, which has apparently hitherto escaped the collectors of Fielding's *Works*, seems worthy of a reprint here, if only for its characteristic sympathy with virtue and distress 'in humble state,' and for the opening tribute to 'Shakespeare's nature' and to 'Fletcher's ease.'

PROLOGUE TO THE FATAL CURIOSITY

"The Tragic Muse has long forgot to please
With Shakespeare's nature or with Fletcher's ease:
No passion mov'd, thro' five long acts you sit,
Charm'd with the poet's language or his wit.
Fine things are said, no matter whence they fall;
Each single character must speak them all.

"But from this modern fashionable way
To-night our author begs your leave to stray.
No fustian hero rages here to-night,
No armies fall to fix a tyrant's right:
From lower life we draw our scenes' distress:
—Let not your equals move your pity less!
Virtue distrest in humble state support;
Nor think she never lives without the court.

"Tho' to our scenes no royal robes belong
And tho' our little stage as yet be young
Throw both your scorn and prejudice aside;
Let us with favour not contempt be try'd,
Thro' the first act a kind attention lend
The growing scene shall force you to attend:
Shall catch the eyes of every tender fair,
And make them charm their lovers with a tear.
The lover too by pity shall impart
His tender passion to his fair one's heart:
The breast which others' anguish cannot move
Was ne'er the seat of friendship or of love."

Notwithstanding all the manager's friendly efforts, the play met at first with very little success, a failure in Davies' opinion "owing in all probability to its being brought on in the latter part of the season, when the public had been satiated with a long run of *Pasquin*," but, he adds, "it is with pleasure I observe that Fielding generously persisted to serve the man whom he had once espoused; he tacked the 'Fatal Curiosity' to his Historical Register which was played with great success in the ensuing winter." [3] We owe no inconsiderable debt to Tom Davies in that he has preserved for us this picture of Fielding, actively engaged in the stage-management of his little theatre; a picture, moreover, that does equal honour to the brilliant wit, the successful political satirist, and to that modest, gentle Nonconformist poet, the man of whom it was said that he "had the spirit of an old Roman joined to the innocence of a Primitive Christian," George Lillo.

A few weeks before the production of Lillo's tragedy, and while *Pasquin* was still in the full tide of political success, an event occurred of closer import to Fielding's affectionate nature than all the applause of the Opposition and the town. This was the birth, in April, 1736, of his daughter Charlotte. No English writer has left more charming pictures of mother and child than those we owe to the tenderness and simplicity of Fielding's pen. When we find Squire Western turning, in his latter days, to Sophia's nursery, and hear him declaring that the prattling of his granddaughter is "sweeter Music than the finest Cry of Dogs in *England*" when we see Captain Booth stretched at full length on the floor of his poor lodgings, with his "little innocents" jumping over him, we are almost inclined to forgive alike the brutalities of the old foxhunter, and the weaknesses of the young soldier. Fielding's affection for his children, his apprehensions for their ultimate provision, his anxiety in their sickness, his grief at the loss of a little daughter, are manifest in his pages. If anything could exceed the satisfaction which the brilliant success of *Pasquin* must have given to his buoyant nature, it would be the birth of this, the first child apparently, of his marriage with the beautiful Charlotte Cradock. The entry in the registers of St Martin's in the Fields runs as follows: Baptized May 19th, 1736 Charlotte Fielding, of Henry and Charlotte, Born April 27th.

The dates of *Pasquin*, of Lillo's tragedy, and of the *Historical Register*, cover a considerable portion of the years 1736, 1737, and their production in a theatre under Fielding's own management practically presupposes his presence in London at that time. This by no means fits in with Murphy's implication that Fielding retired to Stour on his marriage, and that, remaining there, he ran through his "little patrimony," in "less than three years." A complete country retirement cannot be assigned to those busy years in the Haymarket; and in 1736 the journey from London to Dorsetshire was no trifling undertaking. But it seems quite possible that Fielding and his wife went down to their small estate in Dorsetshire for part or all of the summer, autumn and winter of both 1736 and 1737. This would cover the hunting months, and "hounds and horses," according to Murphy, filled a large part in Fielding's country life at Stour; the time would be that of the comparatively dull season for the theatre in the Haymarket; and, with the year immediately preceding *Pasquin*, we should thus, perhaps, account sufficiently for Murphy's "three years". Certain passages in the *Miscellanies*, published long after the pleasant meadows and the modest house at Stour—no less than the turmoil of the green-room and the crowded political audiences in the Haymarket—were things of the past, have a personal ring, reminiscent perhaps of such months of "sweet Retirement" in Dorsetshire. Thus one of the characters in the *Journey from this World to the next* recalls the change, from a life of "restless Anxieties," to a "little pleasant Country House, where there was nothing grand or superfluous, but everything neat and agreeable"; and how, after a little time, "I began to share the Tranquillity that visibly appeared in everything round me. I set myself to do Works of Fancy and to raise little Flower-Gardens, with many such innocent rural Amusements; which altho' they are not capable of affording any great Pleasure, yet they give that serene Turn of the Mind, which I think much preferable to anything else Human Nature is made susceptible of." To this pleasant picture of "rural Amusements," and tranquillity, it is surely not impertinent to add this further passage, as a possible echo of Charlotte Fielding's thought, well acquainted as she must have been both with the "sweetly winding banks of Stour" and with the clamorous successes of political drama: "in all these various Changes I never enjoyed any real Satisfaction, unless in the little time I lived retired in the Country free from all Noise and Hurry."

In the summer or autumn of 1737 the curtain was finally rung down on all the 'noise and hurry,' the achievements and audacities of Fielding's "little stage"; a few months later, and the country retirement at Stour had also become but a memory of that short life into which he managed to compress "more variety of Scenes than many People who live to be very old."

[1] *Life of Garrick.* T. Davies, vol. ii.

[2] *Works of Henry Fielding,* edited by Edmund Gosse. Introduction, p. xxix.

[3] *The Works of Mr George Lillo, with some Account of his Life,* T. Davies.

CHAPTER VI

BAR STUDENT. JOURNALIST

"the ... Covetous, the Prodigal, the Ambitious, the Voluptuous,
the Bully, the Vain, the Hypocrite, the Flatterer, the Slanderer,
call aloud   for the *Champion's* Vengeance."
—The *Champion*, Dec. 22, 1739.

There is no record of when or how Fielding disposed of his share in the management of the New Theatre in the Haymarket. But on June 21 1737, Walpole's Bill for regulating the stage received, as we have seen, the royal assent; and there can be no doubt that Sir Robert would at once apply his newly acquired powers to removing the dances of the fiddler, Mr Quiddam, and the drunken consolations of Mr Pillage, from the Haymarket boards, if indeed these gentlemen had not anticipated events by already removing themselves. We may safely assume that Henry Fielding's career as political dramatist came to an abrupt conclusion some time in the summer of 1737. [1]

It remains a matter for speculation why, after seven years spent in producing a stream of not unsuccessful social comedies and farces, leading up to a final and brilliant success in the field of political satiric drama, Fielding should have thrown up the stage as a whole, when suddenly debarred from those party onslaughts which had occupied but a fraction of his dramatic energies. The cause was not any lack of popularity. "The farces written by Mr Fielding," wrote Murphy in 1762, "were almost all of them very successful, and many of them are still acted every winter, with a continuance of approbation." And it is obvious that the fashionable vices and follies of the time afforded ample inducement to a satiric dramatist to continue 'laying about him,' even when Ministerial offences had been rendered inviolate by Act of Parliament. Neither was Fielding's sanguine temperament likely to be daunted by the single failure of his farce *Eurydice*, which had been damned at Drury Lane on February 19 of this same year: "disagreeable impressions," Murphy tells us, "never continued long upon his mind." The most satisfactory solution of the matter seems to be that now, in the approaching maturity of his powers, the 'Father of the English Novel' was becoming conscious that the true field for his genius lay in a hitherto unattempted form of imaginative narration, and not within the five acts of comedy or farce. The entirely original conceptions of a *Joseph Andrews* and a *Jonathan Wild* may already have begun to captivate the vigorous energies of his mind. We have his own word for assigning "some years" to the writing of *Tom Jones*; it is therefore not unreasonable to suppose that the conception of the first English "Comic Epic Poem in Prose" may date as far back as the summer of 1737.

Leaving surmise for fact, it is certain that this year marks the dividing line in Fielding's life.

Henceforth he ceases to be the witty, facile, popular dramatist; and he enters slowly on his birthright as the first in time, if not in genius, of English novelists. To this complete severance from the theatre belongs his own remark that "he left off writing for the stage when he ought to have begun." Arrived at a late maturity, and with accumulated stores of observation and insight,—"he saw the latent sources of human action," says Murphy—his genius happily turned into a channel carved, with splendid originality, for itself alone. After nine years of servitude to the limitations of dramatic construction, limitations he was wont to relieve, as his friend James Harris tells us, by "pleasantly though perhaps rather freely" *damning the man who invented fifth acts*, Fielding was now soon to discover his freedom in the spacious, hitherto unadventured, regions of prose fiction. But genius, especially genius with wife and child to support, cannot maintain life on inspiration alone; and, accordingly, the ex-dramatist now flung himself, with characteristic impetuosity and courage, into a struggle for independence at the Bar, perhaps the most arduous profession, under all the circumstances, that he could have chosen. For a reputation as the writer of eighteen comedies, and as the reckless political dramatist whose boisterous energies had set the town ringing with *Pasquin* and the *Register*, the fame in short of being the successful manager of *The Great Mogul's Company of Comedians*, was surely the last reputation in the world to bring a man briefs from cautious attorneys. And, with whatever hopes of political patronage, any temperament less buoyant might well have hesitated to embark on reading for the Bar at the age of thirty. But "by dificulties," says his earliest biographer, "his resolution was never subdued; on the contrary they only roused him to struggle through them with a peculiar spirit and magnanimity." So, within six months of the closing down of his little theatre under Walpole's irate hand, Fielding had formally entered himself as a student at the Middle Temple.

The entry in the books of that society runs as follows:—
[574 G] 1 Nov'ris. 1737.

Henricus Fielding, de East Stour in Com Dorset Ar, filius et haeres apparens Brig: Gen'lis: Edmundi Fielding admissus est in Societatem Medii Templi Lond specialiter at obligatur una cum &c.

Et dat pro fine 4. 0. 0.

Of the ensuing two and a half years of student life in the Temple we know practically nothing, beyond one vivacious picture of Harry Fielding's attack upon the law. "His application while a student in the Temple," writes Murphy, "was remarkably intense; and though it happened that the early taste he had taken of pleasure would occasionally return upon him, and conspire with his spirits and vivacity to carry him into the wild enjoyments of the town, yet it was particular in him that amidst all his dispositions nothing could suppress the thirst he had for knowledge, and the delight he felt in reading; and this prevailed in him to such a degree, that he has been frequently known by his intimates, to retire late at night from a tavern to his chambers, and there read and make extracts from the most abstruse authors, for several hours before he went to bed; so powerful were the vigour of his constitution and the activity of his mind."

One of the few pages of Fielding's autograph that have come down to us is presumably a relic of these student days. In the catalogue of the *Morrison Manuscripts* occurs this description of two undated pages in his hand: "List of offences against the King and his state immediately, which the Law terms High Treason. Offences against him in a general light as touching the Commonwealth at large, as Trade etc. Offences against him as supreme Magistrate etc." Were ever genius and wit more straitly or more honourably shackled than that of Henry Fielding, gallantly accepting such toil as this, toil moreover that must have weighed with double weight on a man who had spent nine years in the company of those charming if 'fickle jades' the Muses.

All efforts have failed to trace where Fielding and his wife and child (or children—the date of the birth of his daughter Harriet is not known) lived during these laborious months; but that money was needed in the summer following his entry at the Middle Temple may be inferred from the sale of the property at Stour. According to the legal note of this transaction, [2] "Henry ffeilding and Charlotte his wife" conveyed, in the Trinity Term of 1738, to one Thomas Hayter, for the sum of £260, "two messuages, two dove-houses, three gardens, three orchards, fifty acres of Land, eighty acres of meadow, one hundred and forty acres of pasture, ten acres of wood and common and pasture for all manner of cattle with the appurtenances in East Stour." It does not need a very active imagination to realise the keen regret with which Fielding must have parted with his gardens and orchards, his pastures, woods and commons. Sixty years ago the barn and one of the "dove-houses" had been but recently pulled down; and to this day the estate is still known as "Fielding's Farm." [3]

It has been stated, on what authority does not appear, that, after leaving Stour, Fielding went to Salisbury, and there bought a house, his solicitor being a Mr John Perm Tinney. Whatever be the fact as to the Salisbury residence, it is certain that a full year after the sale of the Dorsetshire property the Temple student was by no means at the end of his resources. For in the following letter [4] to Mr Nourse, the bookseller, dated July 1739, we find him requiring a London house at a rent of forty pounds and with a large "eating Parlour."

"Mr Nourse,

Disappointments have hitherto prevented my paying y'r Bill, which, I shall certainly do on my coming to Town which will be next Month. I desire the favour of y'u to look for a House for me near the Temple. I must have one large eating Parlour in it for the rest shall not be very nice.

Rent not upwards of £40 p. an: and as much cheaper as may be. I will take a Lease for Seven years. Yr Answer to this within a fortnight will much oblige. Y'r Humble Serv't

Henry Ffielding.

I have got Cro: Eliz. [5]

"July 9th 1739."

This note, written a year before Fielding's call to the Bar, suggests that his early married life was by no means spent in the "wretched garrett" of Lady Louisa Stuart's celebrated reminiscence.

In the September following the sale of his Dorsetshire estate Fielding had to regret the death of George Lillo, to whose success he had devoted so much personal care and energy, when staging Lillo's tragedy *Fatal Curiosity* on the boards of the little theatre in the Haymarket. The close relationship in intellectual sympathy between Lillo's talent and the genius of Fielding has already been noticed. But apart from this intellectual sympathy, the personal worth and charm of the good tradesman is noteworthy, as affording striking proof of the quality of man chosen by the 'wild Harry Fielding' for regard and friendship. And it should be remembered that in those days to bridge the social gulf between the kinsman of the Earl of Denbigh and a working jeweller, required courage as well as insight. Some time after Lillo's death a generous memorial notice of him appeared in Fielding's paper the *Champion*. The writer detects in his work "an Heart capable of exquisitely Feeling and Painting human Distresses, but of causing none"; and declares that his title to be called the best tragic poet of his age, "was the least of his Praise, he had the gentlest and honestest Manners, and, at the same Time, the most friendly and obliging. He had a perfect Knowledge of Human Nature, though his Contempt of all base Means of Application, which are the necessary Steps to great Acquaintance, restrained his Conversation within very narrow Bounds: He had the Spirit of an old *Roman*, joined to the Innocence of a primitive Christian; he was content with his little State of Life, in which his excellent Temper of Mind gave him an Happiness, beyond the Power of Riches, and it was necessary for his Friends to have a sharp Insight into his Want of their Services, as well as good Inclinations or Abilities to serve him. In short he was one of the best of Men, and those who knew him best will most regret his Loss." [6] In the excellent company of Henry Fielding's friends George Lillo may surely take his stand beside the 'good Lord Lyttelton,' the munificent and pious Allen, and not far from 'Parson Adams' himself.

No record has survived of Fielding's share in the political struggles of his party, during his first two years of "intense application" to the law. Walpole's power had been sensibly lessened by the death of the Queen, and he was losing the support of the country and even of the trading classes. The Prince of Wales, now openly hostile to the "great man," was the titular head of an Opposition numbering almost all the men of wit and genius in the kingdom. Lyttelton, Fielding's warmest friend, had become secretary to the Prince, and was recognised as a fluent leader of the Opposition in the House of Commons. Another friend, John Duke of Argyll, had joined the ranks of the Opposition in the Lords. On the whole the author of *Pasquin*, may well have hoped for a speedy fall of the "Colossos," with "its Brains of Lead, its Face of Brass, its Hands of Iron, its Heart of Adamant," and the accession to power of a party not without obligations to the fearless manager of the little theatre in the Haymarket. During these years the Opposition, even though supported by Pope and

Chesterfield, Thomson and Bolingbroke, could scarcely fail to utilise the trenchant scorn, the whole-hearted vigour, the boisterous humour, of Fielding's genius; and Murphy, speaking vaguely of Fielding's legal years, says that a "large number of fugitive political tracts, which had their value when the incidents were actually passing on the great scene of business, came from his pen." It is not however till November 1739, two years and a half after the pillorying of Walpole on the Haymarket boards, that Fielding is again clearly seen, 'laying about' him, in those clamourous eighteenth-century politics.

His choice of a new weapon of attack is foreshadowed in the noble concluding words of the *Introduction* to the *Historical Register*; words written on the very eve of the Ministerial Bill gagging that and all other political plays: "If nature hath given me any talents at ridiculing vice and imposture, I shall not be indolent, nor afraid of exerting them, while the liberty of the press and stage subsists, that is to say while we have any liberty left among us." A few weeks after these words were published the liberty of the stage was triumphantly stifled by Walpole's Licensing Bill. But even "old Bob" himself dared not lay his hand on the liberty of the British Press; and so we find Mr Pasquin reappearing under the guise, or in the company, of the *Champion and Censor of Great Britain*, otherwise one *Captain Hercules Vinegar*, a truculent avenger of wrong and exponent of virtue, in whose fictitious name a political, literary, and didactic newspaper entered the field of party politics on November 15, 1739. The paper, under the title of the *Champion*, was issued three times a week, and consisted of one leading article, an anti-Ministerial summary of news, and literary notices of new books. The first number announced that the author and owner was the said Captain Hercules Vinegar, and that the Captain would be aided in various departments by members of his family. Thus the Captain's wife, Mrs Joan Vinegar, a matron of a very loquacious temper, was to undertake the ladies' column, and his son Jack was to have "an Eye over the gay Part of the Town." The criticism was to be conducted by Mr Nol Vinegar who was reported to have spent one whole year in examining the use of a single word in Horace. And the politics were to be dealt forth by the Captain's father, a gentleman intimately versed in kingdoms, potentates and Ministers, and of so close a disposition that he "seldom opens his Mouth, unless it be to take in his Food, or puff out the Smoke of his Tobacco."

The paper bore no signed articles; but judging from an attack levelled against it in a pamphlet of the following year, [7] Fielding and his former not very worshipful partner in the Haymarket management, James Ralph, were the reputed "authors," Ralph being in a subordinate position. Thus, it is stated that Ralph, "is now say'd to be the 'Squire of the *British* CHAMPION"; the writer identifies *Captain Vinegar* and the author of *Pasquin* as one and the same person; he describes Pasquin and Ralph as the "Authors of the Champion"; he asserts that the old Roman statues of Pasquin and Marfario, "are now dignified and distinguished (by The CHAMPION and his doughty Squire RALPH), under the Names [*sic*] of Captain Hercules Vinegar."; he prints an address to the "*Self-dubb'd Captain* Hercules Vinegar," and his "Man *Ralph*"; and appends some doggerel verse entitled "Vinegar and his gang." But from all this nothing definite emerges as to the precise part taken by Fielding in the authorship of the *Champion*. The pamphleteer accredits a fragment of a paper signed C. to the *Captain*, and attributes two papers, [8] signed C. and L., to "Mr Pasquin"—*i.e.* Fielding; and as the reprint of the *Champion*, which appeared in 1741, announces that all papers so signed are the "Work of one Hand," there is so much external proof that all such pages in these volumes (numbering some sixty essays) are by Fielding. Dr Nathan Drake, writing in 1809, more than sixty years after the appearance of the paper, asserts, without stating his reasons, that the numbers marked "C." and "L." "were the work of Fielding." This view is further supported by the opinion of Mr Austin Dobson, that many of the papers signed *C.* "are unmistakably Fielding's."

On the other hand Murphy, writing only twenty-two years after the appearance of the paper, but often with gross inaccuracy, states that the *Champion* "owed its chief support to his [Fielding's] abilities," but that "his essays in that collection cannot now be so ascertained as to perpetuate them in this edition of his works." Boswell refers to Fielding as possessing a "share" in the paper. A manuscript copy of some of the Minutes of meetings of the *Champion* partners, written out in an eighteenth-century handwriting, and now in the possession of the present writer, confirms Boswell's note, in as far as an entry therein records that "Henry Fielding Esq. did originally possess Two Sixteenth Shares of the Champion as a Writer in the said paper." One of the lists of the partners of the *Champion* which occur in the same manuscript, is headed by the name of "Mr Fielding." Finally, a contemporary satirical print shows Fielding with his "length of nose and chin" and his tall figure, acting as standard-bearer of the *Champion*; the paper being represented in its political capacity of a leading Opposition organ. There is, moreover, the internal evidence of style and sentiment. Thus the matter rests; and although it is exceedingly tempting to use the *Champion* for inferences as to the manner in which Fielding approached his new craft of journalism, and as to his attitude on the many subjects, theological, social, political and personal, handled in these essays, the evidence seems hardly sufficient to warrant such deductions. It does, however, seem clear, taking as evidence the shilling pamphlet already mentioned,[9] that Harry Fielding, the intrepid and audacious Mr Pasquin of 1736-7 reappeared, laying about him with his ever ready cudgel now raised to the dignity of a miraculous Hercules club, as the *Champion* of 1739-41. To all lovers of good cudgelling, whether laid on the shoulders of the incorrigible old cynic Sir Robert, or on those of the egregious Colley Cibber, or falling on the follies and abuses of the day, the "Pasquinades and Vinegarades" of *Captain Hercules Vinegar*, and his "doughty Squire Ralph," may be commended. And no fault can be found with the *Captain's* declaration, when establishing a Court of Judicature for the trial and punishment of sundry offenders in his pages, that "whatever is wicked, hateful, absurd, or ridiculous, must be exposed and punished, before this Nation is brought to that Height of Purity and good Manners to which I wish to see it exalted." [10]

One personal sketch of Fielding himself deserves quotation, whether drawn by his own hand or that of another. The *Champion* for May 24, 1740, contains a vision of the Infernal Regions, where Charon, the ghostly boatman, is busy ferrying souls across the River Styx. The ferryman bids his attendant Mercury see that all his passengers embark carrying nothing with them; and the narrator describes how, after various Shades had qualified for their passage, "A tall Man came next, who stripp'd off an old Grey Coat with great Readiness, but as he was stepping into the Boat, *Mercury* demanded half his Chin, which he utterly refused to comply with, insisting on it that it was all his own." Fielding's length of chin and nose was well known; and not less familiar, doubtless, was the 'old Grey Coat,' among the purlieus of the Temple.

The beginning of the year 1740, when the lusty *Champion* and his cudgel were well established, and *Captain Hercules'* private legal studies were drawing to a close, was marked by a fresh outburst of the old feud with Colley Cibber. Cibber, already notorious as actor, dramatist, manager, the Poet Laureat of "preposterous Odes," and the 'poetical Tailor' who would even cut down Shakespeare himself, now appeared in the character of historian and biographer, publishing early in 1740 the famous *Apology for the Life of Mr Colley Cibber, Comedian, and late Patentee of the Theatre Royal. With an Historical View of the Stage during his Own Time.*

Cibber, soon to be scornfully chosen by Pope as dunce-hero of the *Dunciad*, had, for the past six years, been pilloried by Fielding; and, not unmindful of these onslaughts, he inserted in his new work a virulent attack on the late manager of the New Theatre in the Haymarket. The tenor of *Pasquin* was here grossly misrepresented. Fielding was described as being, at the time of entering on his management, "a Broken Wit"; he was accused of using the basest dramatic means of profit, since "he was in haste to get money"; and the final insult was added by Cibber's stroke of referring to his enemy anonymously, as one whom "I do not chuse to name."

Looking back across two centuries on to the supreme figures of Pope and Fielding, it is matter for some wonder that these giants of the intellect should have greatly troubled to annihilate a Colley Cibber. A finer villain, it seems to us, might have been chosen by Pope for the six hundred lines of his *Dunciad* a worthier target might have drawn the arrows of Fielding's *Champion*. But Cibber possessed at least the art of arousing notable enmities; and the four slashing papers in which the *Champion* [11] promptly parried the scurrilities of the *Apology* still make pretty reading for those who are curious in the annals of literary warfare. It is noteworthy that these *Champion* retorts are honourably free from the personalities of an age incredibly gross in the use of personal invective. Fielding's journal, even under the stinging provocation of the insults of the *Apology*, was still true to the standard set in the *Prologue* of his first boyish play

'No private character these scenes expose.'

It is Cibber's ignorance of grammar, his murder of the English tongue, his inflated literary conceit, rather than his 'private character' that are here exposed.

Some time during the latter half of 1740 the whole feud between Cibber, Pope, Fielding and Ralph was reprinted in the shilling pamphlet, already referred to, entitled *The Tryal of Colley Cibber.* The collection concludes as follows:

"ADVERTISEMENT

"If the Ingenious *Henry Fielding* Esq.; (Son of the Hon.
Lieut. General *Fielding,* who upon his Return from his
Travels entered Himself of the *Temple* in order to study
the Law, and married one of the pretty Miss *Cradocks* of
Salisbury) will *own* himself the AUTHOR of 18
strange Things called Tragical *Comedies* and Comical
Tragedies, lately advertised by *J. Watts,* of
Wild-Court, Printer, he shall be *mentioned* in
Capitals in the *Third* edition of Mr CIBBER'S *Life,*
and likewise be placed *among* the *Poetae minores*
Dramatici of the Present Age; then will both his *Name and*
Writings be remembered on Record in the immortal *Poetical*
Register written by Mr Giles Jacob."

The whole production affords a lively example of the full-blooded pamphleteering of 1740; and throws valuable light on Fielding's repute as the *Champion.*

As regards Ralph's collaboration with Fielding at this period (a collaboration further affirmed by Dr Nathan Drake's assertion, written in 1809, that James Ralph was Fielding's chief coadjutor in that paper) it may be recalled that ten years previously this not very reputable American had provided a prologue for Fielding's early play, the *Temple Beau;* and that he appears again as Fielding's partner in the management of the Little Theatre in the Haymarket. Gradually relinquishing his theatrical ambitions, Ralph appears to have turned his talents to political journalism, and according to Tom Davies was becoming formidable as a party writer for the Opposition in these last years of Walpole's administration. Boswell tells us that Ralph ultimately succeeded Fielding in his share of the *Champion;* [12] but we have no definite knowledge of what precise part was taken by him in the earlier numbers. No continued trace occurs of his collaboration with Fielding; and indeed it is difficult to conceive any permanent alliance between Fielding's manly, independent, and generous nature, and the sordid and selfish character, and mediocre talents of James Ralph.

[1] The fullest newspaper for theatrical notices at this date, preserved in the British Museum, the *London Daily Post,* is unfortunately missing for this year.

[2] Now first printed, from documents at the Record Office.

[3] A table inscribed by a former owner as having belonged to Henry Fielding, Esq., novelist, is now in the possession of the Somersetshire Archaeological Society. The inscription adds that Fielding "hunted from East Stour Farm in 1718." He would then be eleven years old!

[4] From the hitherto unpublished original, in the library of Alfred Huth, Esq.

[5] "Cro: Eliz." is the legal abbreviation for Justice Croke's law reports for the reign of Elizabeth.

[6] *Champion*, February 26, 1740.

[7] *The Tryal of Colley Cibber, Comedian etc.* 1740.

[8] Those of April 22, and April 29, 1740.

[9] And see *Daily Gazeteer*, Oct. 9, 1740.

[10] *Champion*, December 22, 1739.

[11] For April 22, April 29, May 6, and May 17.

[12] Boswell's *Johnson*, edited by Birkbeck Hill. Vol. i. p. 169. n. 2: "Ralph ... as appears from the minutes of the partners of the *Champion* in the possession of Mr Reed of Staple Inn, succeeded Fielding in his share of the paper before the date of that eulogium [1744]."

CHAPTER VII

"COUNSELLOR FIELDING"

"Wit is generally observed to love to reside in empty pockets." *Joseph Andrews.*

The last retort on Colley Cibber had scarcely been launched from the columns of the *Champion*, when that intrepid 'Censor of Great Britain' and indefatigable law student, *Captain Hercules Vinegar*, attained the full dignities of a barrister of the Middle Temple. On June 20, 1740, Fielding was called to the Bar; and on the same day the Benchers of his Inn assigned to him chambers at No. 4 Pump Court, "up three pair of stairs." This assignment, according to the wording of the Temple records, was "for the term of his natural life." These chambers may still be seen, with their low ceilings and panelled walls, very much to all appearance as when tenanted by Harry Fielding. The windows of the sitting-room and bedroom look out on to the beautiful old buildings of Brick Court, and from the head of the staircase one looks across to the stately gilded sundial of Pump Court, old even in Fielding's day, with its warning motto:

"Shadows we are and like shadows depart."

Here, in these lofty chambers, up their "three pair" of worn and narrow stairs, Fielding donned his barrister's gown, and waited for briefs; and, possessing as he did an imagination "fond of seizing every gay prospect," and natural spirits that gave him, as his cousin Lady Mary tells us, cheerfulness in a garret, this summer of 1740 must have been full of sanguine hopes. He was now thirty-three, and his splendid physique had not yet become shattered by gout. He had gained, Murphy observes, no inconsiderable reputation by the *Champion*; his position as a brilliant political playwright had been long ago assured by *Pasquin*; the party to whose patriotic interests he had devoted so much energy and wit was now rapidly approaching power; and two years of eager application had equipped him with 'no incompetent share of learning' for a profession in which, we are told, he aspired to eminence. The swift disappointment of these brave hopes, the fast coming years of sickness, distress, and grief endow the old chambers with something of tragedy; but in June, 1740, the shadows were still but a sententious word on the dial.

There is practically no surviving record of Fielding's activity as a barrister. From Murphy we learn that his pursuit of the law was hampered by want of means; and that, moreover, even his indomitable energies were soon often forced to yield to disabling attacks of illness. So long as his health permitted him he "attended with punctual assiduity" on the Western circuit, and in term time at Westminster Hall. But gout rapidly "began to make such assaults upon him as rendered it impossible for him to be as constant at the bar as the laboriousness of his profession required," and he could only follow the law in intervals of health. Under such "severities of pain and want" he yet made efforts for success; and the tribute rendered by his first biographer to the courage of those efforts deserves quotation in full: "It will serve to give us an idea of the great force of his mind, if we consider him pursuing so arduous a study under the exigencies of family distress, with a wife and children, whom he tenderly loved, looking up to him for subsistence, with a body lacerated by the acutest pains, and with a mind distracted by a thousand avocations and obliged for immediate supply to produce almost extempore a farce, a pamphlet, or a newspaper." Murphy's careless pen seems here to confuse the student years with those of assiduous effort at the Bar; and the extempore farces are, judging by the dates of Fielding's collected plays, no more than a rhetorical flourish: but there seems no reason to doubt the essential truth of this picture of the vigorous struggles of the sanguine, witty, and not unlearned barrister, ambitious of distinction, and always sensitively anxious as to the maintenance of his wife and children. We may see him attending the Western circuit in March and again in August, riding from Winchester to Salisbury, thence to Dorchester and Exeter, and on to Launceston, Taunton, Bodmin, Wells or Bristol as the case might be; constant in his appearance at Westminster; and supplementing his briefs by political pamphlets written in the service of an Opposition supported by the intellect and integrity of the day.

It is inexplicable that no records, in the letters or diaries of his brother lawyers, should have come down to us of circuits, enlivened by the wit of Harry Fielding; that practically all traces of his professional work should be lost; and that concerning the many friendships which he is recorded to have made at the Bar we should know practically nothing beyond his own cordial acknowledgment of the lawyers' response, three years after his call, to the subscription for the *Miscellanies*. In the preface to those volumes he writes: "I cannot however forbear mentioning my sense of the Friendship shown me by a Profession of which I am a late and unworthy Member, and from whose Assistance I derive more than half the Names which appear to this subscription." All that we have to add to this, is the unconscious humour of Murphy's observation that the friendships Fielding met with "in the course of his studies, and indeed through the remainder of his life from the gentlemen of the legal profession in general, and particularly from some who have since risen to be the first ornaments of the law, will ever do honour to his memory." Had the names of these worthy 'ornaments' been preserved, posterity could now give them due recognition as having been honoured by the friendship of Henry Fielding. [1]

Fielding in his habit, as he lived, is for ever eluding us. His tall figure vanishes behind the prolific playwright, the exuberant politician, the truculent journalist, the indefatigable magistrate, the great creative genius. But at no point does the wittiest man of his day, and a lawyer of some repute—'Mr Fielding is allowed to have acquired a respectable share of jurisprudence'—escape us so completely as during these years of 'punctual assiduity' at the Bar. His very domicile is unknown, after the surrender of those pleasant chambers in Pump Court, on November 28 1740.

The political activities of "Counsellor Fielding" stand out far more clearly than do the legal labours of these years of struggle at the Bar. The year of his call, 1740, was one of constant embarrassment for Sir Robert Walpole, whose long enjoyment of single power was now at last drawing to a miserable close. The conduct of the Spanish War was arraigned, and suggestions were made that the Government were in secret alliance with the enemy. When the news came, in March, that Walpole's parliamentary opponent, the bluff Admiral Vernon, had captured Porto Bello from Spain, with six ships only, the public rejoicing and votes of congratulation were so many attacks on the peace-at-any-price Minister. A powerful fleet, designed against Spain, lay inactive in Torbay the greater part of the summer, through (alleged) contrary winds. And when Parliament met in November 1740, an onslaught by the Duke of Argyll in the Lords paved the way for the celebrated attack on Sir Robert in the Commons, known as "The Motion" of February 13, 1741. A fine political cartoon published in the following month, and here reproduced, in which Walpole appears as mocking at the death and burial of this same "Motion" of censure (which the House had rejected), places Fielding in the forefront of the Opposition procession. The dead "Motion" is being carried to the "Opposition" family vault, already occupied by Jack Cade and other "reformers"; and the bier is preceded by five standard-bearers, sadly carrying the insignia of the party's papers. Among these, and second only to the famous *Craftsman*, comes Fielding's tall figure, bearing aloft a standard inscribed *The Champion*, and emblazoned with that terrible club of *Captain Hercules Vinegar*, which, we may recall, was always ready to "fall on any knave in company." Behind the bier hobbles, clearly, the old Duchess of Marlborough; and Walpole's fat figure stands in the foreground, laughing uproariously at this "Funeral of Faction." In the doggerel verses beneath this cartoon, it is very plainly hinted that "old Sarah," and the Opposition, were in league with the Stewarts. In this historic debate, for which members secured seats at six o'clock in the morning, the vote of censure on "the *one person*" arraigned was defeated, Sir Robert once again securing a majority, and so "the Motion" as the cartoonist depicts, died "of a Disappointment." Another cartoon commemorating this ill-fated effort is instructive as showing, again in the foreground of the fight, a figure wearing a barrister's wig, gown, and bands, and inscribed with the words *Pasquin* and *The Champion*. The Opposition Leader, Pulteney, leads both the *Pasquin* figure, and another representing the paper *Common Sense*, literally by the nose with the one hand, while with the other he neatly catches, on his drawn sword, Walpole's organ the *Gazetteer*. In doggerel verses attached to the print Fielding is complimented with the following entire verse to himself:—

"Then the Champion of the Age,
Being Witty, wise, and Sage,
Comes with Libells on the Stage."

This *Pasquin* figure has none of the personal characteristics of Fielding, neither his "length of nose" nor his stately stature, so well suggested in the former print; but, lay figure though it be, it symbolises no less clearly the prominent part he played in these final political struggles of 1741. Also the lawyer's dress with which Fielding is here signified is noteworthy; and similar acknowledgment of his new dignities may be seen in the reference (in a copy of Walpole's *Gazetteer* for 1740) to the attacks levelled on Sir Robert by "Captain Vinegar—*i.e.* Counsellor F—d—g."

These popular indications of Fielding's activity in the fighting ranks of the Opposition, during this last year of Walpole's domination, are supplemented by the evidence of his own pen. As early as January 1741, and while the grand Parliamentary attack of the 13th of February was but brewing, he published an eighteenpenny pamphlet, in verse, satirising Sir Robert's lukewarm conduct of the war with Spain. To the title of *The Vernoniad*, there was added a lengthy mock-title in Greek, the whole being presented as a lost fragment by Homer, describing, in epic style, the mission of one "Mammon" sent by Satan to baffle the fleets of a nation engaged in war with *Iberia*. "Mammon" is a perfectly obvious satirical sketch of Walpole himself, in the execution of which the hand that had drawn the corrupt fiddler "Mr Quidam" and the tipsy "Mr Pillage" for the Haymarket stage, has in no wise lost its cunning. "Mammon" (Walpole was reputed to have amassed much wealth) hides his palace walls by heaps of "ill-got Pictures." The pictures collected at Houghton, the Minister's pretentious Norfolk seat, were famous; and the notes to the "Text" are careful to depict, in illustration, "some rich Man without the least Taste having purchased a Picture at an immense Price, lifting up his eyes to it with Wonder and Astonishment, without being able to discover wherein its true Merit lies." "Mammon" declares virtue to be but a name, and his wonted eloquence is bribery. Sir Robert asserted that every man has his price. "Mammon" preserves dulness and ignorance, "while Wit and Learning starve." Walpole's illiterate tastes were notorious. At the close of the poem, "Mammon" accomplishes the behest of his master, Satan, by bribing contrary winds to drive back the English ships (a satire on Walpole's conduct of the war); and he finally returns to hell, and "in his Palace keeps a *three Weeks'* Feast." Sir Robert it may be noted usually entertained for three weeks, in the spring, at Houghton. The whole is a slashing example of the robust eighteenth-century political warfare, polished by constant classical allusions and quotations; and doubtless it was read with delight in the coffee houses of the Town in that critical winter of 1740-1741. Two characteristic allusions must not be omitted. Even in the heat of party hard hitting Fielding finds time for a thrust at Colley Cibber, whose prose it seems was in several places by no means to be comprehended till "explained by the *Herculean* Labours of Captain *Vinegar*" And there is a pleasant reference to "my friend Hogarth the exactest Copier of Nature."

In this first month of 1741, Fielding published yet another poetical pamphlet for his party, but of a less truculent energy. *True Greatness* is a poem inscribed to a recruit in the Opposition ranks, the celebrated George Bubb Dodington; and when the eulogiums offered by the poet to his political leaders, Argyll, Carteret, Chesterfield, and Lyttelton, to all of whom are ascribed that "True Greatness" which "lives but in the Noble Mind," are completed by a description of

Dodington as irradiating a blaze of virtues, this particular pamphlet becomes somewhat rueful reading. For Dodington was, if report speaks true, a pliant politician as well as an ineffable coxcomb, although it must be admitted that he won eulogies and compliments alike from the perfect integrity of Lyttelton, and the honourable pen of James Thomson. Even Fielding's glowing lines do not outstrip Thomson's panegyric in *The Seasons.*

A more enduring interest however than the merits or demerits of a Dodington, lies in this shilling pamphlet. In it is clearly foreshadowed Fielding's great ironic outburst on false greatness, given to the world a few years later in the form of the history of that Napoleon in villany, the "great" Mr Jonathan Wild. In the medium of stiff couplets (verse being "a branch of Writing" which Fielding admits "I very little pretend to") the subject-matter of the magnificent irony of *Jonathan Wild* is already sketched. Here the spurious "greatness" of inhuman conquerors, of droning pedants, of paltry beaus, of hermits proud of their humility, is mercilessly laid bare; and something is disclosed of the "piercing discernment" of that genius which, Murphy tell us, "saw the latent sources of human actions."

We have seen indications in Murphy's careless pages that these few years of Fielding's assiduous efforts at the Bar were years burdened by "severities of want and pain." It is difficult not to admit a reference to some such personal experiences in a passage in this same poem. The lines in question describe the Poet going hungry and thirsty

"As down Cheapside he meditates the Song"....

a "great tatter'd Bard," treading cautiously through the streets lest he meet a bailiff, oppressed with "want and with contempt," his very liberty to "wholesome Air" taken from him, yet possessing the greatness of mind that no circumstances can touch, and the power to bestow a fame that shall outlive the gifts of kings. This latter claim foreshadows the magnificent apostrophe in *Tom Jones* on that unconquerable force of genius, able to confer immortality both on the poet, and the poet's theme. Was the 'great tatter'd Bard,' cautiously treading the streets, little esteemed, and yet the conscious possessor of true greatness (did not the author of *Tom Jones* rely with confidence on receiving honour from generations yet unborn), none other than the tall figure of Fielding himself? At least we know that soon after this year he writes of having lately suffered accidents and waded through distresses, sufficient to move the pity of his readers, were he "fond enough of Tragedy" to make himself "the Hero of one."

One of the rare fragments of Fielding's autograph, [2] refers both to this pamphlet, and to the *Vernoniad*:

"Mr Nourse,

"Please to deliver Mr Chappell 50 of [crossed out: my] [*sic*] True Greatness and 50 of the Vernoniad.

Y'rs

"Hen. Ffielding.

"*April* 20 1741."

In June of this year occurred the death of General Edmund Fielding, briefly noticed in the *London Magazine* as that of an officer who "had served in the late Wars against *France* with much Bravery and Reputation." The General's own struggles to support his large family probably prevented his death affecting the circumstances of his eldest son. In the same month Fielding appears as attending a "Meeting of the Partners in the Champion," held at the Feathers Tavern, on June 29. The list of the partners present at the Feathers is given as follows:—[3]

Present

Mr Fielding
Mr Nourse
Mr Hodges
Mr Chappelle
Mr Cogan
Mr Gilliver
Mr Chandler

The business recorded was the sale of the "Impressions of the Champion in two Vollumes, 12'o, No. 1000." The impression was put up to the Company by auction, and was knocked down to Mr Henry Chappelle for £110, to be paid to the partners. The majority of the partners are declared by the Minutes to have confirmed the bargain; the minority, as appears from the list of signatures, being strictly that of one, Henry Fielding. After this dissension Fielding's name ceases to appear at the *Champion* meetings; and as he himself states that he left off writing for the paper from this very month the evidence certainly points to a withdrawal on his part in June 1741 from both the literary and the business management of the paper. The edition referred to in the Minutes is doubtless that advertised in the *London Daily Post* a few days before the meeting of the partners, as a publication of the *Champion* "in two neat Pocket Volumes." [4]

Meanwhile the whole force of the Opposition was thrown into the battle of a General Election; and it is interesting to note that Pitt stood for the seat for Fielding's boyish home, and the home of his wife, that of Old Sarum. The elections went largely against Walpole, and by the end of June defeat was prophesied for a Minister who would only be supported by a majority of sixteen.

It is somewhat inexplicable that at this, the very moment of the approaching victory of his party Fielding appears to have withdrawn from all journalistic work. "I take this Opportunity to declare in the most solemn Manner," he writes, in after years, "I have long since (as long as from *June* 1741) desisted from writing one Syllable in the *Champion*, or any other public Paper." And yet more unexpected is the fact that six months later, during the last weeks of Walpole's failing power, a rumour should be abroad that Fielding was assisting his old enemy. In one of his rare references to his private life, that in the Preface to the *Miscellanies*, he seeks to clear himself from unjust censures "as well on account of what I have not writ, as for what I have"; and, as an instance of such baseless aspersions, he relates that, in this winter of 1741, "I received a letter from a Friend, desiring me to vindicate myself from two very opposite Reflections, which two opposite Parties thought fit to cast on me, *viz.* the one of writing in the *Champion* (tho' I had not then writ in it for upwards of half a year) the other, of writing in the Gazetteer, in which I never had the honour of inserting a single Word." What can have occurred, in the bewildering turmoil of that eighteenth-century party strife, that the author of *Pasquin*, the possessor of "Captain Vinegar's" Herculean Club, should have to vindicate himself from a charge of writing in the columns of Walpole's *Gazetteer.* During these last months of Sir Robert's power his Cabinet was much divided, and two of his Ministers were in active revolt; possibly rumour assigned the services of the witty pen of Counsellor Fielding to these Opposition Ministerialists. But that some change did indeed take place in Fielding's political activities, in these last six months of 1741 is obvious from his withdrawal from writing in any "Public" paper; and from passages in the last political pamphlet known to have come from his pen. This pamphlet, entitled *The Opposition. A Vision,* was published in the winter of 1741, a winter of severe illness, and of "other circumstances" which, as he tells us, "served as very proper Decorations" to the sickbeds of himself, his wife, and child. It is a lively attack on the divided councils and leaders of the Opposition, thrown into the form of a dream, caused by the author's falling asleep over "a large quarto Book intituled 'An apology for the Life of Mr Colley Gibber, Comedian.'" In his dream Fielding meets the Opposition, in the form of a waggon, drawn by very ill-matched asses, the several drivers of which have lost their way. The luggage includes the Motion for 1741, and a trunk containing the *Champion* newspaper. One passenger protests that he has been hugely spattered by the "Dirt" of the "last Motion," and that he will get out, rather than drive through more dirt. A gentleman of "a meagre aspect" (is he the lean Lyttelton?) leaves the waggon; and another observes that the asses "appear to me to be the worst fed Asses I ever beheld ... that long sided Ass they call *Vinegar,* which the Drivers call upon so often to *gee up,* and *pull lustily,* I never saw an Ass with a worse Mane, or a more shagged Coat; and that grave Ass yoked to him, which they name *Ralph,* and who pulls and brays like the Devil, Sir, he does not seem to have eat since the hard Frost. [5] Surely, considering the wretched Work they are employed in, they deserve better Meat."

The longsided ass, Vinegar, with the worst of manes and the most shagged coat, short even of provender, recalls the picture, drawn twelve months previously, of the great hungry tatter'd Bard; and the inference seems fair enough that for Fielding politics were no lucrative trade. A more creditable inference, in those days of universal corruption, it may be added, would be hard to find. The honour of a successful party writer who yet remained poor in the year 1741, must have been kept scrupulously clean. The *Vision* proceeds to show the waggon, with two new sets of asses from Cornwall and Scotland (the elections had gone heavily against Walpole in both these districts), suddenly turning aside from the "Great Country Road" (the Opposition was known as the

Country Party); and the protesting passengers are told that the end of their journey is "St James." Some of the asses, flinching, are "well whipt"; but the waggon leaves the dreamer and many of its followers far behind. Suddenly a Fat Gentleman's coach stops the way. The drivers threaten to drive over the coach, when one of the asses protests that the waggon is leaving the service of the country, and going aside on its own ends, and that "the Honesty of even an Ass would start" at being used for some purposes. The waggon is all in revolt and confusion, when the Fat Gentleman, who appeared to have "one of the pleasantest and best natured Countenances I ever beheld," at last had the asses unharness'd, and turned into a delicious meadow, where they fell to feeding, as after "long Abstinence." Finally, the pleasant-faced fat gentleman's coach proceeds on the way from which the waggon had deviated, carrying with it some of the former drivers of the same; the mob burn the derelict obstructing vehicle; and their noise, and the stink and smoke of the conflagration wake the dreamer.

In this last word of Fielding's active political career (for his later anti-Jacobite papers are concerned rather with Constitutional and Protestant, than with party strife), a retirement from political collar-work is certainly signified. His reasons for such a step escape us in the mist of those confused and heated conflicts. His detestation of Walpole's characteristic methods may very well have roused his ever ready fighting instincts, whereas, once Walpole's fall was practically assured the weak forces of the Opposition (William Pitt being yet many years from power) could have availed but little to enlist his penetrating intellect. And he may by now have found that politics afforded, in those days, but scanty support to an honourable pen.

But supposition, in lack of further evidence, is fruitless; all that we can clearly perceive is that this winter of sickness and distress marks a final severance from party politics. The hungry 'hackney writer' of the lean sides and shagged coat, if not, indeed, turned to graze in the fat meadow of his dream, was at last freed from an occupation that could but shackle the genius now ready to break forth in the publication of *Joseph Andrews*.

[1] A tantalising reference to one such acquaintance occurs in Lord Campbell's *Lives of the Chancellors*. Vol. v. p. 357. In notes made by Lord Camden's nephew, George Hardinge, for a proposed Life of the Lord Chancellor there is this entry: "formed an acquaintance ... with Henry Fielding ... called to the Bar."

[2] Now in the possession of W. K. Bixby, Esq., of St Louis, U.S.A.

[3] In a manuscript copy of the Minutes, in the possession of the present writer.

[4] *London Daily Post*, June 18-26, 1741.

[5] The hard frost would be the terrible preceding winter of 1739-40, a winter long remembered for the severity of the cold, the cost of provisions, and the suffering of the poor.

CHAPTER VIII

JOSEPH ANDREWS

"This kind of writing I do not remember to have seen hitherto
attempted in our language."
Preface to *Joseph Andrews*.

On the 2nd of February 1742 Sir Robert Walpole, the 'Colossos' of popular broadsides, under whose feet England had lain for exactly thirty years, received his final defeat; and the intrepid wit, who for the past eight years had heartily lashed the tyrannies and corruptions of that 'Great Man,' enjoyed at last the satisfaction of witnessing the downfall of the *Mr Quiddam* and *Mr Pillage* of his plays, of the *Plunderer* and *Mammon* of his pamphlets, of the *Brass* on whom many a stinging blow had fallen in the columns of his *Champion*.

With the retirement of Walpole, Fielding's vigorous figure vanishes from active political service. No more caustic Greek epics, translated from the original "by Homer," no more boisterous interludes with three-bottle Prime Ministers appearing in the part of principal boy, come from his pen. But scarcely is the ink dry on the page of his last known political pamphlet, when Fielding reappears, in this Spring of 1742, not as the ephemeral politician, but as the triumphant discoverer of a new continent for English literature; as the leader of a revolution in imaginative writing which has outlived the Ministries and parties, the reforms, the broils, and warfares of two centuries. For, to-day, the fierce old contests of Whig and Tory, the far-off horrors of eighteenth-century gibbets, jails, and streets, the succession of this and that Minister, the French Wars and Pragmatic Sanctions of 1740 are all dead as Queen Anne. But the novel based on character, on human life, in a word on 'the vast authentic Book of Nature' is a living power; and it was by the publication, in February 1742, of *The Adventures of Mr Joseph Andrews and his Friend Mr Abraham Adams*, that Fielding reveals himself as the father of the English novel. Henceforth we can almost forget the hard-hitting political *Champion*; we may quite forget the facile 'hackney writer' of popular farces, and the impetuous studies of the would-be barrister. With the appearance of these two small volumes Henry Fielding reaches the full stature of his genius as the first, and perhaps the greatest, of English novelists.

It is difficult, at the present day, to realise the greatness of his achievement. Fielding found, posturing as heroines of romance, the *Clelias, Cleopatras, Astraeas*; he left the living women, Fanny Andrews, Sophia Western, Amelia Booth. "Amelia," writes his great follower Thackeray, "... the most charming character in English fiction,—Fiction! Why fiction? Why not history? I know Amelia just as well as Lady Mary Wortley Montagu." Again, Fielding found a world of polite letters, turning a stiff back on all "low" naturalness of life. He taught that world (as his friend Lillo had already essayed to do in his tragedy of a *London Merchant*) that the life of a humble footman, of a poor parson in a torn cassock, of the poverty-hunted wife of an impoverished army-captain, of a country lad without known parentage, interest or fortune, may make finer reading than all the Court romances ever written; and, moreover, that "the highest life is much the dullest, and affords very little humour or entertainment." And, having rediscovered this world of natural and simple human nature, his genius proceeded to the creation of nothing less than an entirely new form of English literary expression, the medium of the novel.

The preface to *Joseph Andrews* shows that Fielding was perfectly conscious of the greatness of his adventure. Such a species of writing, he says, "I do not remember to have seen hitherto attempted in our language." We can but wonder at, and admire, the superb energy and confidence which could thus embark on the conscious production of this new thing, amid want, pain, and distress. And wonder and admiration increase tenfold on the further discovery that this fresh creation in literature, fashioned in circumstances so depressing, is overflowing with an exuberance of healthy life and enjoyment. Having entered on his fair inheritance of this new world of human nature, Fielding pourtrays it from the standpoint of his own maxim, that life "everywhere furnishes an accurate observer with the ridiculous." So, into this, his newly-cut channel for imaginative expression (to use Mr Gosse's happy phrase) he poured the strength of a genius naturally inclined to that "exquisite mirth and laughter," which as he declared in his preface to these volumes, "are probably more wholesome physic for the mind and conduce better to purge away spleen, melancholy, and ill affections than is generally imagined." No book ever more thoroughly carried out this wholesome doctrine. The laughter in *Joseph Andrews* is as whole-hearted, if not as noisy, the practical jokes are as broad, as those of a healthy school-boy; and the pages ring with a spirit and gusto recalling Lady Mary's phrase concerning her cousin "that no man enjoyed life more than he did." To quote again from Mr Gosse: "A good deal in this book may offend the fine, and not merely the superfine. But the vitality and elastic vigour of the whole carry us over every difficulty... and we pause at the close of the novel to reflect on the amazing freshness of the talent which could thus make a set of West country scenes, in that despised thing, a novel, blaze with light like a comedy of Shakespeare."

So original in creation, so humane, so full of a brave delight in life, was the power that, mastering every gloomy obstacle of circumstance, broke into the stilted literary world of 1742; and Murphy's Irish rhetoric is not too warm when he talks of this sunrise of Fielding's greatness "when his genius broke forth at once, with an effulgence superior to all the rays of light it had before emitted, like the sun in his morning glory."

Any detailed comment on the literary qualities of the genius which thus disclosed itself would exceed the limits of this memoir; and indeed such comment is, now, a thrice-told tale. To Sir Walter Scott, Fielding is the "father of the English novel"; to Byron, "the prose Homer of human nature." The magnificent tribute of Gibbon still remains a towering monument, whatever experts may tell us concerning the Hapsburg genealogy. "Our immortal Fielding," he wrote, "was of the younger branch of the Earls of Denbigh, who drew their origin from the Counts of Hapsburg. The successors of Charles V. may disdain their brethren of England; but the romance of *Tom Jones*, that exquisite picture of human manners, will outlive the palace of the Escurial and the Imperial Eagle of Austria." Smollett affirmed that his predecessor painted the characters, and ridiculed the follies, of life with equal strength, humour and propriety. The supreme autocrat of the eighteenth century, Dr Johnson himself, though always somewhat hostile to Fielding, read *Amelia* through without stopping, and pronounced her to be 'the most pleasing heroine of all the romances.' "What a poet is here," cries Thackeray, "watching, meditating, brooding, creating! What multitudes of truths has that man left behind him: what generations he has taught to laugh wisely and fairly." Finally we may turn neither to novelist nor historian, but to the metaphysical philosopher, "How charming! How wholesome is Fielding!" says Coleridge, "to take him up after Richardson is like emerging from a sick-room, heated by stoves, into an open lawn on a breezy day in May." Such are some estimates of the quality of Fielding's genius, given by men not incompetent to appraise him. To analyse that genius is, as has been said, beyond the scope of these pages. But Fielding's first novel is not only a revelation of genius. It frankly reveals much of the man behind the pen; and in its pages, and in those of the still greater novels yet to come, we may learn more of the true Fielding than from all the fatuities and surmises of his early biographers.

Thus in *Joseph Andrews* for the first time we come really close to the splendid and healthy energy, the detachment, the relentless scorn, the warmth of feeling, that characterised Henry Fielding under all circumstances and at all times of his life. This book, as we have seen, was written under every outward disadvantage, and yet its pages ring with vigour and laughter. Here is the same militant energy that had nerved Fielding to fight the domination of a corrupt (and generally corrupting) Minister for eight lean years; and which in later life flung itself into a chivalrous conflict with current social crime and misery. Here is a detachment hardly less than that which fills the pages of the last *Journal of a Voyage to Lisbon* with a courage, a gaiety, a serenity that no suffering and hardship, and not even the near approach of death itself, could disturb. Here, again, Fielding consciously avows a moral purpose in his art; the merciless scorn of his insight in depicting a vicious man or woman is actuated, he expressly declares, by a motive other than that of 'art for art's sake.' And as this motive is scarce perceptible in the lifelike reality of the figures whom we see breathing in actual flesh and blood in his pages, and yet is of the first importance for understanding the character of their creator, the great novelist's confession of this portion of his literary faith may be quoted in full. The passage occurs in the preface to Book iii. of *Joseph Andrews*. Fielding is afraid, he explains, that his figures may be taken for particular portraits, whereas it is the type and not the individual that concerns him. "I declare here," he solemnly affirms, "once for all, I describe not Men, but Manners; not an Individual, but a Species." And he proceeds to make example of the lawyer in the stage coach as not indeed confined "to one Profession, one Religion, or one Country; but when the first mean selfish

Creature appeared on the human Stage, who made Self the Centre of the whole Creation; would give himself no Pain, incur no Damage, advance no Money to assist, or preserve his Fellow-Creatures; then was our Lawyer born; and while such a Person as I have described, exists on Earth, so long shall he remain upon it." Not therefore "to mimick some little obscure Fellow" does this lawyer appear on Fielding's pages, but "for much more general and noble Purposes; not to expose one pitiful Wretch, to the small and contemptible Circle of his Acquaintance; but to hold the Glass to thousands in their Closets that they may contemplate their Deformity, and endeavour to reduce it."

Yet another characteristic of Fielding's personality appears in the conscious control exercised over all the humorous and satiric zest of *Joseph Andrews*. Here is no unseemly riot of ridicule. The ridiculous he declares in his philosophic preface is the subject-matter of his pages; but he will suffer no imputation of ridiculing vice or calamity. "Surely," he cries, "he hath a very ill-framed Mind, who can look on Ugliness, Infirmity, or Poverty, as ridiculous in themselves"; and he formally declares that such vices as appear in this work "are never set forth as the objects of Ridicule but Detestation." What then were the limits which Fielding imposed on himself in treating this, his declared subject matter of the ridiculous? Hypocrisy and vanity, he says, appearing in the form of affectation; "Great Vices are the proper Object of our Detestation, smaller Faults of our Pity: but Affectation appears to me the only true Source of the Ridiculous." Such is Fielding's sensitive claim for the decent limits of ridicule; and such the consciously avowed subject of his work. But the force of his genius, the depth of his insight, the warmth of his detestations and affections, soon carried him far beyond any mere study in the ridicule of vain and hypocritical affectation. The immortal figure of Parson Adams, striding through these pages, tells us infinitely much of the character of his creator, but nothing at all of the nature of affectation. The "rural innocence of a Joseph Andrews," to quote Miss Fielding's happy phrase [1] and of his charming Fanny, are as natural and fresh as Fielding's own Dorsetshire meadows, but instruct us not at all in vanity or hypocrisy.

To turn to the individual figures of *Joseph Andrews*; what do they tell us of the man who called them into being. First and foremost, it is Parson Adams who unquestionably dominates the book. However much the licentious grossness of Lady Booby, the shameless self-seeking of her waiting-woman, Mrs Slipslop, the swinish avarice of Parson Trulliber, the calculating cruelty of Mrs Tow-wouse, to name but some of the vices here exposed, blazon forth that 'enthusiasm for righteousness' which constantly moved Fielding to exhibit the devilish in human nature in all its 'native Deformity,' it is still Adams who remains the central figure of the great comic epic. Concerning the good parson, appreciation has stumbled for adequate words, from the tribute of Sir Walter Scott to that of Mr Austin Dobson. "The worthy parson's learning," wrote Sir Walter, "his simplicity, his evangelical purity of heart, and benevolence of disposition, are so admirably mingled with pedantry, absence of mind, and with the habit of athletic and gymnastic exercise, ... that he may be safely termed one of the richest productions of the Muse of Fiction." And to Mr Austin Dobson, this poor curate, compact as he is of the oddest contradictions, the most diverting eccentricities, is "assuredly a noble example of primitive goodness, and practical Christianity." We love Adams, as Fielding intended that we should, for his single-hearted goodness, his impulsiveness, his boundless generosity, his muscular courage; we are never allowed to forget the dignity of his office however ragged be the cassock that displays it; we admire his learning; we delight in his oddities. But above all he reflects honour on his creator by the inflexible integrity of his goodness. A hundred tricks are played on him by shallow knaves, and the result is but to convince us of the folly of knavery. His ill-clad and uncouth figure moves among the vicious and prosperous, and we perceive the ugliness of vice, and the poverty of wealth. With his nightcap drawn over his wig, a short grey coat half covering a torn cassock, the crabstick so formidable to ruffians in his hand, and his beloved AEschylus in his pocket, Adams smoking his pipe by the inn fire, or surrounded by his "children" as he called his parishioners vying "with each other in demonstrations of duty and love," fully justifies John Forster's comment on Fielding's manly habit of "discerning what was good and beautiful in the homeliest aspects of humanity." Before the true dignity of Abraham Adams, whether he be publicly rebuking the Squire and Pamela for laughing in church, or emerging unstained from adventures with hogs-wash and worse, the accident of his social position as a poor curate, contentedly drinking ale in the squire's kitchen, falls into its true insignificance.

Rumour assigned to Fielding's friend and neighbour at East Stour, the Rev. William Young, the honour of being the original of Parson Adams; and it is a pleasant coincidence that the legal assignment for *Joseph Andrews*, here reproduced in facsimile, should bear the signature, as witness, of the very man whose "innate goodness" is there immortalised. If there be any detractors of Fielding's personal character still to be found, they may be advised to remember the truism that a man is known by his friends, and to apply themselves to a study of William Young in the figure of Parson Adams.

Of the charming picture of rustic beauty and innocence presented in the blushing and warmhearted Fanny less need be said; for Fielding's ideal in womanhood was soon to be more fully revealed in the lovely creations of Sophia and Amelia. And honest Joseph himself, his courage and fidelity, his constancy, his tenderness and chivalrous passion for Fanny, his affection for Mr Adams, his voice "too musical to halloo to the dogs," his fine figure and handsome face, concerns us here chiefly as demonstrating that Fielding, when he chose, could display both virtue and manliness as united in the person of a perfectly robust English country lad.

These then, are some of the figures that Fielding loved to create, breathing into their simple virtues a vigorous human life, fresh as Coleridge said, as the life of a Spring morning. In these joyous creations of his heart and of his genius, the great novelist assuredly gives us a perfectly unconscious revelation of his own character. And among the changing scenes of this human comedy one incident must not be forgotten. In the famous episode of the stage coach, all Fielding's characteristic and relentless hatred of respectable hypocrisy, all his love of innate if ragged virtue is betrayed in the compass of a few pages: in those pages in which we see the robbed, half-murdered, and wholly naked Joseph lifted in from the wayside ditch amid the protests and merriment of the respectable passengers; and his shivering body at last wrapped in the coat of the postilion,— "a Lad who hath since been transported for robbing a Hen-roost,"—who voluntarily stripped off a greatcoat, his only garment, "at the same time swearing a great Oath (for which he was rebuked by the Passengers) 'that he would rather ride in his Shirt all his Life, than suffer a Fellow-Creature to lie in so miserable a Condition.'"

Much has been written concerning the notorious feud between Fielding and Richardson, a feud ostensibly based upon the fact that *Joseph Andrews* was, to some extent, frankly a parody of Richardson's famous production *Pamela*. In 1740, two years before the appearance of *Joseph Andrews* that middle-aged London printer had published *Pamela, or Virtue Rewarded*, achieving thereby an enormous vogue. That amazing mixture of sententious moralities, of prurience, and of mawkish sentiment, became the rage of the Town. Admirers ranked it next to the Bible; the great Mr Pope declared that it would "do more good than many volumes of Sermons"; and it was even translated into French and Italian, becoming, according to Lady Mary Wortley Montagu, who did not love Richardson, "the joy of the chambermaids of all nations." That all this should have been highly agreeable to the good Richardson, a 'vegetarian and water-drinker, a worthy, domesticated, fussy, and highly nervous little man,' ensconced in a ring of feminine flatterers whom he called 'my ladies,' is obvious; and proportionate was his wrath with Fielding's *Joseph Andrews*, of which the early chapters, at least, are a perfectly frank, and to Richardson audacious, satire on *Pamela*. The caricature was indeed frank. Joseph is introduced as Pamela's brother; he writes letters to that virtuous maid-servant; and the Mr B. of Richardson becomes the Squire Booby of Fielding. But there can be hardly two opinions as to such ridicule being an entirely justified and wholesome antidote to the pompous and nauseous original. To Fielding's robust and masculine genius, says Mr Austin Dobson, "the strange conjunction of purity and precaution in Richardson's heroine was a thing unnatural and a theme for inextinguishable Homeric laughter." To Thackeray's sympathetic imagination the feud was the inevitable outcome of the difference between the two men. Fielding, he says "couldn't do otherwise than laugh at the puny cockney bookseller, pouring out endless volumes of sentimental twaddle, and hold him up to scorn as a moll-coddle and a milksop. His genius had been nursed on sack posset, and not on dishes of tea. His muse had sung the loudest in tavern choruses, and had seen the daylight streaming in over thousands of empty bowls, and reeled home to chambers on the shoulders of the watchman. Richardson's goddess was attended by old maids and dowagers, and fed on muffins and bohea. 'Milksop!' roars Harry Fielding, clattering at the timid shop-shutters. 'Wretch! Monster! Mohock!'

shrieks the sentimental author of *Pamela*; and all the ladies of his court cackle out an affrighted chorus."

Looking back on the incident it seems matter for yet more Homeric laughter that Richardson should have called the resplendent genius of Fielding "low." But the feud, it may be surmised, led to much of the odium that seems to have attached to Fielding's name amongst some of his contemporaries. Feeling ran high and was vividly expressed in those days; and when cousinly admiration for Fielding was coupled by an excellent comment on Richardson's book as the delight of the maidservants of all nations, personal retorts in favour of the popular sentimentalist were but too likely to ensue. Apart from this aspect of the matter the ancient quarrel does not seem a very essential incident in Fielding's life.

The lack of means indicated by Fielding himself, in his reminiscence of this winter of 1741-2 as darkened by the illness of himself, his wife and of a favourite child, attended "with other Circumstances, which served as very proper Decorations to such a Scene," received but little alleviation from the publication of *Joseph Andrews*. The price paid for the book by Andrew Millar was but £183, 11s.; and there is no record that Millar supplemented the original sum, as he did in the case of *Tom Jones*, when the sale was assured. The first edition appears to have consisted of 1,500 copies. A second edition, of 2,000 copies was issued in the same summer,[2] and a third edition followed in 1743.

Fielding's formal declaration that he described "not men but manners"; his solemn protest, in the preface to this very book, that "I have no Intention to vilify or asperse anyone: for tho' everything is copied from the Book of Nature, and scarce a Character or Action produced which I have not taken from my own Observations and Experience, yet I have used the utmost Care to obscure the Persons by such different Circumstances, Degrees, and Colours, that it will be impossible to guess at them with any degree of Certainty"—represent rather his intention than the result. The portraits of "manners" by the "prose Homer of human nature" were too lifelike to escape frequent identification. Thus not only was the prototype of Parson Adams discovered, but that of his antithesis, the pig-breeding Mr Trulliber, was thought to exist in the person of the Rev. Mr Oliver, the Dorsetshire curate under whose tutelage Fielding had been placed when a boy. Tradition also connects Mr Peter Pounce with the Dorsetshire usurer Peter Walter. [3]

Two echoes have come down to us of the early appreciation of this novel. A translation of *Joseph Andrews*, "par une Dame Angloise," and bound for Marie Antoinette by Derome le Jeune, was placed on the shelves of her library in the Petit Trianon. [4] And, seven years after the appearance of *Joseph Andrews*, Lady Mary Wortley Montagu, when sixty years old, writes from her Italian exile: "I have at length received the box with the books enclosed, for which I give you many thanks as they amuse me very much. I gave a very ridiculous proof of it, fitter indeed for my granddaughter than myself. I returned from a party on horseback; and after having rode 20 miles, part of it by moonshine, it was ten at night when I found the box arrived. I could not deny myself the pleasure of opening it; and falling upon Fielding's works was fool enough to sit up all night reading. I think Joseph Andrews better than his Foundling." [5]

[1] *Cleopatra and Octavia.* Sarah Fielding. Introduction.

[2] See the ledgers of Woodfall, the printer, quoted in *Notes and Queries*, Series vi. p. 186.

[3] It is interesting to note that Samuel Rogers was heard to speak with great admiration of chapter xiii. of Book iii., entitled "A curious Dialogue which passed between Mr Abraham Adams and Mr Peter Pounce." (MS. note by Dyce, in a copy of *Joseph Andrews*, now in the South Kensington Museum.)

[4] This copy, published in Amsterdam in 1775, is now in the possession of Mr Pierpont Morgan.

[5] Letters and Works of Lady Mary Wortley Montagu. Vol. ii. p. 194.

CHAPTER IX

THE Miscellanies AND Jonathan Wild

"Is there on earth a greater object of contempt than the poor
scholar to a splendid beau; unless perhaps the splendid beau to
the poor scholar."
Covent Garden Journal, No. 61.

If the 'sunrise' of Fielding's genius did indeed shine forth on the publication
of *Joseph Andrews*, it was a sunrise attended by dark clouds. For, with the
appearance of these two little volumes, we enter on the most obscure period of
the great novelist's life, and on that in which he appears to have suffered the
severest 'invasions of Fortune.'

As regards the winter immediately preceding the appearance of that joyous
epic of the highway, he himself has told us that he was 'laid up in the gout, with
a favourite Child dying in one Bed, and my Wife in a Condition very little better,
on another, attended with other Circumstances, which served as very proper
Decorations to such a Scene.' In the following February, an entry in the registers
of St Martin's in the Fields records the burial of a child "Charlott Fielding." So it
is probable that the very month of the appearance of his first novel brought a
private grief to Fielding the poignancy of which may be measured by his
frequent betrayals of an anxious affection for his children.

To such distresses of sickness and anxiety, there was now, doubtless, added
the further misery of scanty means. For a few months later an advertisement
(hitherto overlooked) appears in the *Daily Post*, showing that Fielding was already
eagerly pushing forward the publication of the *Miscellanies*, that incoherent
collection which is itself proof enough that necessity alone had called it into
being. "The publication of these Volumes," he says, "hath been hitherto retarded
by the Author's indisposition last Winter, and a train of melancholy Accidents,
scarce to be parallel'd; but he takes this opportunity to assure his Subscribers
that he will most certainly deliver them within the time mentioned in his last
receipts, viz. by the 25th December next." [1]

We may take it, then, that the first six months of 1742 were attended by no
easy circumstances; and, accordingly, during these months Fielding's hard-
worked pen produced no less than three very different attempts to win
subsistence from those humoursome jades the nine Muses. To take these efforts
in order of date, first comes, in March, his sole invocation of the historic Muse,
the *Full Vindication of the Dutchess Dowager of Marlborough*, published almost before
Joseph Andrews was clear of the printers, and sold at the modest price of one
shilling. We learn from the title page that the *Vindication* was called forth by a
"late *scurrilous* Pamphlet," containing "*base* and *malicious* Invectives" against Her
Grace. Together with Fielding's natural love for fighting, a family tie may have
given him a further incitement to draw his pen on behalf of the aged Duchess.

For his first cousin, Mary Gould, the only child of his uncle James Gould, M.P. for Dorchester, had married General Charles Churchill, brother to the great Duke. Whether this cousinship by marriage led to any personal acquaintance between 'old Sarah' and Harry Fielding we do not know; and the muniment room at Blenheim affords no trace of any correspondence between the Duchess and her champion. But certainly the *Vindication* lacks nothing of personal warmth. Fielding tells us that he has never contemplated the character of that 'Glorious Woman' but with admiration; and he defends her against the attacks of her opponents through forty strenuous pages, in which the curious may still hear the echoes of the controversies that raged round the Duke and his Duchess, their mistress Queen Anne, and other actors of the Revolution. The *Vindication* appeared in March; and a second edition was called for during the year. As far as Millar's payment goes Fielding, as appears from the assignment in *Joseph Andrews*, received only £5; and it is to be feared that the Duchess (who is said to have paid the historian Hooke £5000 for his assistance in the production of her own celebrated pamphlet) placed but little substantial acknowledgment in Fielding's lean purse. Her champion at any rate had, within three years, modified the views expressed in this *Vindication*, concerning the munificence of Her Grace's private generosity; for in his journal the *True Patriot*, there occurs the following obituary notice, "A Man supposed to be a Pensioner of the late Duchess of Marlborough.... He is supposed to have been Poor."

This same month of March marked Fielding's final severance with the *Champion*. The partners of that paper, meeting on March the 1st, ordered "that Whereas Henry Fielding Esq., did Originally possess Two Sixteenth Shares of the Champion as a Writer in the said paper and having withdrawn himself from that Service for above Twelve Months past and refused his Assistance in that Capacity since which time Mr Ralph has solely Transacted the said Business. It is hereby Declared that the said Writing Shares shall devolve on and be vested in Mr James Ralph." [2] It is curious that Fielding did not add to his impoverished exchequer by selling his *Champion* shares.

Having sought assistance from the Muse of history in March, Fielding returns to his old charmer the dramatic Muse in May; assisting in that month to produce a farce, at Drury Lane, entitled *Miss Lucy in Town*. In this piece, he tells us, he had a very small share. He also received for it a very small remuneration; £10, 10s. being recorded as the price paid by Andrew Millar.

In the following month Fielding's inexhaustible energies were off on a new tack, producing, in startling contrast to *Miss Lucy*, a classical work, executed in collaboration with his friend the Rev. William Young, otherwise Parson Adams. The two friends contemplated a series of translations of all the eleven comedies of Aristophanes; adorned by notes containing "besides a full Explanation of the Author, a compleat History of the Manners and Customs of the Ancient Greeks particularly of the Athenians"; and in June they inaugurated their scheme with the work in question, a translation of the Plutus.[3] William Young, says Hutchins, "had much learning which was the cement of Mr Fielding's connexion with him"; and Fielding's own scholarship, irradiated by his wit, would assuredly have made him an ideal translator of Greek comedy. But the public of 1742 appears to have afforded very little encouragement to this scheme, preferring that "pretty, dapper, brisk, smart, pert, Dialogue" of their own comedies, to which allusion is made in the authors' preface.

The rest of the year shows nothing from a pen somewhat exhausted perhaps with the production of *Joseph Andrews* of the historical *Vindication*, and of parts of a Drury Lane farce and of the *Plutus*, all within five months. And the winter following, in which the promised *Miscellanies* should have appeared, brought, in the renewed illness of his wife, an anxiety that paralysed even Fielding's buoyant vigour. This we learn from his own touching apology for the further delay of those volumes; a delay due, their author tells us, to "the dangerous Illness of one from whom I draw all the solid Comfort of my Life, during the greatest Part of this Winter. This, as it is most sacredly true, so will it, I doubt not, sufficiently excuse the Delay to all who know me." [4] Early in the following year, after this second winter of crushing anxiety, and under an urgent pressure for means, Fielding tried again his familiar *rôle* of popular dramatist, giving his public the husks they preferred, in the comedy of the *Wedding Day*. This comedy was produced at Drury Lane on the 17th of February 1743.

If Fielding had failed to descend to the taste of the Town in offering them Aristophanes, he flung them in the *Wedding Day* something too imperfect for acceptance, even by the 'critic jury of the pit,' And the bitter humour in which he was now shackling his genius to the honourable task of immediate bread-winning, or in his own words to the part of "hackney writer," comes out clearly enough in the well-known anecdote of the first night of this comedy. In Murphy's words, Garrick, then a new player, just taking the Town by storm, "told Mr Fielding he was apprehensive that the audience would make free in a particular passage; adding that a repulse might so flurry his spirits as to disconcert him for the rest of the night, and therefore begged that it might be omitted. 'No, d—mn 'em,' replied the bard, 'if the scene is not a good one, let them find *that* out.' Accordingly the play was brought on without alteration, and, just as had been foreseen, the disapprobation of the house was provoked at the passage before objected to; and the performer alarmed and uneasy at the hisses he had met with, retired into the green-room, where the author was indulging his genius, and solacing himself with a bottle of champaign." Fielding, continues Murphy, had by this time drank pretty plentifully, and "'*What's the matter, Garrick?*' says he, '*what are they hissing now?*' Why the scene that I begged you to retrench; I knew it would not do; and they have so frightened me that I shall not be able to collect myself again the whole night. *Oh! d—mn 'em*, replies the author, *they HAVE found it out, have they!*" That Fielding should be scornfully indifferent to the judgment of the pit on work forced from him by overwhelming necessities, and which his own judgment condemned, is a foregone conclusion; but that he suffered keenly in having to produce imperfect work, and was jealously anxious to clear his reputation, as a writer, in the matter of this particular comedy, is no less apparent from the very unusual personal explanation he offered for it, soon after the brief run of the play was over. For no man was more shy of autobiographical revelations. His biographers are continually reduced to gleaning stray hints, here and there, concerning his private life. [5] And therefore we can measure by this emergence from a habitual personal reticence the soreness with which he now published work unworthy of his genius. "Mr Garrick," Fielding tells us, speaking of this distressed winter of 1742-3 "... asked me one Evening, if I had any play by me; telling me he was desirous of appearing in a new Part [and] ... as I was full as desirous of putting Words into his Mouth, as he could appear to be of speaking them, I mentioned [a] Play the very next morning to Mr *Fleetwood* who embraced my Proposal so heartily, that an Appointment was immediately made to read it to the Actors who were principally to be concerned in it." On consideration, however, this play appeared to Fielding to need more time for perfecting, and also to afford very little opportunity to Garrick. So, recollecting that he still had by him a play which, although 'the third Dramatic Performance' he ever attempted, contained a character that would keep the audience's "so justly favourite Actor almost eternally before their Eyes," he decided, with characteristic impetuosity, to a change at the last moment. "I accordingly," he writes, "sat down with a Resolution to work Night and Day, owing to the short Time allowed me, which was about a Week, in altering and correcting this Production of my more Juvenile Years; when unfortunately the extreme Danger of Life into which a Person, very dear to me, was reduced, rendered me incapable of executing my Task. To this Accident alone I have the vanity to apprehend, the Play owes most of the glaring Faults with which it appeared.... Perhaps, it may be asked me why then did I suffer a Piece which I myself knew was imperfect, to appear? I answer honestly and freely, that Reputation was not my Inducement; and that I hoped, faulty as it was, it might answer a much more solid, and in my unhappy situation, a much more urgent Motive." This hope was, alas, frustrated; not even the brilliancy of a cast which included Garrick, Mrs Pritchard, Macklin, and Peg Woffington, could carry the *Wedding Day* over its sixth night; and the harassed author received 'not £50 from the House for it.' The comedy is a coarsely moral attack on libertinism, a fact which probably, in no wise added to the popularity of the play in the pit and boxes of 1743.

A doggerel prologue, both written and spoken by Macklin, gives an excellent picture of the playhouse humours, and of the wild pit, of those exuberant days; and contains moreover the following sound advice, addressed to Fielding

"Ah! thou foolish follower of the ragged Nine
You'd better stuck to honest Abram Adams, by half;
He, in spite of critics can make your Readers laugh."

The next publication of these lean years was the *Miscellanies*, a collection of mingled prose, verse, and drama, of which the only connecting link seems to be the urgent need of money which forced so heterogenous a medley from so great an artist. These long delayed volumes appeared, probably, in April, and were, says Fielding, composed with a frequent "Degree of Heartache." They include the lover's verses of his early youth; philosophical, satiric, and didactic essays; a reprint of the political effusion dedicated to Dodington; a few plays; the fragment entitled *A Journey from this World to the Next*; and the splendid ironic outburst on villany, *Jonathan Wild*.

The *Preface*, largely occupied as it is with those private circumstances which forced the hasty production of the *Wedding Day*, has other matter of even greater interest for the biographer. Thus Fielding's sensitive care of his reputation in essential matters appears in the fiery denial here given to allegations of publishing anonymous scandals: "I never was, nor will be the Author of anonymous Scandal on the private History or Family of any Person whatever. Indeed there is no Man who speaks or thinks with more detestation of the modern custom of Libelling. I look on the practice of stabbing a Man's Character in the Dark, to be as base and as barbarous as that of stabbing him with a Poignard in the same manner; nor have I ever been once in my Life guilty of it." Here too, he marks his abhorrence of that 'detestable Vice' hypocrisy, which vice he was, before long, to expose utterly in the person of Blifil in *Tom Jones*. His happy social temperament is betrayed in the characteristic definition of good breeding as consisting in "contributing with our utmost Power to the Satisfaction and Happiness of all about us." And in these pages we have Fielding's philosophy of *goodness* and *greatness*, delivered in words that already display an unrivalled perfection of style. Speaking of his third volume, that poignant indictment of devilry the *Life of Mr Jonathan Wild the Great*, it is thus that Fielding exposes the iniquity of villains in "great" places:—"But without considering *Newgate* as no other than Human Nature with its mask off, which some very shameless Writers have done, a Thought which no Price should purchase me to entertain, I think we may be excused for suspecting, that the splendid Palaces of the Great, are often no other than *Newgate* with the Mask on. Nor do I know anything which can raise an honest Man's Indignation higher than that the same Morals should be in one Place attended with all imaginable Misery and Infamy and in the other with the highest Luxory and Honour. Let any impartial Man in his Senses be asked, for which of these two Places a Composition of Cruelty, Lust, Avarice, Rapine, Insolence, Hypocrisy, Fraud and Treachery, was best fitted, surely his Answer must be certain and immediate; and yet I am afraid all these Ingredients glossed over with Wealth and a Title, have been treated with the highest Respect and Veneration in the one, while one or two of them have been condemned to the Gallows in the other."

Here is the converse of that insight which could discern goodness under a ragged cassock, or in a swearing postilion. And, having discerned the true nature of such Great Men, Fielding proceeds to point out that "However the Glare of Riches and Awe of Title may terrify the Vulgar; nay however Hypocrisy may deceive the more Discerning, there is still a Judge in every Man's Breast, which none can cheat or corrupt, tho' perhaps it is the only uncorrupt thing about him"; that nothing is so preposterous as that men should laboriously seek to be villains; and that this Judge, inflexible and honest "however polluted the Bench on which he sits," always bestows on the spurious Great the penalty of fear, an evil which "never can in any manner molest the Happiness" of the "Enjoyments of Innocence and Virtue."

The subsequent philosophic dissertation on the qualities of goodness and greatness is interesting for such passages as the definition of a good man as one possessing "Benevolence, Honour, Honesty, and Charity"; and the fine declaration that of the passion of Love "goodness hath always appeared to me the only true and proper Object." And the very springs of action underlying half at least of each of the three great novels, and almost every page of *Jonathan Wild*, are revealed in the final declaration of the writer's intention to expose in these pages vice stripped of its false colours; to show it "in its native Deformity." As the native and stripped deformity of vice is perhaps not often fully apprehended and certainly is very seldom exposed in our own age, Fielding, by the very sincerity and fire of his morality, doubtless loses many a modern reader.

It is in the third volume of the *Miscellanies*, a volume completely occupied by *Jonathan Wild*, that Fielding first fully reveals himself as public moralist. And in this Rogue's progress to the gallows he displays so concentrated a zeal, that nothing short of his genius and his humour could have saved these pages from the dullness of the professional reformer. For the little volume consists of a relentless exposure of the deformity and folly of vice. Here the foul souls of Wild and his associates, stripped of all the glamour of picturesque crime, stand displayed in their essential qualities, with the result that even the pestilential air of thieves' slums, of 'night cellars,' and of Newgate purlieus, an air which hangs so heavy over every page, falls back into insignificance before the loathsomeness of the central figure. A few years later, in the preface to *Tom Jones*, Fielding formally asserted his belief that the beauty of goodness needed but to be seen 'to attract the admiration of mankind'; in *Jonathan Wild* he appears to be already at work on the converse doctrine, that if the deformity of vice be but stripped naked, abhorrence must ensue. Such a naked criminal is Wild; and in the contemplation of his vices, as in the case of the arch hypocrite Blifil, in *Tom Jones*, and of the shameless sensualist "My Lord," in *Amelia*, Fielding's characteristic compassion for the faults of hard pressed humanity is, for the time, scorched up in the fierceness of his anger and scorn at deliberate cruelty, avarice and lust. Under the spell of Fielding's power of painting the devil in his native blackness, we feel that for such as Wild hanging is too handsome a fate. It is easy for his Newgate chaplain to assert that "nothing is so sinful as sin"; it takes a great genius and a great moralist to convince us, as in this picture, that nothing is so deformed or so contemptible. The dark places of *Jonathan Wild* receive some light in the character of the good jeweller, in the tender scenes between that honest ruined tradesman and his wife and children, and in the devoted affection of his apprentice. But the true illumination of the book, and its personal value for the biographer, lie in the white heat of anger, the "sustained and sleepless irony" to adopt Mr Austin Dobson's happy phrase, with which Fielding, with a force unwavering from the first page to the last, here assails his subject. An underlying attack on the Ministerial iniquity of "Great Men" in high places seems to be often suggested; if this be a true inference, it does but give us further proof of Fielding's energies as a political, no less than as a moral, reformer. Certainly, through all the squalid scenes of the book, the contention is insisted on that criminals of Wild's tyrannical stamp may as easily be found in courts, and at the head of armies, as among the poor leaders of Newgate gangs. To the wise moralist it is the same rogue, whether picking a pocket or swindling his country.

And not to forget the wit in the moral reformer, we may leave Mr Jonathan Wild listening to one of the reasons given by the Newgate chaplain for his Reverence's preference for punch over wine: "Let me tell you, Mr Wild there is nothing so deceitful as the spirits given us by wine. If you must drink let us have a bowl of punch; a liquor I the rather prefer as it is nowhere spoken against in Scripture."

After *Jonathan Wild* the most interesting fragment of the *Miscellanies* is the *Journey from this World to the Next*. In this essay Fielding reveals his philosophy, his sternness, his affections, and his humour, as a man might do in intimate conversation. His warm humanity breathes in the conception that "the only Business" of those who had won admission to Elysium 'that happy Place,' was to "contribute to the Happiness of each other"; and again in the stern declaration of Heaven's doorkeeper, the Judge Minos, that "no Man enters that Gate without Charity." And indeed the whole chapter devoted to the judgments administered by Minos on the spirits that come, confident or trembling, before him, and are either admitted to Heaven, sent back to earth, or despatched to the "little Back Gate" opening immediately into the bottomless pit, is full of personal revelation. We feel the glee with which Fielding consigns the "little sneaking soul" of a miser to diabolically ingenious torments; the satisfaction with which he watches Minos apply a kick to the retreating figure of a duke, possessed of nothing but "a very solemn Air and great Dignity"; and the pleasure it gave him to observe the rejection accorded to "a grave Lady," the Judge declaring that "there was not a single Prude in Elysium." Again, nothing could be more true to Fielding's nature than the account of the poet who is admitted, not for the moral value he himself places on his Dramatic Works (which he endeavours to read aloud to Minos), but because "he had once lent the whole profits of a Benefit Night to a Friend, and by that Means had saved him and his Family from Destruction"; unless it were the account of the poverty driven wretch, hanged for a robbery of eighteen-pence, who yet could plead that he had supported an aged Parent with his labour, that he had been a very tender Husband, and a Kind Father, and that he had ruined himself for being Bail for a Friend. "At these words," adds the historian, "the gate opened, and *Minos* bid him enter, giving him a slap on the Back as he passed by him."

When the author's own turn came, he very little expects, he tells us, "to pass this fiery Trial. I confess'd I had indulged myself very freely with Wine and Women in my Youth, but had never done an Injury to any Man living, nor avoided an opportunity of doing good; but I pretended to very little Virtue more than general Philanthropy and Private Friendship." Here Minos cut the speaker short, bidding him enter the gate, and not indulge himself trumpeting forth his virtues. Whether or no we may here read the reflections of Fielding's maturity, looking honestly back over his own forty years and forward with humble fear into the future, we may certainly see reflected in both confession and judgment much of the doctrine and the practice of his life.

After the failure, early in 1743, of the *Wedding Day*, and the subsequent publication of the *Miscellanies*, Fielding seems to have thrown his energies for twelve months into an exclusive pursuit of the law. This appears from his statement, made a year later, in May 1744, that he could not possibly be the author of his sister's novel *David Simple*, which had been attributed to him, because he had applied himself to his profession "with so arduous and intent a diligence that I have had no leisure, if I had inclination, to compose anything of this kind." Clearly, in the period that covers the publication of *Joseph Andrews* an historical pamphlet, parts of a farce and of *Plutus*, and of the *Miscellanies*, Fielding found both leisure and inclination for writing; so this sudden immersion in law must relate to the twelve months or so intervening between these works and the publication of his statement. Murphy corroborates this bout of hard legal effort. After the *Wedding Day* says that biographer "the law from this time had its hot and cold fits with him." The cold fits were fits of gout; and inconveniences felt by Fielding from these interruptions were, adds Murphy "the more severe upon him, as voluntary and wilful neglect could not be charged upon him. The repeated shocks of illness disabled him from being as assiduous an attendant at the bar, as his own inclination and patience of the most laborious application, would otherwise have made him."

Mr Counsellor Fielding follows his retrospect of this strenuous attack on the law with a declaration that, henceforth, he intends to forsake the pursuit of that 'foolscap' literary fame, and the company of the 'infamous' nine Muses; a decision based partly on the insubstantial nature of the rewards achieved, and partly it would seem due to the fact that at Fielding's innocent door had been laid, he declares, half the anonymous scurrility, indecency, treason, and blasphemy that the few last years had produced. [6] In especial he protests against the ascription to his pen of that 'infamous paltry libel' on lawyers, the *Causidicade*, an ascription which, as he truly says, accused him "not only of being a bad writer and a bad man, but with downright idiotism in flying in the face of the greatest men of my profession." He also declares that no anonymous work had issued from his pen since his promise to that effect; and that these false accusations had injured him cruelly in ease, reputation and interest. This solemn declaration that the now detested Muses shall no longer beguile Fielding's pen affords excellent reading in view of the fact that this absorbed barrister must, within a year or two, have been at work on *Tom Jones*. The whole emphatic outburst was probably partly an effort to assert himself as now wholly devoted to the law, and partly an example of one of those "occasional fits of peevishness" into which, Murphy tells us, distress and disappointment would betray him.

The preface to his sister's novel *David Simple*, in which Fielding took occasion to announce these protests and assertions, is his only extant publication for this year of 1744; and apart from its biographical value is not of any great moment. Ample proof may be found in it of brotherly pride and admiration for the work of a sister "so nearly and dearly allied to me in the highest friendship as well as relation." There is the noteworthy declaration that the "greatest, noblest, and rarest of all the talents which constitute a genius" is the gift of "a deep and profound discernment of all the mazes, windings, and labyrinths which perplex the heart of man." The utterance concerning style, by so great a master of English, is memorable—"a good style as well as a good hand in writing is chiefly learned by practice." And a delightful reference should not be forgotten to the carping ignorant critic, who has indeed, "had a little Latin inoculated into his tail," but who would have been much the gainer had "the same great quantity of birch been employed in scourging away his ill-nature."

Disabled by gout and harassed by want of money, a yet greater distress was now fast closing on Fielding in the prolonged illness of his wife. "To see her daily languishing and wearing away before his eyes," says Murphy, "was too much for a man of his strong sensations; the fortitude with which he met all other calamities of life [now] deserted him." In the autumn of 1744 Mrs Fielding was at Bath, doubtless in the hope of benefit from the Bath waters. And here, in November, she died. Her body was brought to London for burial in the church of St. Martin's in the Fields; receiving on the 14th of November, 1744, honourable interment in the chancel vault, to the tolling of the great tenor bell, and with the fullest ceremonial of the time. Indeed it is evident, from the charges still preserved in the sexton's book, that Fielding rendered to his wife such stately honours as were occasionally accorded to the members of the few great families interred in the old church.

The death of this beloved wife, Murphy tells us, brought on Fielding "such a vehemence of grief that his friends began to think him in danger of losing his reason." When we remember that he himself has explicitly stated that lovely picture of the 'fair soul in the fair body,' the Sophia of *Tom Jones*, to have been but a portrait of Charlotte Fielding, we can in some measure realise his overwhelming grief at her death. And that the exquisite memorial raised to his wife by Fielding's affection and genius was not more beautiful in mind or face than the original, is acknowledged by Lady Bute, a kinswoman of the great novelist. Lady Bute was no stranger, "to that beloved first wife whose picture he drew in his Amelia, where, as she said, even the glowing language he knew how to employ did not do more than justice to the amiable qualities of the original, or to her beauty. He loved her passionately, and she returned his affection; yet had no happy life for they were almost always miserably poor, and seldom in a state of quiet and safety. His elastic gaiety of spirit carried him through it all; but meanwhile, care and anxiety were preying upon her more delicate mind, and undermining her constitution. She gradually declined, caught a fever and died in his arms." That Fielding's married life was unhappy, whatever were its outward conditions, is obviously a very shallow misstatement; but, for the rest, the picture accords well enough with our knowledge of his nature. The passionate tenderness of which that nature was capable appears in a passage from those very *Miscellanies*, which, he tells us, were written with so frequent a "Degree of Heartache." In the *Journey from this World to the Next*, Fielding describes how, on his entrance into Elysium, that "happy region whose beauty no Painting of the Imagination can describe" and where "Spirits know one another by Intuition" he presently met "a little Daughter whom I had lost several years before. Good Gods! What Words can describe the Raptures, the melting passionate Tenderness, with which we kiss'd each other, continuing in our Embrace, with the most extatic Joy, a Space, which if Time had been measured here as on Earth, could not have been less than half a Year."

The fittest final comment on Henry Fielding's marriage with Charlotte Cradock is, perhaps, that saying of a member of his own craft of the drama, "Now to love anything sincerely is an act of grace, but to love the best sincerely is a state of grace."

[1] *Daily Post*, June 5, 1742.

[2] MS. copy of the Minutes of the Meetings of the Partners in the *Champion*, in the possession of the present writer.

[3] See *Daily Post*. May 29, 1742.

[4] Preface to the *Miscellanies*.

[5] Such as the inscription on some verses, published in the *Miscellanies*, as "Written *Extempore* in the Pump-room" at Bath, in 1742.

[6] Preface to *David Simple*.

CHAPTER X

PATRIOTIC JOURNALISM

"he only is the *true Patriot* who always does what is in
his Power for his Country's Service without any selfish Views or
Regard to private Interests."—The *True Patriot*.

Fielding's active pen seems to have been laid aside for twelve months after
the death of his wife; and it is perfectly in accord with all that we know of his
passionate devotion to Charlotte Cradock that her loss should have shattered his
energies for the whole of the ensuing year. Murphy, as we have seen, speaks of
the first vehemence of his grief as being so acute that fears were entertained for
his reason. According to Fielding's kinswomen, Lady Mary Wortley Montagu
and Lady Bute, the first agonies of his grief approached to frenzy; but "when the
first emotions of his sorrow were abated" his fine balance reasserted itself, and
to quote again from Murphy, "philosophy administered her aid; his resolution
returned, and he began again to struggle with his fortune."

As we hear no more of exclusive devotion to the law, it may be assumed that
the attempt of the previous year to live by that arduous calling alone was now
abandoned; and to a man of Fielding's strong Protestant and Hanoverian
convictions the year of the '45, when a Stewart Prince and an invading Highland
army had captured Edinburgh and were actually across the border, could not fail
to bring occupation. Fielding believed ardently that Protestant beliefs, civil
liberty, and national independence of foreign powers were best safeguarded by a
German succession to the English throne; so by the time Prince Charles and
6,000 men had set foot on English soil, the former 'Champion of Great Britain'
was again up in arms, discharging his sturdy blows in a new weekly newspaper
entitled the *True Patriot*.

The *True Patriot* is chiefly notable as affording the first sign that Fielding was
now leaving party politics for the wider, and much duller, field of Constitutional
liberty. A man might die for the British Constitution; but to be witty about it
would tax the resources of a Lucian. And, accordingly, in place of that gay young
spark Mr Pasquin, who laid his cudgel with so hearty a good will on the
shoulders of the offending 'Great Man,' there now steps out a very philosophic,
mature, and soberly constitutional *Patriot*; a patriot who explicitly asserts in his
first number, "I am of no party; a word I hope by these my labours to eradicate
out of our constitution: this being indeed the true source of all those evils which
we have reason to complain of." And again, in No. 14, "I am engaged to no
Party, nor in the Support of any, unless of such as are truly and sincerely
attached to the true interest of their Country, and are resolved to hazard all
Things in its Preservation." Here is a considerable change from the personal zest
that placed Mr Quiddam and Mr Pillage before delighted audiences in the Little
Theatre in the Haymarket.

The available copies of the *True Patriot*, now in the British Museum, [1] include only thirty-two numbers, starting from No. 1, which appeared on the 5th of November, 1745, and ending on June 3, 1746. The first number contains a characteristic tribute to Dean Swift, whose death had occurred 'a few days since.' Doctor Jonathan Swift, says the *Patriot*, was "A genius who deserves to be rank'd among the first whom the World ever saw. He possessed the Talents of a Lucian a Rabelais and a Cervantes and in his Works exceeded them all. He employed his Wit to the noblest Purposes in ridiculing as well Superstition in Religion as Infidelity and the several Errors and Immoralities which sprung up from time to time in his Age; and lastly in defence of his Country.... Nor was he only a Genius and a Patriot; he was in Private Life a good and charitable Man and frequently lent Sums of Money, without interest, to the Poor and Industrious; by which means many Families were preserved from Destruction." In No. 2, the *Patriot* reiterates his "sincere Intention to calm and heal, not to blow up and inflame, any Party-Divisions"; but even the task of defending the British Constitution could not stifle Fielding's wit, and he escapes, for breathing space as it were, into a column devoted to the news items of the week, gathered from various papers, and adorned by comments of his own, printed in italics. And in this running commentary on the daily occurences of the time we get nearer, perhaps, to the table-talk of Henry Fielding than by any other means. Thus he faithfully repeats the inflated obituary lists that were then in fashion, but with such a variation as the following, "Thomas Tonkin, ... universally lamented by his Acquaintance. Upwards of 40 Cows belonging to one at Tottenham Court, *universally lamented by all their Acquaintance.*" On a notice of an anniversary meeting of the Society for propagating the Gospel in Foreign Parts there is the pertinent comment "*It is a Pity some Method—was not invented for the Propagation of the Gospel in Great Britain.*" After the deaths of a wealthy banker and factor, comes the obituary of "One Nowns a Labourer, *most probably immensely poor, and yet as rich now as either of the two Preceeding*"; beside which may be placed the very characteristic assertion in No. 6 that "Spleen and Vapours inhabit Palaces and are attired with Pomp and Splendor, while they shun Rags and Prisons."

There is scarcely a personal allusion in all the thirty-two numbers of the *Patriot*, save the charming picture of that gentleman sitting in his study "meditating for the good and entertainment of the public, with my two little children (as is my usual course to suffer them) playing near me." And the ending of his horrid nightmare, in which a Jacobite executioner was placing a rope round his neck, "when my little girl entered my bedchamber and put an end to my dream by pulling open my eyes, and telling me that the taylor had brought home my cloaths for his Majesty's Birthday." The number for January 28 must not be overlooked, containing as it does, a scathing and humourous exposure of the profligate young sparks of the Town, from no less a pen than that of the Rev. Mr. Abraham Adams; and Parson Adams' letter concludes with a paragraph in which may be heard the voice of the future zealous magistrate: "No man can doubt but that the education of youth ought to be the principal care of every legislation; by the neglect of which great mischief accrues to the civil polity in every city." When himself but a lad of twenty, and in the prologue of his first comedy, Fielding had entered his protest against certain popular vices of the time, and had made merry over its follies. The desire to make the world he knew too well a better place than he found it is just as keen in the wit and humourist of thirty-nine; a desire, moreover, undulled by twenty years of vivacious living. Surely not the least amazing feature of Fielding's genius is this dual capacity for exuberant enjoyment, and incisive judgement. "His wit," said Thackeray, "is wonderfully wise and detective; it flashes upon a rogue and brightens up a rascal like a policeman's lantern."

To this time of national ferment belongs a publication of which we know nothing but the title, a *Serious Address*; and also one of our rare glimpses of the novelist's home life. Joseph Warton writes to his brother Tom, on October 29, 1746:—"I wish you had been with me last week when I spent two evenings with Fielding and his sister, who wrote David Simple, and you may guess I was very well entertained. The lady indeed retir'd pretty soon, but Russell and I sat up with the Poet till one or two in the morning, and were inexpressibly diverted. I find he values, as he justly may, Joseph Andrews above all his writings: he was extremely civil to me, I fancy, on my Father's account." Joseph Warton's father was Vicar of Basingstoke, Professor of Poetry at Oxford, and moreover, something of a Jacobite; whereby, we may surmise, that the *True Patriot* did not allow his staunch Hanoverian sentiments too great an invasion into his private society. Alas, that it did not occur to Warton to preserve, for the entertainment of later ages, some fuller record of those two *noctes ambrosianae*.

This sister, Sally Fielding as her cousin Lady Mary Wortley Montagu called her, made some figure in the literary world of the day. Richardson extolled her "knowledge of the human heart"; Murphy writes of her "lively and penetrating genius"; and her classical scholarship is attested by a translation of Xenophon's *Memorabilia*. That she also shared some of the engaging qualities of her brother may be assumed from the lines written to the memory of the "esteemed and loved ... Mrs. Sarah Fielding," by her friend Dr. John Hoadley.

"Her unaffected Manners, candid Mind,
Her Heart benevolent, and Soul resign'd;
Were more her Praise than all she knew or thought
Though Athens Wisdom to her Sex she taught."

Sarah Fielding's name occurs again as living with her brother in that house in Beaufort Buildings with which is associated perhaps the happiest instance of Fielding's warm-hearted generosity. The story may be given as nearly as possible in the words of the narrator, one G. S., writing from Harley Street in 1786. After speaking of the conspicuous good nature of "the late Harry Fielding," G. S. says: "His receipts were never large, and his pocket was an open bank for distress and friendship at all times to draw on. Marked by such a liberality of mind it is not to be wondered at if he was frequently under pecuniary embarrassments.... Some parochial taxes for his house in Beaufort Buildings being unpaid, and for which he had been demanded again and again [we may remember how Mr. Luckless' door was "almost beat down with duns"]...he was at last given to understand by the collector who had an esteem for him, that he could procrastinate the payment no longer." To a bookseller, therefore he addressed himself, and mortgaged the coming sheets of some work then in hand. He received the cash, some ten or twelve guineas, and was returning home, full freighted with this sum, when, in the Strand, within a few yards of his own house, he met an old college chum whom he had not seen for many years. "Harry felt the enthusiasm of friendship; an hundred interrogatives were put to him in a moment as where had he been? where was he going? how did he do? &c. &c. His friend told him in reply he had long been buffeting the waves of adverse fortunes, but never could surmount them." Fielding took him off to dine at a neighbouring tavern, and as they talked, becoming acquainted with the state of his friend's pocket, emptied his own into it; and a little before dawn, he turned homewards "greater and happier than a monarch." Arrived at Beaufort Buildings his sister, who had anxiously awaited him, reported that the collector had called for the taxes twice that day. "Friendship," answered Harry Fielding "has called for the money and had it;—let the collector call again." Well might his cousin Lady Mary say of the man of whom such a story could be told, "I am persuaded he has known more happy moments than any prince upon earth."

During the summer following Warton's visit to the brother and sister, Fielding published a *Dialogue between an Alderman and a Courtier*. And in the following November his second marriage took place, at the little City church of St Bene't's, Paul's Wharf. The story of this marriage cannot be better told than in the words of Lady Mary Wortley Montagu's granddaughter, Lady Louisa Stuart, quoting from the personal knowledge of her mother and grandmother:

"His biographers seem to have been shy of disclosing that after the death of this charming woman [his first wife] he married her maid. And yet the act was not so discreditable to his character as it may sound. The maid had few personal charms, but was an excellent creature, devotedly attached to her mistress, and almost broken-hearted for her loss. In the first agonies of his own grief, which approached to frenzy, he found no relief but from weeping with her; nor solace, when a degree calmer, but in talking to her of the angel they mutually regretted. This made her his habitual confidential associate, and in process of time he began to think he could not give his children a tenderer mother, or secure for himself a more faithful housekeeper and nurse. At least this was what he told his friends; and it is certain that her conduct as his wife confirmed it, and fully justified his good opinion." From a supposed allusion by Smollett, in the first edition of *Peregrine Pickle*, (an allusion afterwards suppressed) it would appear that Fielding's old schoolfellow and lifelong friend 'the good Lord Lyttelton' so far approved the marriage as himself to give Mary Daniel away; and, as the dates in the Twickenham Register of births show that the marriage was one of justice as well as expediency, this well accords with Lyttelton's upright and honourable character. Of Fielding's affectionate and grateful loyalty to his second wife ample evidence appears in the pages of his last book, the *Journal of a Voyage to Lisbon*.

Throughout this touching record of the journey of a dying man, there are references to her tenderness, ability and devotion. At the sad parting from children and friends, on the morning of their departure for Lisbon, he writes of her behaviour as "more like a heroine and philosopher, though at the same time the tenderest mother in the world." When, during the voyage down the Thames, an unmannerly custom house officer burst into the cabin where Fielding and his wife were sitting, the man was soundly rated for breaking "into the presence of a lady without an apology or even moving his hat"; by which we may see his sensitive care that due respect was accorded her. He tells us how he persuaded her with difficulty to take a walk on shore when their vessel was wind bound in Torbay, it being "no easy matter for me to force [her] from my side." With anxious forboding he thinks of his "dear wife and child" facing the world alone after his death, for "in truth I have often thought they are both too good and too gentle to be trusted to the power of any man I know, to whom they could possibly be so trusted." And in a more formal tribute he acknowledges the abilities that accompanied her worth, when he says that "besides discharging excellently well her own and all tender offices becoming the female character; ... besides being a faithful friend, an amiable companion, and a tender nurse, [she] could likewise supply the wants of a decrepit husband and occasionally perform his part." That Fielding suffered socially by the fact of his second marriage is probable. But the fact is proof, if proof were needed, of his courage in reparation, and of the unworldly spirit in which he ultimately followed the dictates of that incorruptible judge which he himself asserted to be in every man's breast.

It was in December 1747, just a month after his second marriage, that Fielding again flung himself into the arena of contentious journalism, 'brandishing' his pen as truculently as ever on behalf of the Protestant and Hanoverian succession, and in despite of the Jacobite cause. He called his new paper "*The Jacobite's Journal*, by John Trott Plaid Esq're.," and the ironic title was accompanied by a woodcut traditionally associated with Hogarth. The ironic mask, Fielding explains, was assumed "in order if possible to laugh Men out of their follies and to make men ashamed of owning or acting by" Jacobite principles.

The *Jacobite's Journal* appeared at a moment when public opinion, and public gossip also, seem to have been immersed in the question whether a notorious pamphlet purporting to have been found among the papers of a late Minister, Mr. Thomas Winnington, were genuine or a libel. Into this fray Fielding promptly plunged, publishing, in December 1747, [2] a shilling pamphlet entitled *A Proper Answer to a Late Scurrilous Libel,... By the Author of the Jacobites Journal.* This little pamphlet, copies of which may be seen in the British Museum, is merely a further vigorous declamation for civil liberty and the Protestant religion, as under King George, and contains hardly any reference either to Winnington or to the author. It was retorted on in two further pamphlets. In one of these a Lady Fanny and her friend, enjoying a 'Chit chat,' discuss the news that Lady Fanny is she "whom F—g represents in a *Plaid Jocket* in the front of his *Jacobite*

Journal." "The Whirling Coxcomb," cries Lady Fanny enraged, "what had he to do with ridiculing any Party, who had travell'd round the whole Circle of Parties and Ministers, ever since he could brandish a Pen." [3] Her Ladyship adds some further sneers on writers pensioned to amuse people with their nonsense. The other counter pamphlet consists of conversations overheard, all over the town, on the subject of Winnington and his *Apology*. Here a mercer and a bookseller abuse Fielding for boxing the political compass, and for selling his pen. Another bookseller insinuates that Fielding's own attack on the *Apology* is but a half-hearted affair—"Ah Sir, you know not what F—g could do if he were willing ... you would have seen him mince and hash it so as to make half the Town weep and the other laugh. Don't you think the Pen that writ *Pasquin, Joseph Andrews*, and the *Champion* could have answered the Apology if he had had the Will?" "But I can't see why the Author of the Jacobite Journal should want that will," protests a Bencher. "Alas Sir!" cries the bookseller, "You forget the Power of *Necessity*. If a Man that wants Bread can establish a Paper by the P—t Off—e [Post Office?] taking off two thousand every week is he not more excusable...." To which the Bencher replies that possibly it is Fielding's 'Wavering Principles' that have "brought him to the Necessity of writing for Bread." [4] From all which we may assume that Fielding's superiority to what he calls the "absurd and irrational Distinction of Parties [which] hath principally contributed to poison our Constitution" [5] was very little understood by the heated party factions of 1747.

To call one's political opponent a 'Whirling Coxcomb,' or a 'pensioned scribbler,' was a very mild amenity in eighteenth century party warfare; and the abuse of such small fry as these anonymous pamphleteers might be wholly disregarded did it not show Fielding's prominence, during these anxious times, as a strenuous Hanoverian, and also the fact that he had now not only largely abjured party politics, but that what party tenets he still held were changed. Indeed as much may surely be deduced from the following philosophic passage in his *True Patriot*. "I have formerly shown in this Paper, that the bare objecting to a Man a *Change* in his *Political Notions*, ought by no means to affect any Person's *Character*; because in a Country like this it is simply impossible that a Man of sound Sense, and strict Honour, should always adhere to the same *Political Creed*." [6] It is very little material to our knowledge of Fielding as an honest man and a great genius to discover, were it possible, precisely what changes his political views underwent. When Sir Robert Walpole essayed to corrupt the nation Fielding fought strenuously in the cause of political honour; when a Stewart invasion threatened (as he thought) both civil liberty and Protestant beliefs he flung himself as zealously into the defence of the Church of England and of the Hanoverian Government. It is clear that the latter exertions stirred up much cheap obliquy; and it must be admitted that such references to his antagonists as "last weeks Dunghill of Papers" were likely to entail unsavory retort.

This abuse seems to have broken out with an excess of virulence not long after the appearance of the *Jacobite's Journal*; a fate, as Fielding observes, little to be expected by the editor of a loyal paper. His dignified protest in the matter is worth recalling. In a leading article he declares that "before my paper hath reached the 20th. number a heavier load of Scandal hath been cast upon me than I believe ever fell to the Share of a Single Man. The Author of the Journal was soon guessed at; Either from some Singularity in Style, or from little care which being free from any wicked Purpose, I have ever taken to conceal my Name. Of this several Writers were no sooner possessed than they attempted to blacken it with every kind of Reproach; pursued me into private Life, *even to my boyish Years*; where they have given me almost every Vice in Human Nature. Again they have followed me with uncommon Inveteracy into a Profession in which they have very roundly asserted that I have neither Business nor Knowledge: And lastly, as an Author they have affected to treat me with more Contempt than Mr. Pope, who hath great Merit and no less Pride in the Character of a Writer hath thought proper to bestow on the lowest Scribbler of his Time. All this moreover they have poured forth in a vein of Scurrility which hath disgraced the Press with every abusive Term in our Language." Although, as Fielding adds, those who knew him would not take their opinion from those who knew him not, it is to be feared that the scurrilous libellers of the day succeeded in creating a prejudice that is hardly yet dispersed. For such petty clamours would be trifling enough round the figure of the creator of the English novel, were it not that in the abuse of the gutter press of his day we may probably find the reason for much of the vague cloud which has so strangely overhung Fielding's name. In his own spirited protest he tells us of the 'ordure' that was thrown at him; and it is an old saying that if enough mud be thrown some will stick.

In the February following the appearance of his new paper Fielding must have been at Twickenham; for the baptism of his son William appears in the Parish Register for that month. A writer of thirty years ago says that the house celebrated as that in which Fielding lived was then still standing, a quaint old fashioned wooden dwelling, in Back Lane; and adds the information that Fielding had two rooms, the house being then let in lodgings. [7] Lysons, however, in his *Environs of London*, published in 1795, says that Fielding "rented a house at this time in the Back-Lane at Twickenham," adding that he received his information from the Earl of Orford. The site is now occupied by a row of cottages. In his *Parish Register for Twickenham* Horace Walpole commemorates the great novelist's residence in that quiet village, so full of eighteenth century memories. Here, he says,

"... Fielding met his bunter Muse,
And, as they quaff'd the fiery juice,
Droll Nature stamp'd each lucky hit
With unimaginable wit."

Bunter was a cant word for a woman who picks up rags about the street; and it may seem to later generations that the epithet fitted far more nicely the *bunter muse* of that "facile retailer of *ana* and incorrigible society-gossip," that rag-picker of anecdotes, Mr. Horace Walpole himself.

When the *Journal* had been running some six months, Fielding formally relinquished his ironic character of a Jacobite, partly because, as he says, the evils of Jacobitism were too serious for jesting and required more open denunciation; partly because the age required more highly seasoned writing, the general taste in reading very much resembling "that of some particular Man in eating who would never willingly devour what doth not stink"; and partly from the ineptitude of the public to appreciate the ironic method. This latter passage is of interest as coming from the author of that great masterpiece in irony, *Jonathan Wild*. Fielding has observed, he tells us that "though Irony is capable of furnishing the most exquisite Ridicule; yet as there is no kind of humour so liable to be mistaken it is of all others the most dangerous to the Writer. An infinite Number of Readers have not the least taste or relish for it, I believe I may say do not understand it; and all are apt to be tired when it is carried to any degree of Length."

The *Jacobite's Journal* is of course mainly occupied with maintaining the Protestant British Constitution; but here, as in the *True Patriot*, Fielding allows himself a pleasant running commentary on the daily news. He also erects a *Court of Criticism* in which, by virtue of his "high Censorial Office," he administers justice in "all matters in the Republic of Literature." By thus adopting the title of "Censor of Great Britain" the editor of the *Jacobites Journal* preserves his identity with that censorial *Champion* who nine years before had essayed to keep rogues in fear of his Hercules' club. Two judgments delivered by the *Court* are of interest. In one, due castigation is given to that incorrigible mimic and wit Foote, who was once threatened by no less a cudgel than that of Dr. Johnson himself. Foote was evading all law and order by his inimitable mimicries at the Little Theatre in the Haymarket; and for these performances at his "scandal-shop" is very properly brought up before Mr. Censor's *Court*. Whereupon Foote begins to mimic the *Court* "pulling a Chew of Tobacco from his Mouth, in Imitation of his Honour who is greatly fond of that weed." The culprit suffers conviction for crime against law and good manners. Having thus seen to the public welfare, Fielding also happily settles a little score of his own on one of his anonymous libellers. "One Porcupine Pillage," he records, "came into the court and threw a great shovelful of dirt at his honour, *but luckily none of it hit him*." His comments on weekly news items are no less characteristic than those hidden in the columns of the *Patriot*. Thus, on a trotting match, he observes, "Trotting is a Sport truly adapted to the English Genius." And on a man found dead in Jewin Street "formerly an eminent Dealer in Buckrams, but [who] being greatly reduced is supposed to have died for Want," he notes, "*either of Common Sense in himself or Common Humanity in his Aquaintance*." His own humanity is shown in the wise appeals, repeated on more than one page of the *Journal*, for some effective provision for the distressed widows and children of the poor clergy. And his unbiassed judgment appears in the *amende honorable* to Richardson, in the form of generous and unstinted praise of *Clarissa*.

The first number of the *Jacobite's Journal* was dated Dec. 5, 1747, and 'Mr. Trott Plaid' formally takes leave of his subject exactly eleven months later, on November 5, 1748, declaring that Jacobites were, by then, little to be feared. [8] Ten days before this last 'brandish' of Fielding's Constitutional pen, on October 26, 1748, his oaths had been received as a Justice of the Peace for Westminster.

[1] These are in the Burney Collection, and are inscribed "These papers are by the celebrated Henry Fielding Esqre."

[2] See the *Gentleman's Magazine*. Dec. 1747.

[3] *A Free Comment on the Late Mr. W-G-N's Apology ... By a Lady ...* 1748.

[4] *The Patriot Analized.* 1748.

[5] *True Patriot No. 14.*

[6] *True Patriot.* No. 29. May 20, 1746.

[7] R. Cobbett. *Memorials of Twickenham*, 1872.

[8] The *Journal's* epitaph was promptly written by a scurrilous opponent in lines showing that the prominences of Fielding's profile were well-known:

Beneath this stone

Lies *Trott Plaid John*

His length of chin and nose.

See the *Gentleman's Magazine*, November 1748.

CHAPTER XI

TOM JONES

"In God's Name let us speak out honestly and set the good against
the bad."
No. 48 of the *Jacobite's Journal.*

The two years of Fielding's life preceding his appointment as a Bow Street
magistrate (an appointment comparable only to the choice of Robert Burns as
an exciseman) were marked, as we have seen, by lively passages in the political
arena, and a steady output of political journalism. Indeed, by this time, the public
must have associated swingeing denunciations of Jacobites, and glowing eulogies
of the British Constitution, with Harry Fielding's name; just as seven years
previously he had been in their eyes the 'Champion' journalist of a brilliant
Opposition; and, for ten years before that, the witty writer of a stream of
popular farces and comedies. For there is no evidence that his audacious
innovation, his splendid adventure in literature, *Joseph Andrews,* really revealed the
existence of a new genius in their midst to the Whigs and Tories of those
factious days, to the gay frequenters of the play-house, to the barristers at
Westminster Hall and on the Western Circuit. In 1748 Fielding must have been,
to his many audiences, a witty and well-born man of letters who, at forty-one,
had as yet achieved no towering success; a facile dramatist; and a master of
slashing political invective, growing perplexingly impartial, alike in his praise and
his condemnation. While, as regards outward circumstances, the struggling
barrister, baffled in his professional hopes by persistent attacks of gout, was now
so far enlisted, to use his own fine image, under the black banner of poverty,
that even the small post and hard duties of a Bow Street magistrate were worth
his acceptance. [1]

Such was Harry Fielding as the world of 1748 knew him, in the Coffee
houses, the Mall, the Green-room and the Law-courts. What that world did not
know was that all this dramatic, journalistic, and political action, was little more
than the surface movement of a vitality far too exuberant to be contained in any
one groove of hackney writing,—of an impetuous 'enthusiasm for righteousness'
far too ardent to pass by any flagrant social, moral, or political abuse without
inflicting some form of chastisement; and that beneath this ever active surface
movement Fielding's genius was slowly maturing in that new continent of
literature the borders of which he had already crossed seven years before. In the
pages of *Joseph Andrews,* he had, as we know, tentatively explored that continent
feeling his way along the unknown paths of this long neglected world of human
nature; bringing back with him one immortal figure, that living embodiment of
simple piety and scholarship, of charity and honest strength, Parson Adams;
disclosing hints of discoveries, not yet perfected, among the humours and
villanies, the virtues and charms, of a dozen other inhabitants of his *terra*

incognita. But there is no sign that the greatness of his discovery, the splendour of his addition to the empire of English literature, was in the least apprehended during the seven years following the appearance of *Joseph Andrews*. Only Fielding himself was conscious that he had created a kind of writing "hitherto unattempted in our language."

And, having crossed the borders of this new continent, he seems, after his first survey, to have deliberately immersed himself in one portion, and that the blackest, of his re-discovered world. For *Jonathan Wild*, with its disclosure of the active spirit of 'diabolism,' of naked vice, is little else than the exploration of those darkest recesses of human nature which can be safely entered only by the sanest and healthiest of intellects. Fielding's strength was equal to his exploit; and from this, his second adventure, he brought back a picture of the deformity and folly of vice, drawn with a just and penetrating scorn unequalled, perhaps, by any English moralist. But neither of these two essays in the new field of writing had covered more than isolated or outlying portions, the first in sunlight, the second in shadow, of that vast territory. And it was not till the perfect maturity of his powers and of his experience, not till he had seen both the 'manners of many men,' and the workings of many hearts, not in a word till he had made himself master of great tracts of that human nature which had so long lain neglected, that Fielding in *Tom Jones* disclosed himself as the creator of the English novel.

Little is known as to when the conception of *Tom Jones* first shaped itself in his mind, of where he lived during the writing of the great Comic Epic, or of the time occupied in its completion. Appropriately for a book expressly designed "to recommend goodness and innocence" the plan of the novel was suggested, many years before its appearance, by the 'good Lord Lyttelton'; and we know, further, that the writing occupied 'some thousands of hours'; but *Tom Jones* does not emerge into definite existence till the summer of 1748.

Legend it is true, attesting to the greatness of the achievement contained in the six little volumes, endows many localities with the fame of their origin. A well-credited contemporary writer, the Rev. Richard Graves, declared that the novelist "while he was writing his novel of Tom Jones" lived at Tiverton (Twerton), one and a half miles from Bath, and dined daily at Prior Park the seat of his munificent and pious friend Ralph Allen. Mr Graves says that Fielding then lived in "the first house on the right hand with a spread eagle over the door." [2] Salisbury is insistent that part at least of the great novel was written at Milford House, near to that city. An anonymous old engraver asserts the same honour for Fielding's Farm at East Stour, an assertion certainly not confirmed by the newly found documents concerning Fielding's sale of property at Stour in 1738. Twickenham claims that the book was wholly composed in the house in Back Lane. And to an ancient building at Tintern Parva in the Wye Valley, said to have once been the lodging of the Abbot of Tintern, was also assigned the reputation of being the birthplace of the English novel. If the latter tradition were true, the fact that it was in the Harlequin chamber of the Abbots of Glastonbury that Henry Fielding was born, becomes strangely matched by the birth, some forty years later, of his masterpiece, in the lodging of the Abbot of Tintern. The one point of real interest in all these traditions is the fact that the fame of *Tom Jones* has been sufficient to create a widespread popular legend. The truth probably is that the book was written in the many shifting scenes of Fielding's life during these years; now at Bath whither his gout and the generous hospitality of Ralph Allen would take him; now in Salisbury, the home of his boyhood, and the scene of his courtship with the lovely original of Sophia Western; possibly in his own county of Somerset; and most probably both at Twickenham, and in London.

From these various legends it is pleasant to be able to disentangle one clear picture of the making of *Tom Jones*. Before the manuscript was placed in the printers' hands Fielding submitted it to the opinion both of the elder Pitt, and of the estimable and pious Lyttelton; and the account of this memorable meeting cannot be better given than in the words of a descendant of the hostess on that occasion, the Rev. George Miller, great-grandson of that Sanderson Miller of Radway, Warwickshire, who numbered many men of note among his acquaintance, and with whom Fielding was on terms of intimate friendship. [3] Writing to the present writer, in 1907, Mr. Miller says: "Lord Chatham and Lord Lyttleton came to Radway to visit my ancestor, when Lord Chatham planted three trees to commemorate the visit, and a stone urn was placed between them. Fielding was also of the party and read 'Tom Jones' in manuscript after dinner for the opinion of his hearers before publishing it. My father told me this often and he had the account from his Grandmother who survived her husband several years and who was the hostess on the occasion." Unhappily no record exists of the comments of one of the greatest of English statesmen when listening to this reading, in manuscript, of indubitably one of the greatest of English novels.

The vagueness which hangs over the places in which *Tom Jones* was written, the certainty that in all of them poverty was constantly present, is in perfect accord with the power of detachment manifested in this book from circumstances that would surely have tinged, if not over-whelmed, a weaker genius. Sickness and poverty are stern sponsors; but neither were suffered to leave more than two traces on the pages destined to outlive so greatly the harsh circumstances in which they had birth. There is the frank acknowledgement of the writer's dependence on Lyttelton's noble generosity, without which the book had never, Fielding says, been completed, since "I partly owe to you my Existence during great Part of the Time which I have employed in composing it." And a touching betrayal occurs of his anxiety for the future provision of the "prattling babes, whose innocent play hath often been interrupted by my labours." Fielding was sensitively anxious for his wife and children; but, for himself, living as he did with visions such as that of the *Invocation* introducing Book xiii of *Tom Jones*, the precise situation of his "little Parlour," or the poorness of its furniture, cannot have appeared very material. "Come bright Love of Fame," he cries "... fill my ravished Fancy with the Hopes of charming Ages yet to come... Do thou teach me not only to foresee, but to enjoy, nay, even to feed on future Praise. Comfort me by a solemn Assurance, that when the little Parlour in which I sit at this Instant, shall be reduced to a worse furnished Box, I shall be read, with Honour, by those who never knew nor saw me, and whom I shall neither know nor see."

This capacity of Fielding for relegating circumstance to its true level, the detached idealism that moulded his genius, are, indeed, shown once for all in the fact that the exquisite picture of virtue, the whole-hearted attack on vice, the genial humour, the sunny portraits of humanity, the splendid cheerfulness of *Tom Jones*, that 'Epic of Youth,' came from a man in middle age, immersed in disheartening struggles, and fighting recurrent ill health. Superficial critics have called Fielding a realist because his figures are so full-blooded and alive that we feel we have met them but yesterday in the street; to eyes so shortsighted life itself must seem merely realistic. As none but an idealist could have conceived Parson Adams, so the creator of Sophia again announced himself an idealist in the Dedication of *Tom Jones*. Here, in language of pure symbolism, he contends that the ideal virtues such as goodness and innocence, may most effectively be presented to men in a figure, for "an Example is a Kind of Picture, in which Virtue becomes as it were an Object of Sight, and strikes us with an Idea of that Loveliness, which *Plato* asserts there is in her naked Charms." [4] To the man who could write thus, and, who, in later pages of his great 'Epic,' could humbly desire of Genius "do thou kindly take me by the Hand, and lead me through all the Mazes, the winding Labyrinth of Nature. Initiate me into all those Mysteries which profane Eyes never beheld,"—to this man the material surroundings of life must have seemed of little greater import than the fittings of that narrow box to the occupation of which he looked forward with so calm a foresight. Indeed he himself acknowledges a carelessness of outward comfort on his own behalf. "Come," he cries, to the spirit of mercenary success, "Thou jolly Substance, with thy shining Face, ... hold forth thy tempting Rewards; thy shining chinking Heap; thy quickly-convertible Bank-bill, big with unseen Riches; thy often-varying Stock; the warm, the comfortable House; ... Come thou, and if I am too tasteless of thy valuable Treasures, warm my Heart with the transporting Thought of conveying them to others." His happy constitution, wrote his cousin Lady Mary, "made him forget everything when he was before a venison pasty or a flask of champagne"; but behind those healthy exhilarations was, assuredly, a serenity based on a clear perception of the values of life. To a man of Fielding's happy social temperament, and who was yet also initiated into mysteries and occupied in converting ideal loveliness into 'an object of sight,' such matters as duns and pawnbrokers would seem precisely fit for oblivion in venison and champagne. In the creator of Tom Jones and of Sophia the most indestructible delight in living, and the keenest discernment of the unsubstantial qualities of that delight, appear to have been admirably interwoven.

By June 11, 1748, the book was far enough advanced for the publisher, Andrew Millar, to pay £600 for it, as appears from a receipt now in the possession of Mr. Alfred Huth. [5] And it is eminently characteristic of the finances of a man who, as Lady Mary said, would have wanted money had his estates been as extensive as his imagination, that the receipt for this £600 is dated more than six months before the publication of the book. For it was not till February 28, 1749, that the *General Advertiser* announced

This day is published, in six vols., 12 mo
THE HISTORY OF TOM JONES,
A FOUNDLING
Mores hominum multorum vidit.
By HENRY FIELDING, *Esqre*

Henceforth Fielding ceases to be the boisterous politician, the witty dramatist; his poverty and his struggles for subsistence fall back, at his own bidding, among the accidents of life; and he stands revealed as the supreme genius, the creator of the English novel, the inheritor of that lasting fame which he had dared so confidently to invoke.

The immediate success of the book, in that eighteenth-century world into which it was launched, is attested by the notice in the *London Magazine* of the very month of its publication. Under the heading of a "Plan of a late celebrated NOVEL," the *Magazine* devotes its five opening pages to a summary of a book "which has given great Amusement and we hope Instruction to the polite Part of the Town." The summary is preceded by a description of *Tom Jones* as a novel "calculated to recommend religion and virtue, to shew the bad consequences of indiscretion, and to set several kinds of vice in their most deformed and shocking light." The reviewer declares that "after one has begun to read it, it is difficult to leave off before having read the whole." And he concludes, "Thus ends this pretty novel, with a most just distribution of rewards and punishments, according to the merits of all the persons who had any considerable share in it." [6] Three months later Horace Walpole wrote, "Millar the bookseller has done very generously by him [Fielding]: finding Tom Jones, for which he had given him £600, sell so greatly, he has since given him another hundred." An admirer breaks out into rhyme, in the *Gentleman's Magazine* for August 1749,—
"let Fielding take the pen!
Life dropt her mask, and all mankind were men."
thereby anticipating Thackeray's famous complaint that in his day no one dared "to depict to his utmost power a Man." Lady Bradshaigh, writing by a happy irony of fate to Richardson, says "as to Tom Jones I am fatigued with the name, having lately fallen into the company of several young ladies, who had each a 'Tom Jones' in some part of the world, for so they call their favourites." The gentlemen also had their Sophias, one indeed having bestowed that all-popular name on his 'Dutch mastiff puppy.' That eccentric eighteenth century philosopher, and enthusiastic Greek scholar, Lord Monboddo declared that *Tom Jones* had more of character in it than any other work, ancient or modern, known to him, adding, "in short, I never saw anything that was so animated, and as I may say, *all alive* with characters and manners as *the History of Tom Jones*"; a criticism that recalls Lady Mary Wortley Montagu's remark that no man enjoyed

life more than did Fielding. Doubtless it was his own magnificent capacity for living that endowed the very creatures of his pen with so abundant a vitality. In her own copy Lady Mary wrote *Ne plus Ultra*.

To turn from the popular voices of the day to the comments of those capable of appraising genius, "What a master of composition Fielding was!" exclaimed Coleridge, "Upon my word I think 'Oedipus Tyrannus,' the 'Alchemist,' and 'Tom Jones' the three most perfect plots ever planned." To Sir Walter Scott *Tom Jones* was "truth and human nature itself." Gibbon described the book as "the first of ancient or modern romances"; and, as we have seen, declared that its pages would outlive the Imperial Eagle of those Hapsburgs from whom Fielding was said to be descended. "There can be no gainsaying the sentence of this great judge," wrote Thackeray. "To have your name mentioned by Gibbon is like having it written on the dome of St Peter's. Pilgrims from all the world admire and behold it." Pilgrims from all the world have likewise admired *Tom Jones*. Translations have appeared in French, German, [7] Spanish, Swedish, Russian, Polish and Dutch; and as for the English editions, they range from the three editions issued within the year of publication to the several noble volumes newly edited in our own day, and the sixpenny copies on our railway bookstalls. So fully has time justified the invocation to future fame sent forth from the little ill-furnished parlour of the struggling barrister.

To analyse the grounds for a chorus of praise ranging from the 'young ladies' of the eighteenth century to the utterances of distinguished critics, and popular authors of our own day, would be to confound literary criticism with biography. But there are some points appertaining to Fielding's great novel which cannot be here disregarded, in that they closely affect his personal character. Such are the light in which he himself regarded his masterpiece, the intention with which he wrote it, and the means which he selected to carry that intention into effect.

All these he himself very plainly sets forth in his *Dedication* to Lyttelton and in other passages of *Tom Jones*. As to his intention. "I declare," he says, in the *Dedication*, "that to recommend Goodness and Innocence hath been my sincere Endeavour in this History." And the means selected for this end, and for the companion object of persuading men from guilt, are as clearly stated. First as we have seen, Fielding plays the part of pure idealist, purposing to create a picture "in which virtue becomes as it were an object of sight." For such pictures we have but to think of Sophia Western, and of that final page of *Tom Jones*, than which no more charming representation of mutual affection, esteem, and well doing can be imagined. But besides this means of reaching his audience Fielding adopted, he tells us, a second method. He argues that no acquisitions of guilt can compensate a man for the loss of inward peace, for the attendant horror, anxiety, and danger, to which he subjects himself; thus endeavouring to enlist man's self-interest no less than his admiration, on the side of virtue. Again, he explains yet another method by which he essays to foil the progress of evil, viz. to show that virtue and innocence are chiefly betrayed "into the snares that deceit and villainy spread for them" by indiscretion; a moral which he has "the more industriously laboured ... since I believe it is much easier to make good

Men, wise than to make bad Men good." For this purpose, he concludes, namely to show, as in a figure, the beauty of virtue, to persuade men that in following innocence and virtue they follow their own obvious interests, to arm them from the snares of villainy and deceit, "I have employed all the Wit and Humour of which I am Master in the following History; wherein I have endeavoured to laugh Mankind out of their favourite Follies and Vices."

And, conscious that wit and humour require a rein quite unneeded by the methods of the professional moralist, Fielding further asserts that in these pages his laughter is worthy of the aim which he sets before him. Here, he carefully insists, are wit and humour wholly void of offence. He assures his reader that in the whole course of the work, he will find "nothing prejudicial to the Cause of Religion and Virtue; nothing inconsistent with the strictest Rules of Decency, nor which can offend even the chastest Eye in the Perusal." As the almost incredible change from the manners of 1749 to those of the following century, and of our own day, has injuriously affected the reputation of Fielding among readers ignorant of past conditions, this protest, in striking accord with the prologue for his first play acted when he was but a lad of twenty, cannot be too emphatically recorded. And no further justification of Fielding's words need be entered than that verdict of the eighteenth century scholar and bishop of the English Church, Doctor Warburton, when he declared that "Mr. Fielding [stands] the foremost among those who have given a faithful and chaste copy of life and manners."

Such were the noble purposes to which Fielding consciously dedicated his genius in *Tom Jones*, and such was the careful restraint with which he exercised his chosen methods of wit and humour. That these purposes, executed by a supreme genius in the language and scenes of his own day, should ever have laid their author open to a charge of immorality is perhaps one of the most amazing pieces of irony in the whole history of English literature. But as this charge of moral laxity has been seriously brought against the pages of *Tom Jones*, and is perhaps not yet quite exploded, it cannot be wholly disregarded. The imputation amounts, briefly, to a too easy forgiveness for the youthful sins of Jones, and the involving that engaging youth in too deep a degradation. The answers to these charges are, firstly, that Fielding held strongly, and here exhibits, the humane and wise doctrine that a man should be judged, not by what he sometimes does, but by what he *is*. And, secondly, that as Sir Walter Scott pointed out, when dealing with this very matter, "the vices into which Jones suffers himself to fall are made the direct cause of placing him in the distressful situation which he occupies during the greater part of the narrative; while his generosity, his charity, and his amiable qualities become the means of saving him from the consequences of his folly." Fielding was not wholly concerned with the acts of a man; to him the admission of the Penitent Thief into Paradise, at the eleventh hour, could have been no stumbling block. And, further, Tom Jones not only suffers for his ill doing, but wins no heaven until he wholly purges himself from the sin which did so easily beset him.

The distinction between doing and being is very fully enunciated by Fielding himself, in the *Introduction* to Book vii. "A single bad Act," he says, "no more constitutes a Villain in Life, than a single bad Part on the Stage". And again, "Now we, who are admitted behind the Scenes of this great Theatre of Nature, (and no Author ought to write any Thing besides Dictionaries and Spelling-Books who hath not this Privilege) can censure the Action, without conceiving any actual Detestation of the Person, whom perhaps Nature may not have designed to act an ill Part in all her Dramas: For in this Instance, Life most exactly represents the Stage, since it is often the same Person who represents the Villain and the Heroe". Coleridge has expressed the same truth in words written in a copy of *Tom Jones*, "If I want a servant or mechanic I wish to know what he *does*—but of a Friend I must know what he *is*. And in no writer is this momentous distinction so finely brought forward as by Fielding. We do not care what Blifil does ... but Blifil *is* a villain and we feel him to be so." [8]

It is true that, as Scott regrets the depth of degradation into which Tom Jones is suffered to fall, so Coleridge expresses a wish, "relatively to Fielding himself" that the great novelist had emphasised somewhat more the repentance of his hero: but this may be balanced by that other noble tribute to his morality, "I dare believe who consulted his heart and conscience only without adverting to *what the world* would say could rise from the perusal of Fielding's *Tom Jones, Joseph Andrews* and *Amelia* without feeling himself the better man—at least without an intense conviction that he could not be guilty of a base act." [9] To be forced to watch the temporary degradation of a noble nature, and the miseries ensuing, is surely one of the most effective means of rousing a hatred of vice. That such an exhibition should ever have been construed into moral laxity on the part of the author, especially when the restoration of the hero's character is drawn as entirely due to his ingrained worship of innocence and virtue, is almost incredible.

In exact accordance with Fielding's character as moralist in intent, although supreme artist in execution, is the fact of the dedication of *Tom Jones* to his life-long friend Lyttelton. George Lyttelton, statesman, scholar, and orator, was a friend of whom any man might be proud. It was said of him that he "showed the judgment of a minister, the force and wit of an orator, and the spirit of a gentleman." As theologian he wrote a treatise on *The Conversion of St. Paul* which, a hundred years later, was described as being "still regarded as one of the subsidiary bulwarks of Christianity." As poet he won the praise of Gray for his tender and elegiac verse. Thomson sang of his "sense refined," and adds
Serene yet warm, humane yet firm his mind
As little touch'd as any man's with bad;

And Pope drew his character as "Still true to virtue and as warm as true."

It was to this devout scholar, this refined gentleman, this warm-hearted follower of virtue, that *Tom Jones* was dedicated, nay more, to him it owed both origin and completion. "To you, Sir," Fielding writes in his *Dedication*, "it is owing that this History was ever begun. It was by your Desire that I first thought of such a Composition.... Again, Sir, without your Assistance this

History had never been completed.... I partly owe to you my Existence during great Part of the Time in which I have employed in composing it." And that Lyttelton cordially approved the book which owed so much to his own insight and generosity is evident from the references, in the *Dedication*, to his favourable judgment.

With the appearance of *Tom Jones* Fielding steps into his own place among the immortals. But lofty as his genius was, his feet were firmly planted in the world which he relished so keenly. To no man could be applied more happily the motto chosen by him for his title page, *mores hominum multorum vidit*—he saw the manners of many men. This characteristic emerges in a personal reminiscence of the novelist, at the very moment when the sheets of *Tom Jones* were passing through the press. The great-nephew of his intimate friend Mrs Hussey relates; "Henry Fielding was fond of colouring his pictures of life with the glowing and variegated tints of Nature, by conversing with persons of every situation and calling, as I have frequently been informed by one of my great aunts, the late Mrs Hussey, who knew him intimately. I have heard her say, that Mr Fielding never suffered his talent for sprightly conversation to mildew for a moment; and that his manners were so gentlemanly, that even with the lower classes, with which he frequently condescended particularly to chat such as Sir Roger de Coverley's old friends, the Vauxhall water-men, they seldom outstepped the limits of propriety. My aunt ... [was] a fashionable sacque and mantua-maker, and lived in the Strand, ... One day Mr Fielding observed to Mrs Hussey, that he was then engaged in writing a novel, which he thought would be his best production; and that he intended to introduce into it the characters of all his friends. Mrs Hussey, with a smile, ventured to remark, that he must have many niches, and that surely they must already be filled. 'I assure you, my dear madam,' replied he, 'there shall be a bracket for a bust of you.' Some time after this, he informed Mrs Hussey that the work was in the press; but, immediately recollecting that he had forgotten his promise to her, went to the printer, and was time enough to insert, in vol. iii. p. 17, where he speaks of the shape of Sophia Western—'Such charms are there in affability, and so sure is it to attract the praises of all kinds of people.... It may indeed be compared to the celebrated Mrs Hussey.' To which observation he has given the following note: 'A celebrated mantua-maker in the Strand, famous for setting off the shapes of women.'" [10]

Here is yet further proof, that Fielding loved not only to see the manners of many men, but also to render them whatever service lay within his power. Never were the warmest heart and the loftiest genius more happily united than in the creator of the English novel.

Lyttelton not only suggested and approved the great Comic Epic, and enabled distressed genius to live while composing it; his own worth and benevolence, together with those of the generous Allen, afforded Fielding, as he tells us, the materials for the picture here presented of Allworthy. "The World," he says, speaking of this picture, "will not, I believe, make me the Compliment of thinking I took it from myself. I care not: This they shall own, that the two

Persons from whom I have taken it, that is to say, two of the best and worthiest Men in the World, are strongly and zealously my Friends." And a point of still closer personal interest is the fact, already noticed, that in the lovely character and person of Sophia Western, Fielding raised an enduring memorial to that beloved wife whose death had occurred a few years before the publication of *Tom Jones*. The authenticity of the portrait is explicitly stated in the *Invocation* prefixed to Book xiii. Apostrophizing that 'gentle Maid,' bright 'Love of Fame,' Fielding bids her, in the eighteenth century phrase that falls so strangely on a modern ear, "Foretell me that some tender Maid, whose Grandmother is yet unborn, hereafter, when under the fictitious Name of *Sophia* she reads the real worth which once existed in my *Charlotte*, shall, from her sympathetic Breast, send forth the *Heaving Sigh*." Then follows, immediately, his own desire that he too may live in the knowledge and honour of far distant readers. Fielding lies buried under southern skies, far from his wife's English grave; but in the immortal pages of his masterpiece they are not divided.

[1] The Fiat appointing Fielding as Magistrate for the City and Borough of Westminster, now in the House of Lords, is dated July 30, 1748.

[2] On the house identified with Mr Graves' description, and now known as "Fielding's Lodge," a tablet has recently been placed, through the energy of Mr R. G. Naish of Twerton.

[3] See *Life of the Earl of Hardwicke*. G. Harris. 1847. Vol. II. pp. 456-7.

[4] *Tom Jones*. Dedication.

[5] See Appendix for this, hitherto unpublished, receipt.

[6] *London Magazine*. Feb. 1749.

[7] In Germany an edition of 1771 was followed by a second in 1780, and a third in 1786. In 1765 a lyrical comedy founded on the famous novel was acted in Paris; and the same year it was transformed into a German comedy by J.H. Steffens.

[8] S. T. Coleridge. Manuscript notes in a copy of *Tom Jones*, now in the British Museum.

[9] Ibid.

[10] J. T. Smith. *Nollekens and his Times*. Vol. i. pp. 124-5.

CHAPTER XII

MR JUSTICE FIELDING

"The principal Duty which every Man owes is to his Country." *Enquiry into the ... Increase of Robbers.*

To have created the English novel were, it might seem, achievement enough to tire for a while the most vigorous of intellects; but to the author of *Tom Jones* the apathy of repose was unknown. At no period of Fielding's short life can he be discerned as doing nothing; and, indeed, to an insight so penetrating, to an ardour so irrepressible, the England of George the Second can have afforded but very little inducement to inaction.

Thus, in the one month of October 1748, the pages of *Tom Jones* must have been nearing completion, if indeed the sheets were not already passing through the press. The Hanoverian philippics of "Mr Trott-Plaid" were still resounding in the *Jacobite's Journal.* While, on the 26th. of the month, Fielding's oaths were received for an entirely new rôle, that of a Justice of the Peace for Westminster. [1] Ten days later the *Jacobite's Journal* had ceased to exist; and that a rumour was abroad connecting this demise of the *Journal* with the bestowal of a new and arduous post on its editor appears from a paragraph in the *London Evening Post.* On Nov. 8, that organ prepares its readers for the fact that the now defunct "Mr Trott-Plaid" may possibly "rise awful in the Form of a Justice." Within four weeks of this announcement 'Justice Fielding's' name appears for the first time in the Police-news of the day, in a committal dated December 10th [2]. And two days later he is sending three thieves to the Gatehouse, and admitting a suspected thief to bail, "after an Examination which lasted several hours." And it is interesting to notice that throughout this first month of his magisterial work the now 'awful form' of Justice Henry Fielding was kept constantly tempered in the public mind by the fact of his still undiminished popularity as a dramatist. In this December his comedies, with the inimitable 'romp' Kitty Clive as *Miss Lucy*, or the *Intrigueing Chambermaid* or *Chloe*, as the case might be, were played no fewer than nine times on the Drury Lane boards.

Scarcely had Fielding bent his genius to these new responsibilities of examining Westminster suspects and sending the rogues of that city to prison, than he appears preparing for an extension of those duties over the county of Middlesex. To be a county magistrate in 1750, however, necessitated the holding of landed estate worth £100 per annum; and Fielding's estate, for many years, seems to have been his pen. In this difficulty he turned to the Duke of Bedford, whose public virtues, and private generosity, were so soon to be acknowledged in the Dedication of *Tom Jones*. It was but three weeks after his appointment that the Westminster magistrate wrote as follows to the giver of those "princely Benefactions":

"Bow Street. Decr. 13. 1748.

"My Lord,

"Such is my Dependence on the Goodness of your Grace, that before my Gout will permit me to pay my Duty to you personally, and to acknowledge your last kind Favour to me, I have the Presumption to solicite your Grace again. The Business of a Justice of Peace for Westminster is very inconsiderable without the Addition of that for the County of Middlesex. And without this Addition I cannot completely serve the Government in that office. But this unfortunately requires a Qualification which I want. Now there is a House belonging to your Grace, which stands in Bedford St., of 70l. a year value. This hath been long untenanted, and will I am informed, require about 300l. to put in Repair. If your Grace would have the Goodness to let me have a Lease of this House, with some other Tenement worth 30l. a year, for 21 years, it would be a complete Qualification. I will give the full Worth for this lease, according to the valuation which any Person your Grace shall be pleased to appoint sets upon it. The only favour I beg of your Grace is, that I be permitted to pay the Money in two years, at four equal half-yearly Payments. As I shall repair the House as soon as possible, it will be in Reality an Improvement of that small Part of your Grace's estate, and will be certain to make my Fortune.

"Mr Butcher will acquaint your Grace more fully than perhaps I have been able to do; and if Your Grace thinks proper to refer it to him, I and mine will be eternally bound to pray for your Grace tho I sincerely hope you will not lose a Farthing by doing so vast a service to,

"My Lord your Grace's

"Most obliged most obed' humble servant

"H. Ffielding." [3]

It seems probable that the Duke found better means of helping wit and genius, than by the leasing of the dilapidated tenement in Bedford Street. At any rate a month later, on January 11, we find Fielding duly swearing to an estate as consisting of "several Leasehold Messuages or Tenements Lying or being in the several parishes of St Paul Covent Garden, St Martin in the ffields, St Giles in the ffields, and St Georges Bloomsbury ... now in the possession or occupation of [my] Tennants or Undertennants, for and during the Term of Twenty one years of the clear yearly value of £100...." This statement, which is preserved in the Middlesex Records, is followed by Fielding's signature, appended to an oath that his qualification to serve as a Justice of the Peace for the county is as above described. [4]

On the day following this sworn statement, January 12, 1749, his oaths were received as a Justice of the Peace for Middlesex. [5] But even this did not satisfy all the requirements of those days of doctrinal inquisitions and Jacobite risings. The certificate may still be seen among the Middlesex Records, duly certified by Charles Tough, Minister of the Parish and Church of St Pauls, Covent Garden, and 'Sworn in Court,' that "Henry Fielding Esq. on Sunday the 26th day of March, 1749, did receive the Sacrament of the Lord's Supper in ye Parish

Church aforesaid, immediately after Divine Service and Sermon, according to the usage of the Church of England." [6] And among the same archives the dusty *Oath Roll* is preserved, bearing, under date of April 5, 1749, the signature of *Henry ffielding* to a declaration of disbelief in the doctrine of Transubstantiation; a comprehensive oath of faithful service to King George and abjuration of King James; an oath directed against the power of the Holy See; and an oath of true allegiance to King George. All which oaths and declarations, it appears from the endorsement of the *Roll*, were taken immediately after the administration of Holy Communion, as attested by two credible witnesses.[7]

It is with this second Commission in the Peace that we enter on the last five years of Fielding's crowded life, years full of that valiant struggle with eighteenth century crime to which the health of the great novelist was ultimately sacrificed. For no magistrate ever fulfilled more faithfully, or at greater personal cost, the first obligation of his Oath, "Ye shall swear that as Justice of Peace ... ye shall do equall right to the Poor and to the Rich, after your Cunning Witt and Power and after the Laws and Customes of the Realm...." And Fielding brought to his new post something more than a zealous discharge of the daily and nightly duties of an eighteenth century police magistrate. His genius and his patriotism found opportunity in the squalid Bow Street Court-room for advocating reforms as yet untouched by the slow hand of the professional philanthropist. The names of those reformers, of the men and women who swept away the pestilential horrors of eighteenth century prisons, of the statesmen who abolished laws that hung a man for stealing a handkerchief, and destroyed the public gallows that gave the mob their *Tyburn holiday*, of the creators of our temperance legislation, of our poor-law system, of our model dwellings,—all these are held high in honour. Because Henry Fielding was above all things a great creative genius his wise and strenuous efforts to raise social conditions, and to eradicate social sores, have been unduly forgotten.

"Whatever he desired, he desired ardently," says Murphy. We soon have evidence of Justice Henry Fielding's ardent desire to cleanse London from some of the crying evils of his time. Of these evils none pressed more cruelly on the honest citizens than the prevalence and brutality of street robberies. To the well-protected Englishman of to-day the London of 1750 would seem a nightmare of lawlessness. Thieves, as Fielding tells us, attacked their victims with loaded pistols, beat them with bludgeons and hacked them with cutlasses; and as to the murderers of the period, he has recorded how he himself was engaged on *five* different murders, all committed by different gangs of street robbers within the space of one week. The exploit of one such gang may be quoted, from a newspaper paragraph of the first month of Fielding's administration at Bow Street. "On Friday evening," says the *General Advertiser* for January 23, 1749, "about twenty fellows arm'd with Pistols, Cutlasses, Hangers, &c. went to the Gatehouse and one of them knocking at the Door, it was no sooner open'd than they all rush'd in, and struck and desperately wounded the Turnkey, and all that oppos'd them, and in Triumph carried off the Fellow who pick'd General

Sinclaire's pocket of his watch as he was going into Leicester House." Surely, cries the indignant newspaper, "this instance of Daring Impudence must rouse every Person of Property to assemble and consult means for their own Security at least; for if Goals can be forc'd in this manner, private Houses can make but little resistance against such Gangs of Villains as at present infest this Great Metropolis." It was admitted that the numbers and arms of street robbers rendered it ordinarily impossible to arrest them in the act; and Fielding tells us how "Officers of Justice have owned to me that they have passed by [men] with Warrants in their Pockets against them without daring to apprehend them; and indeed they could not be blamed for not exposing themselves to sure Destruction: For it is a melancholy Truth, that at this very Day a Rogue no sooner gives the Alarm within certain Purlieus, than twenty or thirty armed Villains are found ready to come to his Assistance." And the new Justice found no effectual means at his disposal for coping with what he very aptly calls the enslaved condition of Londoners, assaulted, pillaged, and plundered; unable to sleep in their own houses, or to walk the streets, or to travel in safety. There were the Watch, who, we learn from *Amelia* were "chosen out of those poor old decrepid People, who are from their Want of bodily Strength rendered incapable of getting a Livelihood by Work. These Men, armed only with a Pole, which some of them are scarce able to lift, are to secure the Persons and Houses of his Majesty's Subjects from the Attacks of Gangs of young, bold, stout, desperate and well-armed Villains.... If the poor old Fellows should run away from such Enemies, no one I think can wonder, unless he should wonder that they are able even to make their Escape." [8] These lineal descendants of Dogberry were supplemented by constables who it appears had to apply to the military when called upon to cope with the mere suppression of a gaming-house; and by "Thief-catchers," individuals so popularly odious that "the Thief-catcher is in Danger of worse Treatment from the Populace than the Thief." While the law was thus handicapped, the thief, on his side, had the advantage of the irregular buildings and the immense number of lanes, alleys, courts, and bye-places of London and Westminster, which, says Fielding, "had they been intended for the very purpose of concealment, they could scarce have been better contrived. Upon such a view the whole appears as a vast Wood or Forest, in which a Thief may harbour with as great Security as Wild Beasts do in the Desarts of Africa or Arabia." Also the thief's organisation was excellent: "there are at this Time," Fielding observes, "a great Gang of Rogues whose Number falls little short of a Hundred, who are incorporated in one Body, have Officers and a Treasury; and have reduced Theft and Robbery into a regular System." Further, he could generally bribe or deter the prosecutor. And in a last resource "rotten Members of the Law" forged his defence, and abundant false witnesses supported it. An illuminating example of the methods employed by our Georgian ancestors towards "deterring" prosecution occurs in a smuggling case of 1748, perpetrated shortly before Fielding first took office. A party of smugglers caught a custom-house officer and a shoemaker on their way to give evidence. The officer had 'every joint of him' broken; and after other torture, the description of which is more suitable for eighteenth century pages than our own, was dispatched. The less fortunate shoemaker was hung by the middle over a dry well, and left there. Several days afterwards the smugglers, returning and hearing him groan, cut the rope, let him drop to the bottom, and threw in logs and stones to cover him. And it was not only from the common thief that the Londoner of 1750 suffered. That fine flower of eighteenth century lawlessness, the gentleman of the road, carried his audacities into the heart of the Town itself. "I was sitting in my own dining-room on Sunday night," writes Horace Walpole, to a friend, "the clock had not struck eleven, when I heard a loud cry of 'stop thief!' A highwayman had attacked a postchaise in Piccadilly: the fellow was pursued, rode over the watchman, almost killed him, and escaped."

It was into a conflict with this epidemic of crime that Fielding, at forty-three, and with already broken health, flung his energies, to such purpose that in these last five years of his life it is but too easy to forget the creator of *Joseph Andrews*, of *Tom Jones*, and of *Amelia*, in his last 'ardent desire,' as ardently pursued, to purify the sorely diseased body politic. His method of attack was twofold. He dealt vigorously with the individual criminal; and he sought to remove some of the causes by which those criminals were engendered. The individual attack is, for the most part, but sordid reading. Thus from a fragment of the Westminster *Committment Books*, preserved with the Middlesex Records, we may see how in January and February of this year 1749 'Henry Fielding Esq.' committed to the New Prison such cases as:

Thomas Thrupp	for riot
Thomas Trinder	for burglary
T. Chamberlain and Terence Fitz Patrick	for assault
C. O'Neal	for assaulting two Watchmen
Mary Hughes and Caterine Edmonds	for assault and beating
John Smithson	for exercising the art of pattenmaker without having been brought up thereto for seven years
Cornelius York	for filing guineas
Christo Kelsey	for ill fame
Bryan Park	for assault

This sorry list, interspersed with cases of murder, of robbery with violence, and of smuggling, may doubtless be extended over the entire five years of Fielding's work on the Bench; and to reiterate the details of such work would be as tedious now as the monotonous discharge of these duties must once have been to the author of *Tom Jones*. [9] Of much more enduring interest is the great novelist's second line of attack on the problem confronting him.

For Henry Fielding's insight was far too profound for him to fail to strike at the root of individual crime, in those conditions which bred the criminal as surely as, to use his own favourite simile, unclean surroundings breed disease. And he had not been six months on the Bench before finding his first opportunity in a *Charge* delivered, as their Chairman, to the Westminster Grand Jury, on June 29, 1749. [10] This "very loyal, learned, ingenious, excellent and useful" Charge was published "By Order of the Court, and at the unanimous Request of the Gentlemen of the Grand Jury"; and it is, Mr Austin Dobson tells us, "still regarded by lawyers as a model exposition." It is also a stirring appeal to the worthy jurors to discharge their duties as befitted men called upon to exercise one of the most ancient and honourable of English liberties: "Grand Juries, Gentlemen," declared their new Chairman, "are in Reality the only Censors of this Nation. As such, the Manners of the People are in your Hands, and in yours only. You, therefore, are the only Correctors of them.... To execute this Duty with Vigilance, you are obliged by the Duty you owe both to God and to your Country." Here is the same zeal, now directed to stimulating the conscience of the Westminster Jurors, which moved *Captain Vinegar* to lay about him so lustily on all the abuses within reach of his newspaper, and which inspired the 'father of the English Novel' with the admitted motive,—"I declare, that to recommend Goodness and Innocence hath been my sincere Endeavour in this History"—if not with the consummate art of his pages.

Fielding specially directs the energies of his jurors to the repression of open profligacy, the more as, through the 'egregious folly' of their parents, the *Town* had then become the 'seminaries of education' for youths of birth and station. And he bids them attend to those 'temples of iniquity' the masquerade rooms of the time, with a side glance at Foote's scandalous performances; to the gaming houses; to the prevalent vice of profane swearing, that "detestable Crime, so injurious to the Honour of God, so directly repugnant to His positive Commands, so highly offensive to the Ears of all good Men, and so very scandalous to the Nation in the Ears of Foreigners"; and to the libeller, a species of 'Vermin' whom "men ought to crush wherever they find him, without staying till he bite them." It is noteworthy also, that to the genius of Fielding, 'watching, brooding, creating,' the characteristic feature of his age seemed to be a "fury after licentious and luxurious pleasures." "Gentlemen," he cries, "our News-Papers, from the Top of the Page to the Bottom, the Corners of our Streets up to the very Eves of our Houses, present us with nothing but a View of Masquerades, Balls, and Assemblies of various Kinds, Fairs, Wells, Gardens, &c. tending to promote Idleness, Extravagance and Immorality, among all Sorts of People." Many of the public, he declares, make diversion "no longer the Recreation or Amusement, but the whole Business of their Lives"; and not content with three theatres they must have a fourth. What would he have said to a London in which not four but a hundred and twenty theatres draw nightly, and sometimes twice a day, their crowded audiences.

Two days after the delivery of this *Charge* (which the *General Advertiser* praises as "excellent and learned") a three days street riot broke out, which it fell to Fielding to subdue. On Saturday July 1 a mob had gathered in the Strand, about a disorderly house where a sailor was said to have been robbed. Beadle Nathaniel Munns, arriving on the scene, found the mob crying out "Pull down the house, pull down the house!"; and sent for the constables. Meanwhile the mob broke open the house and demolished and stripped the same; and throwing the goods out of the windows, set fire to them, causing such danger of a general conflagration that 'the parish engines' were sent for. A constable, *not being able to find any magistrate in Town*, went to Somerset House to procure assistance from the military, and on his returning with a corporal and twelve men, a force that later that night was increased to an officer and forty men, the mob was at last dispersed. On the next day, however, Sunday, they reassembled, and proceeded to demolish a second house, and to burn the goods thereof with an even larger fire than that of the preceding night. Mr Saunders Welch, High Constable for Holborn and, Fielding tells us, "one of the best Officers who was ever concerned in the Execution of Justice, and to whose Care, Integrity and Bravery the Public hath, to my Knowledge, the highest Obligations," passing through Fleet Street at the time, saw this second fire, and was told by the owner of another house that the mob threatened to come to him next. Upon which Mr Welch "well knowing the Impossibility of procuring any Magistrate at that Time who would act," went to the Tilt Yard and procured an officer and some forty men; and returning, found the third house in great part wrecked, the danger of fire here being aggravated by the extreme narrowness of the street on both sides and the fact that the premises of a bank were adjacent. This same Sunday night, also, the mob broke open the night-prison under Beadle Munns' house, rescuing two prisoners; and forced the Watch-house of the Liberty with stones and brick bats, to the imminent danger of the Beadle's life, as "sworn before me, Henry Fielding." Till three in the morning Mr Welch and the soldiers remained on duty, by which time the rioters had again dispersed. All this time Fielding, Mr Welch records, was out of town; but, by noon on Monday, the Justice was back in Bow Street: and, on being acquainted with the riot, immediately dispatched an order for a party of the Guards to bring the prisoners to his house, the streets being then full of a riotous crowd threatening danger of rescue. Fielding proceeded to examine the prisoners, a "vast mob" meanwhile being assembled in Bow Steet, and the streets adjacent. On information of the threatening aspect of the people he applied to the Secretary at War for a reinforcement of the Guards; and from his window, spoke to the mob, informing them of their danger, and exhorting them to disperse, but in vain. Rumours, moreover, came that four thousand sailors were assembling to march to the Strand that Monday night. In view of these rumours and of the riotous state of the streets, Fielding, the officer of the guard, and Mr Welch "sat up the whole night, while a large party of soldiers were kept ready under arms who with the peace officers patrolled the streets." And thanks to this vigorous action on the part of their new magistrate the citizens found peace restored within twelve hours of his return to town.

The same day as that on which Fielding was addressing the riotous mob from his Bow Street windows, and sitting up all night with the officer of a military guard, he found time to write to the Duke of Bedford on his own behalf and on that of his family, concerning the provision for which he betrays so constant an anxiety.

"Bow Street. July 3. 1749.

"My Lord,

"The Protection which I have been honoured with receiving at the Hands of your Grace, and the goodness which you were pleased to express some time toward me, embolden me to mention to your Grace that the Place of Solicitor to the Excise is now vacant by the Death of Mr Selwyn. I hope no Person is better qualified for it, and I assure you, my Lord, none shall execute it with more Fidelity. I am at this Moment busied in endeavouring to suppress a dangerous Riot, or I w'd have personally waited on your Grace to solicite a Favour which will make me and my Family completely happy.

"I am, &c.,

"H. Ffielding." [11]

The vacant post was secured, alas, by another candidate.

A few weeks after the riotous scenes which had enabled Fielding to show himself a man of prompt action in times of popular ferment, the publication is advertised of his *Charge*, published "by order of the Court and at the request of the Gentleman of the Grand Jury." And on the same day he submits to the Lord Chancellor a copy both of this pamphlet, and of a draft of a *Bill for the better preventing Street Robberies &c*, the design of which it appears Lord Hardwick had already encouraged.

"Bow Street, July 21. 1749.

"My Lord,

"I beg your Lordship's acceptance of a Charge given by me to the Grand Jury of Westminster though I am but too sensible how unworthy it is of your notice.

"I have likewise presumed to send my Draught of a Bill for the better preventing street Robberies &c. which your Lordship was so very kind to say you would peruse; I hope the general Plan at least may be happy in your Approbation.

"Your Lordship will have the goodness to pardon my repeating a desire that the name of Joshua Brogden, may be inserted in the next commission of the Peace for Middlesex and Westminster for whose [integrity] and Ability in the Execution of his office. I will engage my credit with your Lordship, an Engagement which appears to me of the most sacred Nature.

"I am,

"My Lord, with the utmost Respect and Devotion,

"Your Lordship's most Obed't

"Most humble Servant

"H. Ffielding. [12]

"To the Right Hon'ble.

"The Lord High Chancellor of G. Britain."

All trace of the text of this draft Bill seems to have been lost; but the fact of the Lord Chancellor's consent to consider its provisions shows clearly enough how rapidly Fielding was adding to his now achieved fame as the author of *Tom Jones* the very different reputation of an authority on criminal legislation.

The application on behalf of Joshua Brogden, later if not at this time the Justice's Clerk, recalls the further pleasant tribute paid to the soundness of Mr Brogden's morals in the *Journal of a Voyage to Lisbon*. If all Fielding's modest magisterial income of £300 a year had gone, as he declares it should have done, to his clerk, that functionary would, he tells us, have been "but ill paid for sitting almost sixteen hours in the twenty four, in the most unwholesome, as well as nauseous air in the universe, and which hath in his case corrupted a good constitution without contaminating his morals." It was Joshua Brogden who had witnessed, a few months earlier, the agreement with Andrew Millar for *Tom Jones*. Could the good clerk but have played the part of a Boswell to his illustrious master we should have something more than our present scanty materials for the personal life of Henry Fielding.

Yet another of Fielding's rare letters belongs to this year; a letter conveying his formal congratulations to Lyttelton, on that model statesman's second marriage, and in which his warm heart again makes application, not on behalf of his own scanty means, but for a friend.

"Bow Street, Aug't 29, 1749.

"Sir,

"Permit me to bring up the Rear of your Friends in paying my Compliments of Congratulation on your late Nuptials. There may perhaps be seasons when the Rear may be as honourable a Post in Friendship as in War, and if so such certainly must be every time of Joy and Felicity. Your present situation must be full of these; and so will be, I am confident, your future Life from the same Fountain. Nothing can equal the excellent character your Lady bears among those of her own Sex, and I never yet knew them speak well of a woman who did not deserve their good words. How admirable is your Fortune in the Matrimonial Lottery! I will venture to say there is no man alive who exults more in this, or in any other Happiness that can attend you than myself; and you ought to believe me from the same Reason that fully persuades me of the satisfaction you receive from any Happiness of mine; this Reason is that you must be sensible how much of it I owe to your goodness; and there is a great Pleasure in Gratitude though it is second I believe to that of Benevolence; for of all the Delights upon Earth none can equal the Raptures which a good mind feels on conferring Happiness on those whom we think worthy of it. This is the sweetest ingredient in Power, and I solemnly protest I never wished for Power, more than a few days ago for the sake of a Man whom I love, and that more perhaps from the esteem I know he bears towards you than from any other Reason. This Man is in Love with a young Creature of the most apparent worth, who returns his affection. Nothing is wanting to make two very miserable People extremely Blessed but a moderate portion of the greatest of human Evils.

118

So Philosophers call it, and so it is called by Divines, whose word is the rather to be taken, as they are, many of them, more conversant with this Evil than ever Philosophers were. The Name of this man is Moore to whom you kindly destined that Laurel, which, though it hath long been withered, may not probably soon drop from the Brow of its present Possessor; but there is another Place of much the same Value now vacant: it is that of Deputy Licensor to the Stage. Be not offended at this Hint; for though I will own it impudent enough in one who hath so many Obligations of his own to you, to venture to recommend another man to your Favour, yet Impudence itself may possibly be a Virtue when exerted on the behalf of a Friend; at least I am the less ashamed of it, as I have known men remarkable for the opposite Modesty possess it without the mixture of any other good Quality. In this Fault then you must indulge me; for should I ever see you as high in Power as I wish, and as it is perhaps more my Interest than your own that you should be, I shall be guilty of the like as often as I find a Man in whom I can, after much intimacy discover no want, but that of the Evil above mentioned. I beg you will do me the Honour of making my Compliments to your unknown Lady, and believe me to be with the highest Esteem, Respect, Love, and Gratitude

"Sir,
"Y'r most obliged
"Most obed't
"humble Servant
    "Henry Fielding.
"To the Hon'ble
"George Lyttelton, Esqr." [13]

This Edward Moore was a poet held worthy, it would seem, to possess the Laureat's 'withered' laurel (even in 1749 Fielding cannot refrain from a thrust at Colley Cibber); a journalist; a writer of whom Dibden declared that the tendency of all his productions was to "cultivate truth and morality"; a tradesman in the linen business; and the son of a dissenting minister: a combination of circumstances closely recalling Fielding's friendship for the good dissenter, jeweller, and poet, George Lillo. And it is to an undated letter by Edward Moore, hitherto overlooked, that we owe one of the rare references to Henry Fielding from a contemporary pen. Moore is writing to a dissenting minister at Taunton, one Mr John Ward, of whom it was said that venerable as he himself was for learning, worth, and piety he deemed it "*an honour to have his name connected with that of Moore*,"—a further proof of the quality of man whom Fielding choose for friend. Moore had been prevented, by Fielding's illness, from appointing an evening on which he might invite the Taunton minister to his lodgings to meet there some of the first wits of the day. "It is not," he writes, "owing to forgetfulness that you have not heard from me before. Fielding continues to be visited for his sins so as to be wheeled about from room to room; when he mends I am sure to see him at my lodgings; and you may depend upon timely notice. What fine things are Wit and Beauty, if a Man could be temperate with one, or a Woman chaste with the other! But he that will confine his acquaintance to the sober and the modest will generally find himself among the dull and the ugly. If this remark of mine should be thought to shoulder itself in without an introduction you will be pleased to note that Fielding is a Wit; that his disorder is the Gout, and intemperance the cause." It is of course idle to contend that Fielding always carried a cool head. Murphy tells us that to him might justly be applied a parody on a saying concerning Scipio,—"always over a social bottle or a book, he enured his body to the dangers of intemperance, and exercised his mind with Studies." But we must in justice remember that the Augustan age of English literature concerned itself but very little with our modern virtue of sobriety. That Fielding, with the other great men of his day, very often drank more than was good for him, amounts to little more than saying that he wore a laced coat when he had one, and carried a sword at his side.

The execution of one of the Strand rioters, Bosavern Penlez by name, in September, had roused much controversy; and as the evidence in the case was in Justice Fielding's possession, and the attacks were levelled at the Government, we find him plunged once more into political pamphleteering in the publication, under the date of 1749, of the learned little treatise entitled "*A True State of the Case of Bosavern Penlez' who suffered on account of the late riot in the Strand. In which the Law regarding these Offences and the Statute of George I. commonly called the Riot Act are fully considered.*" The pamphlet opens with a warm protest against the abuse to which Fielding had been subjected by his political opponents. "It may easily be imagined," he writes, "that a Man whose Character hath been so barbarously, even without the least Regard to Truth or Decency, aspersed, on account of his Endeavours to defend the present Government, might wish to decline any future Appearance as a political Writer"; but more weighty considerations move him to lay the defence of the Riot Act in general, and of this application of it in particular, before a public which had been imposed upon "in the grossest and wickedest manner." We have already quoted the vivid depositions concerning this Strand riot, which were sworn before Fielding, and which he here reproduces; and his historical defence of the public need of suppressing riots, from the days of Wat Tyler onwards, may be left to the curious reader. Needless to say, Fielding makes out an excellent case against the toleration of mob law:— "When by our excellent Constitution the greatest Subject, no not even the King himself, can, without a lawful Trial and Conviction divest the meanest Man of his Property, deprive him of his Liberty, or attack him in his Person; shall we suffer a licentious Rabble to be Accuser, Judge, Jury, and Executioner; to inflict corporal Punishment, break open Men's Doors, plunder their Houses, and burn their Goods?" And, at the close, this pamphlet reveals the warm-hearted magistrate no less than the erudite lawyer. For of the two condemned prisoners, Wilson and Penlez, the case of the former seemed to Fielding "to be the Object of true Compassion." Accordingly he laid the evidence in his possession before "some very noble Persons," and, he adds, "I flatter myself that it might be a little owing to my Representation, that the Distinction between an Object of Mercy, and an Object of Justice at last prevailed". So the felon gained his respite, and a lasting niche for his name, in that he owed his life partly if not wholly to the generous compassion of Henry Fielding. The pamphlet seems to have made its mark, for a second edition was advertised within a month of publication.

This eventful year, the year which had seen the publication of *Tom Jones*, the shackling of Fielding's genius within the duties of a London magistrate, the issue of two pamphlets occupied with criminal reform and administration, the drafting of a proposed Criminal Bill, and the suppression of a riot, closed sadly with the death of Fielding's little daughter, Mary Amelia, when barely twelve months old. She was buried at St Paul's, Covent Garden, on the seventeenth of December, 1749. And some time in the autumn or early winter Fielding himself appears to have been dangerously ill. This we learn from the following paragraph in the *General Advertiser* for December 28: "Justice Fielding has no Mortification in his Foot as has been reported: that Gentleman has indeed been very dangerously ill with a Fever, and a Fit of the Gout, in which he was attended by Dr Thompson, an eminent Physician, and is now so well recovered as to be able to execute his Office as usual."

[1] His Commission in the Peace for Westminster bears date October 25. 1748.

[2] An application is reported for the 2nd of December before "Justice Fielding" of Meards Court, St. Anne's, but for reasons given below this *may* refer to John Fielding.

[3] From the autograph now at Woburn Abbey, and printed in the *Correspondence of John Fourth Duke of Bedford*. Vol. i. p. 589.

[4] Middlesex Records. Volume of *Qualification Oaths for Justices of the Peace*. 1749. From an entry dated July 13, 1749, in the same volume, Fielding appears to have then owned leases in the three first named parishes only.

[5] See the King's Writ, now preserved in the Record Office.

[6] Middlesex Records. *Sacramental Certificates*.

[7] Middlesex Records. *Oath Rolls*.

[8] *Amelia*. Book i. Chapter ii.

[9] The Westminster *Session Rolls*, preserved among the Middlesex Records, contain many recognizances all signed by Fielding.

[10] "On Friday last," announces the General Advertiser for May 17, "Counsellor Fielding, one of his Majesty's Justices of the Peace was chosen Chairman of the Sessions at Hicks Hall for the County of Middlesex"; a statement not very compatible with the incontestable evidence preserved in the *General Orders Books* of the Middlesex Records, by which it appears that John Lane Esq're was elected Chairman of the Middlesex General Sessions and General Quarter Session from Ladyday 1749 to September 1752. The personal paragraphist of 1749 was perhaps no less inaccurate than his descendant of to-day. But a few weeks later this honour of chairmanship was certainly accorded to Fielding by his brethren of the Bench for Westminster. An entry in the *Sessions Book* of Westminster, 1749 runs as follows: "May. 1749, Mr Fielding elected chairman of this present Session and to continue untill the 2nd day of the next." *MSS Sessions Books for Westminster. Vol. 1749*. Middlesex Records.

[11] From the autograph now at Woburn Abbey, and printed in the *Correspondence of John, Fourth Duke of Bedford*, vol. ii. p. 35.

[12] From the hitherto unpublished autograph now in the British Museum.

[13] This letter is now in the Dreer Collection of the Historical Society of Pennsylvania, Philadelphia, U.S.A.

CHAPTER XIII

FIELDING AND LEGISLATION

"The Subject, as well as the Child, should be left without excuse
before he is punished: for, in that case alone, the Rod becomes
the Hand either of the Parent or the Magistrate."
Inquiry Into the Causes of the late Increase of Robbers.

There is no Bill for the suppression of street robberies on the Statute Book
for 1749 or 1750; so the draft which Fielding, with characteristic energy,
despatched to the Lord Chancellor but a few months after his appointment to
the Bench, was, presumably, pigeon-holed. Meanwhile, the criminal conditions
of the metropolis seem to have become, if anything, more scandalous. In
February 1750, the *Penny Post* reports the gaols in and about London to be "now
so full of Felons and desperate Rogues that the Keepers have not fetters enow
to put upon them; so that in some Prisons two or three are chained together to
prevent their escape." And on the fifth of the same month the *General Advertiser*
hears that "near 40 Highwaymen, street Robbers, Burglars, Rogues, Vagabonds,
and Cheats have been committed within a week last past by Justice Fielding."
But however full of business the Bow Street court-room might be, that dreary
routine [1] would make, as we have said, but equally dreary reading. And the fact
that both John and Henry Fielding appear to have been known as 'Justice
Fielding' during the lifetime of the latter, lessens whatever biographical value
might be extracted from the constant newspaper paragraphs recording the
Fielding cases. It is clear that the house in Bow Street was the centre of an active
campaign against the thieves, murderers, professional gamblers, and
highwaymen, who were then so rife. Military guards conducted thither prisoners,
brought for examination from Newgate, for fear of rescue from gangs lurking in
the neighbouring streets. All "Persons who have been robbed" and their
servants, were desired, by public advertisement, to attend Justice Fielding "at his
House in Bow Street," to identify certain prisoners under examination. And
thither came the "porters and beggars," the composing of whose quarrels Henry
Fielding himself has told us, occupied his days. The generous spirit in which he
treated such poor clients, and his tenderness for those driven by want into
crime, are eminently characteristic of the man. By adjusting, instead of inflaming,
these squalid quarrels, and by "refusing to take a shilling from a man who must
undoubtedly would not have had another left," he reduced a supposed income
of £500 a year to £300. And if the picture of the poor wretch, driven to highway
robbery by the sight of his starving family, whom Tom Jones relieved from his
own scanty purse, be not proof enough of the compassion that tempered Justice
Fielding's sternness, we have his own express pleading for these unhappy victims
of circumstance: "what can be more shocking," he cries, "than to see an
industrious poor Creature, who is able and willing to labour forced by mere want

into Dishonesty, and that in a Nation of such Trade and Opulence." So justly could Fielding apportion the contributary negligence of society towards the criminals bred by its apathy.

And it was not only the impoverished porter who found help at Bow Street. "When," says Murphy, "in the latter end of [Mr Fielding's] days he had an income of four or five hundred a-year, he knew no use of money but to keep his table open to those who had been his friends when young, and had impaired their own fortunes." As Mr Austin Dobson says, in commenting on one of Horace Walpole's scurrilous letters, [2] "it must always have been a more or less ragged regiment which met about that kindly Bow Street board." The man who parted with his own hardly won arrears of rent to relieve the yet greater need of a College friend, was little likely to be less generous when the tardy 'jade Fortune' at last put some secured income into his hands.

No special event marks the spring and summer of 1750. On the 11th of January the Westminster General Quarter Sessions opened, and on the following day Fielding was again elected as chairman "for the two next Quarter Sessions"; which election was repeated, "for the two next Sessions, [3]" in July. The Registers of St Paul's Covent Garden record the baptism of a daughter, Sophia, on the 21st of January. And an indication that the zealous magistrate was plunged, personally, into some of the tumults of the time occurs in the following trifling note to the Duke of Bedford.

"My Lord,
"In obedience to the Commands I have the Honour to receive from your Grace, I shall attend tomorrow morning and do the utmost in my Power to preserve the Peace on that occasion.
"I am, with gratitude and Respect,
"My Lord,
"Your Grace's most obliged
"most obedient humble servant.
    "Henry Ffielding. [4]
    "Bow Street,
    "May 14, 1750."

By the autumn, however, a rumour was abroad that the now famous author of *Tom Jones* was engaged on pages of a very different nature. The *General Advertiser*, for October 9, announces:—

"We hear that an eminent Magistrate is now employed in preparing a Pamphlet for the Press in which the several causes that have conspired to render Robberies so frequent of late will be laid open; the Defects of our Laws enquired into, and Methods proposed which may discourage and in a great measure prevent this growing Evil for the future."

This pamphlet, in which many a later reform was urged by Fielding's far-sighted zeal, seems to have been still in preparation for the next two months. And in November the reform of the law had to give place to a more immediate urgency in protecting the Lord Chancellor. The keepers of three gaming houses, closed by his lordship's orders, were reported to be plotting against that exalted dignitary; and the case, as appears from the following letter to a lawyer, Mr Perkins, was in Fielding's hands. [5]

"Sir

"I have made full enquiry after the three Persons and have a perfect account of them all. Their characters are such that perhaps three more likely Men could not be found in the Kingdom for the Hellish Purpose mentioned in the Letter. As the Particulars are many and the Affair of such Importance I beg to see you punctually at six this evening when I will be alone to receive you—and am, Sir, "Yr. most obed;
"humble servant
   "He Ffielding.
   "Bow Street. Nov. 25. 1750."

When the keepers of gambling houses dared to fly at such high game as the person of the Lord Chancellor, there is no wonder that the safety of his Majesty's ordinary lieges was of small account. "Robbery," writes Horace Walpole, a few weeks before the date of the above letter, "is the only thing which goes on with any vivacity." And at the close of the year a Royal Proclamation was actually published, promising £100 over and above other rewards, and a free pardon, to any accomplice who should apprehend offenders committing murder, or robbery by violence, in London streets or within five miles of London, providing such an accomplice had not himself dealt a mortal wound. So startling a confession of impotence on the part of the Government served very fitly to introduce the pamphlet, then on the eve of publication. And if further proof be needed of the conditions of public safety at the beginning of the year 1751, it may be seen in the passage of the King's Speech delivered at the opening of Parliament on the 17th of January, in which his Majesty exhorted the Commons to suppress outrages and violences on life and property; words representing, of course, the policy of the Ministry.

The title of Fielding's little book, dedicated to Lord Hardwick, and published about January 22, is *An Enquiry into the Causes of the late Increase of Robbers &c. with some Proposals for remedying this growing Evil. In which the Present Reigning Vices are impartially exposed; and the Laws that relate to the Provision for the Poor and to the Punishment of Felons are largely and freely examined.* The *Enquiry* opens with a powerful denunciation of the licence then allowed to the three great causes, in Fielding's opinion, of the increasing demoralisation of the 'most useful Part' of the people. These were, first, the immense number of places of amusement, all seducing the working classes to squander both their money and their time; this being "indeed a certain Method to fill the Streets with Beggars and the Goals with Debtors and Thieves." Here, in Fielding's view, new legislation was demanded. The second cause of the late excessive increase of crime, according to the *Enquiry*, was an epidemic of gin drinking, "a new Kind of Drunkenness unknown to our Ancestors [which] is lately sprung up amongst us." Gin, says Fielding, appeared to be the principal sustenance of more than an hundred thousand Londoners, "the dreadful Effects of which I have the Misfortune every Day to see, and to smell too." The crime resulting from such drunkenness was obvious; but Fielding, looking far beyond the narrow confines of his court-room, beheld a future gin-sodden race, and he appeals to the legislature to put a stop to a practice, the consequences of which must alarm "the most sluggish Degree of Public Spirit." It is surely something more than a coincidence that a few weeks after these warnings were published, Hogarth issued his awful plate of *Gin Lane*. A third source of crime, in Fielding's eyes, was the gambling among the 'lower Classes of Life,'—a school "in which most Highwaymen of great eminence have been bred," and a habit plainly tending to the "Ruin of Tradesmen, the Destruction of Youth, and to the Multiplication of every Kind of Fraud and Violence." In this case the 'Eminent Magistrate' finds new legislation less needed than a vigorous enforcement of existing laws; such, he adds, "as hath lately been executed with great Vigour within the Liberty of Westminster." Before long the pages of *Amelia* were to bring home yet more forcibly to Fielding's readers the cruel results of the pleasures (or speculations) of the needy gambler,—the 'Destruction of Familys,' thereby incurred, no less than the breeding of highwaymen. Who does not remember "that famous scene when Amelia is spreading, for the recreant who is losing his money at the Kings Arms, the historic little supper of hashed mutton, which she has cooked with her own hands, and denying herself a glass of white wine to save the paltry sum of sixpence, 'while her Husband was paying a Debt of several Guineas incurred by the Ace of Trumps being in the hands of his Adversary'—a scene which it is impossible to read aloud without a certain huskiness in the throat." [6] The last great cause of crime which the *Enquiry* considers, and with much learning and detail, is the condition of the poor. Here Fielding's views on our modern problem of the unemployed may be read. And here occurs a splendid denunciation of the 'House of Correction' or Bridewell of the period, a prison for idle and disorderly persons where "they are neither to be corrected nor employed: and where with the conversation of many as bad and sometimes worse than themselves they are sure to be improved in the Knowledge and confirmed in the Practice of Iniquity." The most impudent of the wretches brought before him, Fielding tells us, were always "such as have been before acquainted with the Discipline of Bridewell." These prisons, from which the disorderly and idle came out, "much more idle and disorderly than they went in," were, says Fielding, no other than "Schools of Vice, Seminaries of Idleness, and Common-sewers of Nastiness and Disease." A fixed (and lower) rate of wages, it is curious to note, is one remedy advocated in the *Enquiry*, for raising the condition of the poor.

Such were the 'temptations' to robbery that Fielding would have removed, nobly conceiving the highest office of the legislature to be that of prevention rather than cure. The *Enquiry* concludes with offering some more immediate palliatives for the diseased state of the body politic, in the removing of actual 'Encouragement to Robbery.' First among such encouragements Fielding places the fact that "the Thief disposes of his goods with almost as much safety as the honestest Tradesman"; and he urged the need of legislation to prohibit the amazing advertisements by which our ancestors promised to give rewards for the recovery of stolen goods "*and no questions asked.*" Such advertisements he declares to be "in themselves so very scandalous and of such pernicious Consequence, that if Men are not ashamed to own they prefer an old Watch or a Diamond Ring to the Good of [the] Society it is a pity some effectual Law was not contrived to prevent their giving this public Countenance to Robbery for the future." And, under this head, he advocates legislation either for the regulating of pawnbrokers, or for the entire extirpation of a "Set of Miscreants which, like other Vermin, harbour only about the Poor and grow fat sucking their Blood." The subsequent legislation by which prosecutors were recompensed for loss of time and money, when prosecuting the 'wolves in society,' may be added to the measures forseen if not actually promoted by Fielding's enlightened zeal. And in nothing was he more in advance of his age than in his denunciation of that scandal of the eighteenth century, the conduct and frequency of public executions. It has taken our legislators a hundred years to provide the swift, solemn and private executions urged by Henry Fielding, in place of the brutal 'Tyburn holiday' enacted every six weeks for the benefit of the Georgian mob. Another matter demanding legislation was the great probability of escape afforded to thieves by the narrow streets and the common-lodging houses of the day. Of the latter, crowded with miserable beds from the cellar to the garret, let out, at twopence a night the single beds, and threepence the double ones, Fielding draws a picture as terrible as any of his friend Hogarth's plates. And he concludes "Nay I can add what I myself once saw in the Parish of Shoreditch where two little Houses were emptied of near seventy Men and Women," and where the money found on all the occupants (with the exception of a pretty girl who was a thief) "did not amount to one shilling." In all these houses gin, moreover, was sold at a penny the quartern. Housed thus, in conditions destructive of "all Morality, Decency and Modesty," with the street for bed if they fall sick ("and it is almost a Miracle that Stench, Vermin, and Want should ever suffer them to be well"), oppressed with poverty, and sunk in every species of debauchery, "the Wonder in Fact is," cries Fielding, "... that we have not a thousand more Robbers than we have; indeed that all these wretches are not thieves must give us either a very high Idea of their Honesty or a very mean one of their Capacity and Courage." And, leaving for a moment legislative reform, Fielding delivers a vigorous attack on the national sluggishness of public spirit which helped to render robbery a fairly safe profession. With such sluggishness his ardent nature had very little sympathy. "With regard to Private Persons," he protests, "there is no Country I believe in the World where that vulgar Maxim so generally prevails that what is the Business of every Man is the business of no Man; and for this plain Reason, that there is no Country in which less Honour is gained by serving the Public. He therefore who commits no crime against the

Public, is very well satisfied with his own Virtue; far from thinking himself obliged to undergo any Labour, expend any Money, or encounter any Danger on such Account." And in no part of the *Enquiry* does the writer more truly show his wisdom than in the pages on 'false Compassion' that plausible weakness which refuses to prosecute the oppressors of the helpless and innocent, and which at that time, in the person of his Majesty, King George II. was, it appears, very active in pardoning offenders when convicted. Fielding's arguments are incontestable; but his apologue may have found even more favour in the age of wit. He hopes such good nature may not carry those in power so far, "as it once did a Clergyman in *Scotland* who in the fervour of his Benevolence prayed to God that He would be graciously pleased to pardon the poor Devil."

To the devil, whether in man or in society, Fielding was ever a 'spirited enemy'; and his first biographer tells us that "to the unworthy he was rather harsh." But the last page of this little book breathes that spirit of tenderness for hard pressed humanity which in Fielding was so characteristically mingled with a wholesome severity. If the legislature would take proper care to raise the condition of the poor, then he declares the root of the evil would be struck: "nor in plain Truth will the utmost severity to Offenders be justifiable unless we take every possible Method of preventing the offence ... the Subject as well as the child should be left without Excuse before he is punished: for in that Case alone the Rod becomes the Hand either of the Parent or the Magistrate." And his last word is one of compassion for the "many Cart-loads of our Fellow-creatures [who] once in six weeks are carried to Slaughter"; of whom much the greater part might, with 'proper care and Regulations' have been made "not only happy in themselves but very useful Members of the Society which they now so greatly dishonour in the Sight of all Christendom."

Henry Fielding is himself his own best illustration when he declares that the "good Poet and the good Politician do not differ so much as some who know nothing of either art affirm; nor would *Homer* or *Milton* have made the worst Legislators of their Times."

To the reader of to-day the *Enquiry* betrays no party flavour, but its sedate pages clearly stirred up the hot feeling of the times. Early in February the Advertiser announced "*This Day is published A Letter to Henry Fielding Esqre. occasioned by his Enquiry into the causes of the late increase of Robbers &c.*" And about the end of the month there appeared *Considerations*, in two numbers of the *True Briton*, "on Justice Fielding's 'Enquiry,' shewing his Mistakes about the Constitution and our Laws and that what he seems to propose is dangerous to our Properties, Liberties and Constitution." On March 7 was announced *Observations on Mr Fielding's Enquiry*, by one B. Sedgley. Some opposition squib, too, must have been launched, to judge by the following item from an advertisement column of the same date: "a Vindication of the Rights and Privileges of the Commonality of England, in Opposition to what has been advanced by the Author of the Enquiry, or to what may be promulgated by any Ministerial Artifices against the public Cause of Truth and Liberty. *By Timothy Beck the Happy Cobler of Portugal-street.*" [7] Perhaps some collector of eighteenth century pamphlets may be able to reveal these comments of the '*Happy Gobler of Portugal-street*' upon the 'artifices' of Henry Fielding. [8]

In the February following the publication of the *Enquiry* a Parliamentary Committee was appointed "to revise and consider the Laws in being, which relate to Felonies and other Offences against the Peace." [9] The Committee included Lyttelton and Pitt, and there is of course every probability that Fielding's evidence would be taken; but it seems impossible now to discover what share he may have had in this move by the Government towards fresh criminal legislation. There is, however, the evidence of his own hand that in the matter of prison administration his efforts were not limited to academic pamphlets, or to the indictment, so soon to be published, contained in the terrible prison scenes of *Amelia*. The following letter to the Duke of Newcastle [10] shows an anxious endeavour to secure such good government as was possible for at least one of the gaols.

"My Lord

"It being of the utmost consequence to the Public to have a proper Prison Keeper of the new Prison at the Time, I beg leave to recommend Mr William Pentlow a Constable of St George Bloomsbury to your Grace's Protection in the present Vacancy. He is a Man of whose Courage and Integrity I have seen the highest Proofs, and is indeed every way qualified for the charge. I am with the most Perfect Respect,

"My Lord,

"Your Grace's most obedient

"and most humble servant,

"Henry Ffielding

"Bow Street Jan. 15. 1750 [1751]."

A second edition of the *Enquiry* appeared early in the spring; and according to the *Journals of the House of Commons* it was resolved, in April, that a Bill be brought in on the resolution of the Committee appointed two months previously to consider criminal legislation. Again it can only be surmised that Fielding's assistance would be invoked in the drafting of this Bill. That his vigorous denunciations of the national danger of the gin curse were in complete accord with the feeling of the Government is apparent from the fact that two months later, in June 1751, the *Tippling Act* [11] received the royal assent, by which Act very stringent restrictions were imposed on the sale of spirits.

In June Fielding again appears as Chairman of the Westminster Sessions. [12] And in September cases occur as brought before John Fielding and others "at Henry Fielding's house in Bow Street," [13] from which it appears that Fielding's blind half-brother was already acting as his assistant. In the following month John Fielding appears among the Justices of the Westminster Quarter Sessions. [14]

The year that had seen the publication of the *Enquiry*, affords proof enough of Fielding's active labours in criminal and social reform; but the last month of this year is marked by an occurrence of much greater import for English literature, the publication of the third great novel, *Amelia*.

[1] Doubtless faithfully rendered in the old print, here reproduced, of Fielding's blind half-brother, assistant, and successor, Sir John Fielding, hearing a Bow Street case.

[2] See Appendix.

[3] Middlesex Records. *MSS. Sessions Books*. 1750.

[4] From the hitherto unpublished autograph, now at Woburn Abbey.

[5] This hitherto unpublished letter is now in the British Museum. It is addressed to "—Perkins, Esq. at his Chambers No. 7, in Lincolns Inn Square," and is sealed with Fielding's seal, a facsimile of which appears on the cover of the present volume.

[6] *Fielding*. Austin Dobson. p. 156.

[7] *The General Advertiser*. March 7, 1751.

[8] The *London Magazine* for February devoted five columns to an "Abstract of Mr Fielding's Enquiry"; and in the following month the *Magazine* again noticed the book, by printing a long anonymous letter in which Fielding is attacked as a 'trading author' and a 'trading justice,' and in which the writer shows his intellectual grasp by advocating in all seriousness a law prohibiting the sovereign from gambling!

[9] See *Journals of the House of Commons*. Vol. xxii. p. 27, and the *London Magazine*. Vol. xx. p. 82. The *Catalogue of Printed Papers. House of Commons*, 1750-51, includes "A Bill for the more effectual preventing Robberies Burglaries and other Outrages within the City and Liberty of Westminster—" &c.

[10] This hitherto unpublished letter is now in the British Museum. It is endorsed "Jan. 15, 1750(1)."

[11] 24 George II. c. 40. June 1751.

[12] Middlesex Records. *Sessions Book*. 1751.

[13] *General Advertiser*. Sept. 9. 1751.

[14] Middlesex Records. *Sessions Book*. October, 1751.

CHAPTER XIV

AMELIA

"of all my Offspring she is my favourite Child."
The *Covent Garden Journal*. No. 8.

On the 2nd of December 1751 the *General Advertiser* announces that

On Wednesday the 18th of this Month will be published

IN FOUR VOLUMES DUODECIMO

AMELIA

By HENRY FIELDING, Esq;
Beati ter et amplius
Quos irrupta tenet Copula. HOR.

And the puff preliminary of the period may be read in the same columns, declaring that the "earnest Demand of the Publick" had necessitated the use of four printing presses; and that it being impossible to complete the binding in time, copies would be available "sew'd at Half-a-Guinea a Sett." Sir Walter Scott tells us that, at a sale to booksellers before publication, Andrew Millar, the publisher, refused to part with *Amelia* on the usual discount terms; and that the booksellers, being thus persuaded of a great future for the book, eagerly bought up the impression. Launched thus, and heralded by the popularity with which *Tom Jones* had now endowed Fielding's name, the entire edition was sold out on the day of publication; an event which evoked the observation from Dr Johnson that *Amelia* was perhaps the only book which being printed off betimes one morning, a new edition was called for before night. The Doctor gave not only unstinted praise, but also an involuntary tribute to *Amelia*. He read the book through, without pausing, from beginning to end. And he pronounced Amelia herself to be "the most pleasing heroine of all the romances." [1]

But to the majority of readers Amelia is, assuredly, something more than the most charming of heroines. She is the delightful companion; the wise and tender friend; a woman whose least perfection was that dazzling beauty which shone with equal lustre in the 'poor rags' lent her by her old nurse, or in her own clothing, just as the happy purity of her nature only glows more brightly for the dark scenes through which she moves. In the whole range of English literature there is surely no figure more warmly human, and yet less touched with human imperfection; none more simply and naturally alive, and yet truer in every crisis (and there were few of the sorrowful things of life unknown to her) to the best qualities of generous womanhood. And if it is largely for her glowing vitality that we love Amelia, we love her none the less in that she is no fool. It was hardly necessary to tell us, as Fielding is careful to do, that her sense of humour was keen, and that her insight into the ridiculous was tempered only by the deeper insight of her heart. Her understanding of her husband is as perfect as her love for him; and that love is far too profound to allow a moment's suggestion of mere placid amiability. Amelia, whether quizzing the absurdities of the affected fine ladies of her own rank, or cooking her husband's supper in the poor lodgings of their poverty; whether so radiant with happiness after seeing her little children handsomely entertained that with flushed cheeks and bright eyes, "she was all a blaze of beauty," or, pale with distress, bravely carrying her own clothes and the children's trinkets to the pawnbroker; whether betraying her own noble qualities of silence and forgiveness, or losing her temper with Mrs Bennett,—commands equal affection and admiration. "They say," wrote Thackeray, "that it was in his own home that Fielding knew her and loved her: and from his own wife that he drew the most charming character in English fiction—Fiction? Why fiction! Why not history? I know Amelia just as well as Lady Mary Wortley Montagu."

Lady Mary, and her daughter Lady Bute, have left very definite statements concerning this portrait which their cousin was alleged to have hidden under the fair image of Amelia. Lady Bute we are told was no stranger "to that beloved first wife whose picture he drew in his Amelia, where, as she said, even the glowing language he knew how to employ did not do more than justice to the amiable qualities of the original...." [2] And Lady Mary herself writes, "H. Fielding has given a true picture of himself and his first wife, in the characters of Mr and Mrs Booth [Amelia and her husband], some compliments to his own figure excepted; and I am persuaded several of the incidents he mentions are real matters of fact." [3] Against these persuasions we must place the fact that this book contains no such explicit statement as that which in *Tom Jones* assures us of the original of the beautiful Sophia. But we shall not love Amelia the less if we see her, with her courage and her beauty, her happy gaiety of spirit, her tenderness and strength, solacing the distresses and calming the storms of Fielding's restless genius, rather than devoting those qualities to assuaging the misfortunes of Captain William Booth. For indeed Captain Booth has but one substantial title to our regard, and that is his adoration for his wife. True, he is a pretty figure of a man; he has a handsome face; he fights bravely, and would kick a rogue through the world; he believes in and loves his friends; and he plays charmingly with his children. But, deprive him of the good genius of his life, and Captain Booth would very speedily have sunk into the ruin and despair of any other profligate young gamester about the Town; and for this his adoration the culprit wins our forgiveness, even as Amelia not only forgave but forgot, when by virtue of her own unconscious goodness the Captain retrieved himself, at last, from the folly of his ways. Undoubtedly the man whom Amelia loved, and who had the grace to return that passion, was no scoundrel at heart.

It is impossible, now, to discover with any certainty the incidents which Lady Mary was persuaded were matters of fact. The experiences of Captain Booth, when essaying to turn gentleman farmer, have been quoted as copies of

Fielding's own ambitions at East Stour; but surely on very slender evidence. Much more personal seem many of the later scenes in the poor London lodgings, scenes of cruel distress and perfect happiness, of bitter disappointments and sanguine hope. Here, very probably, we have echoes of the struggles of Harry and Charlotte Fielding, in the days of hackney writing and of baffled efforts at the Bar; just as the dry statement by Arthur Murphy, that Fielding was "remarkable for ... the strongest affection for his children," comes to life in the many touching pictures of Amelia and Booth with their little son and daughter. The pursuit of such identity of incident may the more cheerfully be left to the anecdotist, in that the biographical value of *Amelia*, is far more than incidental. For the book is, as has been said, a one-part piece. Round the single figure of Amelia all the other characters revolve; and it was of Amelia that Fielding himself has told us, in words that are a master key to his own character "of all my offspring she is my favourite Child." As surely as a man may be known by his choice in a friend, so is the nature of the artist betrayed when he avows his partiality for one alone among all the creations of his genius.

As to the remaining figures in this "model of human life," to quote Fielding's own descriptive phrase of his book, those which tell us most of their author are that worthy, authoritative, humourous clergyman, Dr Harrison; the good Sergeant Atkinson; and that fiery pedant Colonel Bath, with his kind heart hidden under a ferocious passion for calling out every man whom he conceived to have slighted his honour. Dr Harrison does not win quite the same place in our hearts as the man whom Thackeray calls 'dear Parson Adams'; his cassock rustles a little too loudly; the saint is a trifle obscured in the Doctor. But yet we love him for his warm and protecting affection for his 'children' as he calls Amelia and Booth; for his dry humour; and for that generosity which was for ever draining his ample purse. And perhaps we like him none the less for his scholar's raillery of that early blue-stocking Mrs Bennet; while his dignity never shows to greater advantage than when he throws himself bodily on the villain Murphy, achieving the arrest of that felon by the strength of his own arm, and the nimbleness of his own legs. And to this good Doctor is given a saying eminently characteristic of Justice Fielding himself. We are told that "it was a maxim of his that no man could descend below himself in doing any act which may contribute to protect an innocent person, or to bring a rogue to the gallows." Another trait of the Doctor recalls Fielding's oft reiterated aversion to what he calls grave formal persons: "You must know then, child," said he, to poor Booth, sunk in the melancholy problem of supporting a wife and three children on something less than £40 a year, "that I have been thinking on this subject as well as you; for I can think, I promise you, with a pleasant countenance." Of Amelia's foster-brother Sergeant Atkinson (from whom Major William Dobbin is directly descended) it is enough to say that the noble qualities concealed beneath the common cloth of his sergeant's coat perfectly confirm a sentence written many years before by the hand of his author. "I will venture to affirm," Fielding declares, in his early essay on the *Characters of Men*, "that I have known ... *a Fellow whom no man should be seen to speak to,* capable of the highest acts of Friendship and Benevolence."

Fielding's energies in this his last novel, a novel be it remembered written in the midst of daily contact with the squalid vices exhibited in an eighteenth century court-room, seem to have been almost wholly absorbed in creating the most perfect escape from those surroundings in the person of Amelia. Beside the figure of his 'favourite child,' the vicious criminals of his stage, the malefic My Lord, the loathsome Trent, the debased Justice, the terrible human wrecks in Newgate, are but dark figures in a shadowy back-ground. Still, the great moralist shows no lack of vigour in his delineations of such offspring of vice. The genius that knew how to rouse every reader of *Tom Jones* to 'lend a foot to kick Blifil downstairs,' awards in the last pages of *Amelia*, a yet more satisfying justice to that nameless connoisseur in profligacy, My Lord.

In his Dedication to Ralph Allen, Fielding states that his book "is sincerely designed to promote the Cause of Virtue, and to expose some of the most glaring Evils, as well public as private, which at present infest this Country". The statement seems somewhat needless when prefacing pages which enshrine Amelia; and where also are displayed Blear Eyed Moll in the prison yard of Newgate, as Newgate was twenty years before the prison reforms of Howard were heard of; Justice Thrasher and his iniquities; the 'diabolisms' of My Lord and of his tool Trent; the ruinous miseries of excessive gambling; and the abuses of duelling. Indeed the avowedly didactic purpose of the moralist seems at times to cloud a little the fine perception of the artist. There are passages, in this book which, much as they redound to the honour of their writer, are indisputably heavy reading. But what shall not be forgiven to the creator of Amelia. "To have invented that character," cries Thackeray, also becoming didactic, "is not only a triumph of art, but it is a good action." And he tells us how with all his heart he loves and admires the 'kindest and sweetest lady in the world'; and how he thinks of her as faithfully as though he had breakfasted with her that morning in her drawing-room, or should meet her that afternoon in the Park.

It is recorded that Fielding received from Andrew Millar £1000 for the copyright of *Amelia*. But the reception of the new novel, after the first rush for copies, seems to have done little credit either to the brains or to the heart of the public. And in the month following *Amelia's* appearance, Fielding satirises the comments of the Town, in two numbers of his *Covent Garden Journal*; protesting that though he does not think his child to be entirely free from faults—"I know nothing human that is so,"—still "surely she does not deserve the Rancour with which she hath been treated by the Public." As ironic specimens of the faults complained of in his heroine, he quotes the accusations that her not abusing her husband "for having lost Money at Play, when she saw his Heart was already almost broke by it, was *contemptible Meanness*"; that she condescends to dress her husband's supper, and to dress her children, to whom moreover she shows too much kindness; that she once mentions the DEVIL; that she is a *low* character; and that the beauty of her face is hopelessly flawed by a carriage accident. Such are some of the charges brought against the lovely Amelia by the "Beaus, Rakes, fine Ladies, and several formal Persons with bushy wigs and canes at their Noses," who, in Fielding's satire, crowd the Court where his book is placed on trial for the crime of dullness. Then Fielding himself steps forward, and after pleading for this his 'favourite Child,' on whom he has bestowed "a more than ordinary Pains in her Education," he declares, with the same hasty petulance that characterised that previous outburst in the preface to *David Simple*, that indeed he "will trouble the World no more with any children of mine by the same Muse." Two months later the *Gentleman's Magazine* prints a spirited appeal against this resolution. "His fair heroine's nose has in my opinion been too severely handled by some modern critics," [4] writes Criticulus, after a passage of warm praise for the characterisation, the morality, and the 'noble reflections of the book'; and he proceeds to point out that the writings of such critics "will never make a sufficient recompense to the world, if *Mr Fielding* adheres to what I hope he only said in his warmth and indignation of this injurious treatment, that he will never trouble the public with any more writings of this kind." The words of the enlightened *Criticulus* echo sadly when we remember that in little more than two years the great genius and the great heart of Henry Fielding were to be silenced.

The *London Magazine* for 1751 devotes the first nine columns of its December number to a resume of the novel, and continues this compliment in another nine columns of appendix. With a fine patronage the reviewer concludes that "upon the whole, the story is amusing, the characters kept up, and many reflections which [sic] are useful, if the reader will but take notice of them, which in this unthinking age it is to be feared very few will." Some imperfections he kindly excuses on the score of "the author's hurry of business in administering impartial justice to his majesty's good people"; but he cannot excuse what he declares to be the ridicule of *Liberty* in Book viii.; and he solemnly exhorts the author that as "he has in this piece very justly exposed some of the private vices and follies of the present age" so he should in his next direct his satire against political corruption, otherwise 'he and his patrons' will be accused of compounding the same. [5] It seems incredible that any suggestion should ever have attached to the author of *Pasquin* and the *Register*, as to one who could condone public corruption. And as for the accusation of tampering with "Liberty" the like charge was brought, we may remember, by the "Happy Cobler of Portugal Street" against Fielding's *Inquiry into the Encrease of Robbers*. The literary cobblers who pursued *Amelia* with the abuse of their poor pens may very well be consigned to the oblivion of their political brother. The comment of one hostile pen cannot however be dismissed as coming from a literary cobbler, and that is the 'sickening' abuse, to use Thackeray's epithet, which Richardson dishonoured himself in flinging at his great contemporary. That abuse the sentimentalist poured out very freely on *Amelia*; but, as Mr Austin Dobson says, "in cases of this kind *parva seges satis est*, and Amelia has long since outlived both rival malice and contemporary coldness. It is a proof of her author's genius that she is even more intelligible to our age than she was to her own." [6]

In Fielding's satiric description of the Court before which his Amelia stood her trial, he describes himself as an 'old gentleman.' The adjective seems hardly applicable to a man of forty five; but, to quote again from Mr Austin Dobson, "however it may have chanced, whether from failing health or otherwise, the Fielding of *Amelia* is suddenly a far older man than the Fielding of *Tom Jones*. The robust and irrepressible vitality, the full veined delight of living, the energy of observation and strength of satire, which characterise the one, give place in the other to a calmer retrospection, a more compassionate humanity, a more benignant criticism of life." Murphy's Irish tongue declares a similar feeling in his comparison of the pages of this, the last of the three great novels, to the calm of the setting sun; a sun that had first broken forth in the 'morning glory' of *Joseph Andrews*, and had attained its 'highest warmth and splendour' in the inimitable pages of *Tom Jones*. There is indeed a mature wisdom and patience in Amelia such as none but a pedant could demand of her enchanting younger sister Sophia. In these later pages Sophia has grown up into a gracious womanhood, while losing none of her girlhood's gaiety and charm. That Amelia, his older and wiser though scarce sadder child, was the nearest, as he himself tells us, to Fielding's own heart, is one more indication that here is the perfected image of that beloved wife, from whose youthful grace and beauty his genius had already modelled one exquisite memorial.

[1] *Anecdotes*. Mrs Piozzi. p. 221.

[2] Letters and Works of Lady Mary Wortley Montagu. Introductory Anecdotes, p. cxxiii.

[3] Ibid. Vol. ii. p. 289.

[4] It is curious that to this unlucky incident, based according to Lady Louisa Stuart, Lady Mary Wortley Montagu's grand-daughter, on a real accident to Mrs Fielding, Dr Johnson attributed the failure of the book with the public: "that vile broken nose ruined the sale," he declared. Early in January Fielding himself protests in his *Covent Garden Journal* that every reader of any intelligence would have discovered that the effects of Amelia's terrible carriage accident had been wholly remedied by "a famous Surgeon"; and that "the Author of her History, in a hurry, forgot to inform his Readers of that Particular." The particular has by now fallen into its due insignificance, and, save for Johnson's explanation therein of the poor sale of the book, is scarce worth recalling.

[5] *London Magazine*. December 1751. p. 531 and Appendix.

[6] *Fielding*. Austin Dobson. p. 161.

CHAPTER XV

JOURNALIST AND MAGISTRATE

"However vain or romantic the Attempt may seem I am sanguine
enough to aim at serving the noble Interests of Religion, Virtue,
and good Sense, by these my lucubrations."
The *Covent Garden Journal*. No. 5.

Nothing could be more characteristic of Fielding's active spirit than were the early months of 1752. For, no sooner had he deposited the four volumes of *Amelia* in the hands of the public, essaying to win his readers over to a love of virtue and a hatred of vice, by placing before their eyes that true "model of human life," than we find him launching a direct attack on the follies and evils of the age, by means of his old weapon, the press.

The first number of the *Covent Garden Journal* appeared on the 4th of January, and its pages, produced under Fielding's own management and apparently largely written by his own pen, provided satires on folly, invectives against vice, and incitements to goodness and sense, delivered in the name of one *Sir Alexander Drawcansir, Knt. Censor of Great Britain.* [1] The new paper ran but for seventy-two numbers; perhaps for all the wit and learning, the fire and zest of its columns, the public were reluctant to buy their own lashings. But it may be doubted whether, except in the pages of his three great novels, Henry Fielding ever revealed himself more completely than in these his last informal 'lucubrations.' Here, the active Justice, the accomplished scholar, the lawyer, and man of the world, the first wit of his day, talks to us of a hundred topics, chosen indeed on the spur of the moment, but discussed in his own incomparable words, and with the now mature authority of one, who had "dived into the inmost Recesses of Human Nature." No subject is too abstruse, none too trifling, for *Mr Censor* to illumine. Freed from the political bands of the earlier newspapers, this last *Journal*, produced be it remembered by a man in shattered health, and distracted by the squalid business of a Bow Street Court-room, ranges over an amazing compass of life and manners.

Thus, one January morning, *Sir Alexander's* readers would open their paper to find him deploring the decline of "a Religion sometime ago professed in this Country, and which, if my Memory fails me not was called Christian." The following Saturday they are presented with a learned and pleasant argument to prove that every male critic should be eighteen years of age, and "BE ABLE TO READ." A few days later the pages of writers purveying the prevalent "Infidelity, Scurrility, and Indecency" are ingeniously allotted to various uses. In February the *Journal* accords a noble tribute "to that great Triumvirate Lucian, Cervantes, and Swift"; not indeed "for that Wit and Humour alone, which they all so eminently possesst, but because they all endeavoured with the utmost Force of their Wit and Humour, to expose and extirpate those Follies and Vices which chiefly prevailed in their several Countries." The design of Aristophanes and Rabelais on the other hand, appears to *Mr Censor*, if he may speak his opinion freely, "very plainly to have been to ridicule all Sobriety, Modesty, Decency, Virtue, and Religion out of the world." From such considerations it is an easy passage to a definition of 'real Taste' as derived from a "nice Harmony between the Imagination and the Judgment"; and to these final censorial warnings:—"*Evil Communications corrupt good Manners* is a quotation of St Paul from Menander. EVIL BOOKS CORRUPT AT ONCE BOTH OUR MANNERS AND OUR TASTE." Four days after this learned 'lucubration' the voice of the warm-hearted magistrate speaks in a reminder of the prevailing abject misery of the London poor who "in the most miserable lingering Manner do daily perish for Want in this Metropolis." And in almost the next number his Honour gives his readers letters from the fair *Cordelia*, from *Sarah Scandal*, and from other correspondents, of a wit pleasant enough to drive London's poverty far from their minds. Two days after attending to these ladies, the *Censor* takes up his keenest weapons in an attack on that "detestable vice of slander" by which is taken away the "*immediate Jewel of a Man's Soul*," his good name; a crime comparable to that of murder. Here we have *Sir Alexander* speaking with the same voice as did the playwright and journalist of ten years previously, when he declared, in his *Miscellanies*, that to stab a man's character 'in the dark' is no less an offence than to stab his flesh in the same treacherous manner. Indeed, throughout these last columns of weekly satire, wit, and learning, Fielding remains true to the constant tenor of his genius. He exposes the miser, the seducer of innocence, the self-seeker, the place-hunter, the degraded vendor of moral poison, the 'charitable' hypocrite, with the same fierce moral energy as that with which, when but a lad of one and twenty, he first assailed the vices of the society in which his own lot was cast. His unconquerable energy, an energy that neither sickness nor distress could abate, still assaults that "cursed Maxim ... that Everybody's business is Nobody's." And his wit has lost none of its point when thrusting at the lesser follies of the day; at the fair Clara's devotion to her pet monkey; at the insolence of the Town Beau at the playhouse; at the arrogance of carters in the streets; at the vagaries of fashion according to which Belinda graces the theatre with yards of ruff one day, and on the next discards that covering so entirely that the snowy scene in the boxes "becomes extremely delightful to the eyes of every Beholder."

It is quite impossible to convey, within the limits of a few pages, all that *Sir Alexander* tells us of what he sees and hears, as the tragi-comedy of life passes before his Bow Street windows. For Fielding possessed in the highest degree the art of hearing, to use his own analysis, not with the ear only (an organ shared by man with "other Animals") but also with the head, and with the heart; just as his eye could penetrate beneath the velvet coat of the prosperous scoundrel, the reputation of the illiterate author, or the sorry rags of some honest hero of the gutter. And his *Covent Garden Journal* is, in truth, his journal of eleven months of a life into the forty odd years of which were compressed both the insight of genius, and the activities of twenty average men. Such a record cannot be sifted into a summary. The acknowledged motive of this last of Fielding's newspapers is, however, concise enough; and does equal honour to his patriotism and his humanity. The age, as it seemed to him, was an age of public degradation. Religion was vanishing from the life of the people; politics were a petty question of party jealousy; literary taste was falling to the level of alehouse wit and backstairs scandal; the youth of the nation were completing their education, when fifteen or sixteen years old, by a course of the Town, and then qualifying for a graduate's degree in like knowledge, by a foreign tour; the 'mob' was gaining a dangerous excess of power; the leaders of society were past masters and mistresses of vice and folly; the poor in the streets were sunk in misery, or brutalised into reckless crime. This was the England that *Mr Censor* saw from his house in Bow Street; this was the England which he set out to purify; and the means which he chose were his own familiar weapons of satire and ridicule. Of these, ridicule, he declares, when his *Journal* was but four weeks old, "is commonly a stronger and better method of attacking Vice than the severer kind of Satire." In accordance with which view, *General Sir Alexander* is represented, in a mock historic forecast, as having, in the space of twelve months, entirely cleansed his country from the evils afflicting it, by means of a "certain Weapon called a Ridicule." These evils moreover Fielding held to be most readily combated by assailing "those base and scandalous Writings which the Press hath lately poured in such a torrent upon us that the Name of an Author is in the ears of all good Men become almost an infamous appelation"; and, accordingly, the first number of his new paper discloses *Sir Alexander* in full crusade against these Grub-Street writers. But that he soon perceived the quixotic impolicy of such a campaign, appears very clearly, as early as the fifth number of the *Journal*:— "when Hercules undertook to cleanse the Stables of Augeas (a Work not much unlike my present Undertaking) should any little clod of Dirt more filthy perhaps than all the rest have chanced to bedawb him, how unworthy his Spirit would it have been to have polluted his Hands, by seizing the dirty clod, and crumbling it to Pieces. He should have known that such Accidents were incident to such an Undertaking: which though both a useful and heroic office, was yet none of the cleanliest; since no Man, I believe, ever removed great quantities of Dirt from any Place without finding some of it sticking to his skirts." Such dirty clods were undoubtedly thrown by nameless antagonists, as unworthy of Fielding's steel as was one whose name has come down to us, the despicable Dr John Hill, who once suffered a public caning at Ranelagh; and one clod, "more filthy perhaps than all the rest," soiled the hands of Smollett. [2] But the dirt which was very freely flung on to our eighteenth-century Hercules has, by now, fallen back, with great justice, on to the heads of his abusers. Fielding has placed on record, in the *Journal*, his conviction that the man who reads the works of the five heroic satirists, Lucian, Cervantes, Swift, Moliere and Shakespeare, "must either have a very bad Head, or a very bad Heart, if he doth not become both a Wiser and a better Man." To-day, 'party and prejudice' having subsided, we are ready to say the same of the readers of the *Covent Garden Journal*; perceiving that, if *Mr Censor*, like his five great forerunners, chose to send his satire "laughing into the World," it was that he might better effect the 'glorious Purpose' announced in the fifth number of his paper: "However vain or romantic the Attempt may seem, I am sanguine enough to aim at serving the noble Interests of Religion, Virtue, and good Sense, by these my Lucubrations."

To most men the production, twice a week, of a newspaper so wide in scope as the *Covent Garden Journal* (for its columns included the news of the day, as well as the manifold 'censorial' energies of *Sir Alexander*) would have been occupation enough; especially with a "constitution now greatly impaired and enfeebled," and when "labouring under attacks of the gout, which were, of course, severer than ever."

But there is no hint of either editorial or valetudinarian seclusion in the fragmentary glimpses obtainable of Mr Justice Fielding during these eleven months of 1752. Thus, by an advertisement recurring throughout the *Journal*, he expressly invites to his house in Bow Street, "All Persons, who shall for the Future suffer by Robbers Burglars &c.," that they may bring him "the best Description they can of such Robbers, &c., with the Time, and Place, and Circumstances of the Fact"; and that this invitation was likely to bring half London within his doors appears from Fielding's own description of the condition of the capital at the time. "There is not a street," he declares, speaking of Westminster, "which doth not swarm all day with beggars, and all night with thieves. Stop your coach at what shop you will, however expeditious the tradesman is to attend you, a beggar is commonly beforehand with him; and if you should directly face his door the tradesman must often turn his head while you are talking to him, or the same beggar, or some other thief at hand will pay a visit to his shop!" And nothing could prove more conclusively the arduousness of Fielding's work as a magistrate than the record of the last ten days of January, 1752. On the night of the 17th a peculiarly brutal murder had been perpetrated on a poor higgler in Essex; and the *Journal* for January 28, tells us how Fielding "spent near eight hours," examining, separately, suspected persons, "at the desire of several gentlemen of Fortune in the County of Essex"; having on the previous Friday and Saturday, been engaged "above Twenty hours in taking Depositions concerning this Fact." Then, on the day after the arrival of the murder suspects, we find two of the Shoreditch constables bringing no fewer than ten "idle lewd and disorderly" men and women before the Justice; a woman was charged by a diamond seller on suspicion of feloniously receiving "three Brilliant Diamonds"; Mr Welch, the notable High Constable of Holborn, brought seventeen "idle and lewd Persons" whom he had apprehended the night before; and, to complete this single day's work, an Italian was brought in, "all over covered with [the] Blood" of a brother Italian, whose head he had almost cut off. Twenty-nine cases on one day, and these in the midst of eight hour examinations concerning a murder, were surely work enough to satisfy even Fielding's energies. And, as another entry in his *Journal* mentions the examination of a suspected thief "very late at Night," there seems to have been no hour out of the twenty-four in which the great novelist did not hold himself at the service of the public.

Meanwhile, the criminal licence of the streets was now receiving Ministerial attention. The King's Speech, delivered at the opening of Parliament in the previous November, had contained a passage which might have been inspired by Fielding himself: "I cannot conclude," said His Majesty, "without recommending to you in the most earnest manner, to consider seriously of some effectual provisions to suppress those audacious crimes of Robbery and Violence which are now become so frequent...and which have proceeded in great Measure from that profligate Spirit of Irreligion, Idleness, Gaming, and Extravagance, which has of late extended itself in an uncommon degree, to the Dishonour of the Nation, and to the great Offence and Prejudice of the sober and industrious Part of the People." Six weeks later the first number of the *Journal*, makes comment on the need of fresh legislation to suppress drunkenness; and on the twenty first of the month *Sir Alexander* announces, with something of special information in his tone, that the immediate suppression of crimes of violence "we can with Pleasure assure the Public is at present the chief attention of Parliament."

It must have been with something of the pleasure which he so earnestly desires in one of the last utterances of his pen—"the pleasure of thinking that, in the decline of my health and life, I have conferred a great and lasting Benefit on my Country,"—that Fielding saw the royal assent given, in the following March, to an Act for the "*better preventing Thefts and Robberies and for regulating Places of Public Entertainment, and punishing Persons keeping disorderly Houses.*" [3] For this Act is directed to the suppression of four of the abuses so strongly denounced, twelve months previously, in his own *Enquiry*; and when we recall the fact that he had already submitted, to the Lord Chancellor, draft legislation for the suppression of robberies, it is at least a plausible surmise that here we have a memorial of Henry Fielding's patriotic energy, preserved on the pages of the Statute Book itself. [4] The four points so specially urged in the *Enquiry*, and here made law, are the suppression of the "multitude of places of Entertainment" for the working classes; the better suppression of Gaming Houses; the punishment of the scandalous advertisements offering rewards 'and no questions asked' for stolen goods; and the payment of certain prosecutors for their expenses in time and trouble, when a conviction had been obtained.

In this same month of March another Act, which closely concerned Fielding's official work, received the royal assent. This was an Act "for better preventing the horrid Crime of Murder." [5] The pressing need of such a measure had been already urged in the *Covent Garden journal*. In February the *Journal* declares that *"More shocking Murders have been committed within the last Year, than for many Years before. To what can this be so justly imputed as to the manifest decline of Religion among the lower People. A matter, which even, in a Civil Sense, demands the attention of the Government."* And Mr Censor returns to the subject on March 3: *"More Murders and horrid Barbarities have been committed within the last twelvemonth, than during many preceding years. This as we have before observed, is principally to be attributed to the Declension of Religion among the Common People."* By the end of the month the above-named Act had received the royal assent; and the first clause thereof again yielded Fielding the satisfaction of seeing a measure which he had warmly recommended in his Enquiry now placed on the Statute Book, namely the clause that the execution of the criminal be made immediate on his conviction. This Act, moreover, provides for the abatement of another scandal exposed by Fielding many years previously, in the pages of Jonathan Wild, that of the excessive supply of drink allowed to condemned prisoners.

In the following month Fielding carried out a scheme, conceived he tells us "some time since," for combating this prevalence of murder. This was his shilling pamphlet, published about April 14, entitled "Examples of the Interposition of Providence in the *Detection* and *Punishment* of MURDER. Containing above thirty cases, in which this dreadful crime hath been brought to light in the most extraordinary and miraculous manner." The advertisement describes the *Examples* as *"very proper to be given to all the inferior Kind of People; and particularly to the Youth of both sexes, whose natural Love of Stories will lead them to read with Attention what cannot fail of Infusing in to their tender Minds an early Dread and Abhorrence of staining their Hands with the Blood of their Fellow-creatures"* Low as was the price, a "large allowance" was made by Andrew Millar to those who bought any quantity; and Fielding distributed the little volume freely in Court.

The thirty-three *Examples* are introduced and concluded by Fielding's own denunciation of this, "the blackest sin, which can contaminate the hands, or pollute the soul of man." And from these pages we may learn his own solemnly declared belief in a peculiarly "immediate interposition of the Divine providence" in the detection of this crime; and also his faith in "the fearful and tremendous sentence of eternal punishment" as that divinely allotted to the murderer. He warns the murderer, moreover, that by hurrying a fellow-creature to a sudden and unprepared death he may be guilty of destroying not only his victim's body, but also his soul. And it may be questioned whether Fielding ever put his unrivalled mastery of style to a nobler intention than in the closing words of this pamphlet, words designed to be read by the lowest of the people: "Great courage may, perhaps, bear up a bad mind (for it is sometimes the property of such) against the most severe sentence which can be pronounced by the mouth of a human judge; but where is the fortitude which can look an offended Almighty in the face? Who can bear the dreadful thought of being confronted with the spirit of one whom we have murdered, in the presence of all the Host of Heaven, and to have justice demanded against our guilty soul, before that most awful judgement-seat, where there is infinite justice as well as infinite power?"

The dedication of this pamphlet, dated Bow Street, April 8, 1752, is addressed to Dr Madox, Bishop of Worcester, and in it Fielding recalls a conversation he had some time previously had with that prelate, in which he had mentioned the plan of such a book, and received immediate encouragement from his lordship. A further appreciation of the *Examples* appears in a paragraph in the *Journal* for May 5: "Last week a certain Colonel of the Army bought a large number of the book called *Examples of the Interposition of Providence in the Detection and Punishment of Murder*, in Order to distribute them amongst the private soldiers of his Regiment. An Example well worthy of Imitation!"

Fielding never allows us to forget for any length of time one or another of his contrasting activities, however absorbed he may seem to be in some one field of action. Now, when he is plunged in a hand-to-hand struggle with the criminal conditions of London, when he is admonishing the gayer end of the Town with his weekly censorial satire and ridicule, and while he is watching the enactment of new legislation for which he had so strenously pleaded,—he suddenly reappears in his earlier rôle of classical scholar. On June 17, the columns of the *Journal* advertise proposals for "A New Translation into English of the Works of LUCIAN. From the original Greek. With Notes, Historical, Critical and Explanatory. By Henry Fielding Esquire; and the Rev. Mr William Young." To which notice there is added, a few days later, the assurance that "Everything which hath the least Tendency to the Indecent will be omitted in this Translation." The most delightful, perhaps, of all the leading articles in the *Covent Garden Journal* is that in which the merits of this "Father of True Humour" are delineated. The facetious wit, the "attic Elegance of Diction," the poignant satire, the virtues and abilities of Lucian are here so persuasively presented that scarce a reader but surely would hasten, as he laid his paper down, to Mr Fielding's or Mr Young's house, or to Millar in the Strand or Dodsley in Pall Mall, where orders (with a guinea to be paid on booking the same) were received. And this essay is also memorable for the express declaration therein contained that Fielding had "formed his stile" upon that of Lucian; and, again, as betraying a note of disappointment, an acknowledgment that worldly fortune had indeed treated him somewhat harshly, such as Fielding's sanguine courage very seldom permits him to utter. The concluding words, written on his own behalf and on that of Mr Young, are words of gentle protest to the public for their lack of support to "two gentlemen who have hitherto in their several capacities endeavoured to be serviceable to them without deriving any great Emolument to themselves from their Labours." And when he tells us how that 'glory of human Nature, Marcus Aurelius' employed Lucian "in a very considerable Post in the Government," since that great emperor "did not, it seems, think, that a Man of Humour was below his Notice or unfit for Business of the gravest Kind," we cannot but remember that the business on which the Government of George II. thought fit to employ the inimitable genius of Henry Fielding was that of a Bow Street magistrate.

The onerous drudgery of that business, or else lack of response from a public deaf to its own interests, seems to have brought to nothing the project of this translation; and so English literature is the poorer for the loss of the works of the 'Father of Humour' translated by the incomparable pen of the 'Father of the English Novel.'[6]

Four months after the publication of the proposals for *Lucian*, Fielding took formal leave of the readers of his *Covent Garden Journal*, telling them that he no longer had "Inclination or Leisure," to carry on the paper. His brief farewell words contain an assurance very like that solemnly made, we may remember, five years before the publication of *Tom Jones*. At present, he declares, he has "No intention to hold any further correspondence with the gayer Muses"; just as eight years before he had announced that henceforth the 'infamous' Nine should have none of his company. To this declaration is added a protest against the injustice of attributing abuse to a writer who "never yet was, nor ever shall be the author of any, unless to Persons who are or ought to be infamous." From the tenor of this parting speech it is clear that Fielding was, at the time, feeling keenly the imputation, flung by some of his contemporaries, of producing 'scandalous Writings'; unmindful for the moment of his own calmer and wiser utterance, when he declared that men who engage in an heroic attempt to cleanse their age will undoubtedly find some of the dirt thereof sticking to their coats. "As he disdained all littleness of spirit, where ever he met with it in his dealings with the world, his indignation was apt to rise," says his contemporary Murphy; and we know from earlier protests how cruelly Fielding suffered from the attribution to his pen of writings utterly alien to his character. "... really," he cries, in the last words of the *Journal*, "it is hard to hear that scandalous Writings have been charged on me for that very Reason which ought to have proved the Contrary namely because they have been Scandalous."

The year 1752 closes with the birth of another daughter, born presumably in the house in Bow Street, as her baptism under the name of Louisa is entered in the registers of St Paul's, Covent Garden.

The curtain that, in Fielding's case, hangs so closely over all the pleasant intimate details of life, lifts once or twice during this year of incessant activity, and discloses just those warmhearted acts of kindness that help us to think of Harry Fielding with an affection almost as warm and personal as that we keep for Dick Steele or Oliver Goldsmith. Fielding, we know, had "no other use for money" than to help those even less fortunate than himself; and several incidents of this year show how he turned his opportunities, both as journalist and magistrate, to like generous uses. Thus there is the story of how, one day in March, "A poor girl who had come from Wapping to see the new entertainment at Covent Garden Theatre had her pocket cut off in the crowd before the doors were opened. Tho' she knew not the Pickpocket she came immediately to lay her complaint before the Justice and with many tears lamented not the loss of her Money, but of her Entertainment. At last, having obtained a sufficient Passport to the Gallery she departed with great satisfaction, and contented with the loss of fourteen shillings, though she declared she had not much more in the world." [7] Another day, or night rather, it is a poor troup of amateur players who had good reason to be grateful to the kindly Justice:—"last Monday night an Information was given to Henry Fielding Esquire: that a set of Barber's apprentices, Journeymen Staymakers, Maidservants &c. had taken a large room at the Black House in the Strand, to act the Tragedy of the Orphan; the Price of Admittance One shilling. About eight o'clock the said Justice issued his Warrant, directed to Mr Welch, High Constable, who apprehended the said Actors and brought them before the said Justice, who out of compassion to their Youth only bound them over to their good behaviour. They were all conducted through the streets in their Tragedy Dresses, to the no small diversion of the Populace." [8] And in May both the ample energies and scanty purse of Justice

Fielding were occupied in collecting a subscription for a young baker and his wife and child, who, by a disastrous fire, were suddenly plunged into destitution. For these poor people Fielding obtained no less a sum than £57, within a fortnight of his announcement of their distress in the columns of the *Journal*. The list of subscribers, published on May 16, shows a guinea against his own name, and a like sum, it may be noted, from the wealthy Lyttelton.

The splendour of Fielding's genius has shone, as Gibbon foretold, throughout the world. His indefatigable labours in cleansing England from some of the evils that then oppressed her deserve to be remembered, if not by all the world, at least by the citizens of that country which, in the decline of 'health and life,' he yet strove so eagerly to benefit.

[1] A dramatic satire, advertised in March at Covent Garden Theatre and written (as stated by Dibdin, *History of the Stage.* Vol. v. p. 156), by the actor Macklin, bore for sub-title *Pasquin turned Drawcansir, Censor of Great Britain.* The name, and the further details of the advertisement, recall Fielding's early success with his political *Pasquin*: but all further trace of this 'Satire' seems lost. See Appendix C.

[2] *A faithful Narrative....* By Drawcansir.... Alexander. 1752.

[3] 25. G II. cap 36.

[4] All trace seems now lost of the actual part Fielding may have taken in the drafting of this Act.

[5] 25. G. II. c. 37.

[6] It would seem, from the following advertisement, that Fielding's inexhaustible pen published, about this time, a sixpenny pamphlet on 'a late Act of Parliament'; but all trace of it has been lost:—"A speech made in the Censorial Court of Alexander Drawcansir, Monday, 6th June, 1752, concerning a late Act of Parliament. Printed for the Author. Price 6d." *The General Advertiser*, June 27, 1752.

[7] The *General Advertiser* March 4. 1752.

[8] The *General Advertiser*, April 15, 1752.

CHAPTER XVI

POOR LAW REFORM

"... surely there is some Praise due to the bare Design of doing a Service to the Public."—Dedication of the *Enquiry*.

It is evident that the beginning of the year 1753 found Fielding fully conscious that now he could only anticipate a 'short remainder of life.' But neither that consciousness, nor the increasing burden of ill-health, availed to dull the energies of these last years. Scarcely had that indomitable knight, General Sir Alexander Drawcansir retired from the active public service of conducting the *Covent Garden Journal* when his creator reappeared with an astonishingly comprehensive and detailed plan of poor-law reform; a plan adapted to the whole kingdom, and which according to a legal comment involved "nothing less than the repeal of the Act of Elizabeth and an entire reconstruction of the Poor Laws." [1] Poor-law reform was at this time occupying the attention of the nation, and apparently also of the legislature. And we know, from the *Enquiry into the Increase of Robberies*, that the question of lessening both the sufferings and the criminality of the poor had for years occupied Fielding's warm heart and active intellect. But the extent to which he devoted these last months of his life to the cause of the poorest and most degraded deserves more than a passing recognition. He tells us, in the *Introduction* to the pamphlet embodying his great scheme, that he has applied himself long and constantly to this subject; that he has "read over and considered all the Laws, in anywise relating to the Poor, with the utmost Care and Attention," in the execution of which, moreover, he has been for "many Years very particularly concerned"; and that in addition to this exhaustive study of the laws themselves, he has added "a careful Perusal of everything which I could find that hath been written on this Subject, from the Original Institution in the 43d. of *Elizabeth* to this Day." Such was the laborious preparation, extending presumably over many months, which the author of *Tom Jones*, and the first wit of his day, devoted to solving this vast problem of social reform.

Fielding was far too well skilled in the art of effective construction to present the public with undigested note-books from his voluminous reading. His scheme, based on all the laws, and upon all the comments on all the laws, regarding the poor, enacted and made for two hundred years, is a marvel of conciseness and practical detail; and, together with an *Introduction* and an *Epilogue*, does but occupy the ninety pages of a two-shilling pamphlet.

The pamphlet was published at the end of January 1753, with the title *A Proposal for making an effectual Provision for the Poor, for amending their Morals, and for rendering them useful Members of the Society. To which is added a Plan of the Buildings proposed, with proper Elevations ... By Henry Fielding, Esq.; Barrister-at-Law, and one of His Majesty's Justices of the Peace for the County of Middlesex.* The dedication, dated January 19, is to Henry Pelham, then Chancellor of the Exchequer, and from it we learn that Fielding had personally mentioned his scheme to this Minister. The

Introduction presents an eloquent appeal for some effectual remedy for the intolerably diseased state of the body politic as regarded the distresses and vices of the poor, their unseen sufferings no less than their frequent misdeeds. Fielding protests against the popular ignorance of these sufferings in words that might have been spoken by some pleader for the East End 'Settlements' of to-day. "If we were," he declares, "to make a Progress through the Outskirts of this Town, and look into the Habitations of the Poor, we should there behold such Pictures of human Misery as must move the Compassion of every Heart that deserves the Name of human. What indeed must be his Composition who could see whole Families in Want of every Necessary of Life, oppressed with Hunger, Cold, Nakedness, and Filth, and with Diseases, the certain Consequence of all these; what, I say, must be his Composition, who could look into such a Scene as this, and be affected only in his Nostrils?" As an instance of Fielding's personal knowledge of the London slums of his day, a reference made by Mr Saunders Welch to their joint work is of interest. Writing in the same year, 1753, he mentions assisting "Mr Henry Fielding in taking from under one roof upwards of seventy lodgers of both sexes." [2]

To this little known misery of the poor, who "starve and freeze and rot among themselves," was added the problem of streets swarming with beggars during the day, and with thieves at night. And the nation groaned under yet a third burden, that of the heavy taxes levied for the poor, by which says Fielding "as woeful experience hath taught us, neither the poor themselves nor the public are relieved." To attack such a three-headed monster as this was an adventure better fitted, it might seem, for that club which "Captain Hercules Vinegar" had wielded thirteen years before, when in the full tide of his strength, than for the pen of a man in shattered health, and already serving the public in the daily labours of a principal magistrate. But nothing could restrain the ardour of Fielding's spirit, how frail so ever had become its containing 'crust of clay,' when great abuses and great misery made their call on his powers; or countervail against the hope, with which the *Introduction* to his plan concludes. If that plan fails, he shall indeed, he declares have "lost much Time, and misemployed much Pains; and what is above all, shall miss the Pleasure of thinking that in the Decline of my Health and Life, I have conferred a great and lasting Benefit on my Country."

The *Plan* is that of the erection of a vast combined county workhouse, prison, and infirmary; where the unemployed should find, not only work but *skilled instruction*, the poor relief, and the sick a hospital; where discipline and good order should be stringently enforced; and where two chaplains should labour at that 'correction and amendment' of the mind which "in real truth religion is alone capable of effectually executing." The entire scheme is worked out with extraordinary detail, in fifty-nine clauses; and is preceded by an elaborate architectural plan of the proposed institution (which was to house no less than five thousand six hundred persons) with its workshops, its men's quarters rigorously divided from those for the women, its recreation ground, its provision shops, its cells for the refractory and for prisoners, and its whipping post. And the pamphlet concludes by lengthy arguments in favour of the various clauses; and by a personal protest concerning the disinterestedness of proposals which "some few enemies" might assert to show signs of a design for private profit. Fielding touchingly disavows any thought of occupying, officially, the great house raised by his imagination. To a man in his state of health such a project would, he says, be to fly in the face of the advice of his 'Master,' Horace; "it would be indeed *struere domos immemor sepulchri*." And, he adds, those who know him will hardly be so deceived "by that Chearfulness which was always natural to me; and which, I thank God, my Conscience doth not reprove me for, to imagine that I am not sensible of my declining Constitution." The concluding words of this, Fielding's last legislative effort, betray a like calm assurance that his day's work was drawing to its close. He has now, he tells us, "no farther Design than to pass my short Remainder of Life in some Degree of Ease, and barely to preserve my Family from being the Objects of any such Laws as I have here proposed."

It is wholly in keeping with the genius of Henry Fielding that almost the last endeavour of his intellect should have been devoted to relieving the wretchedness and lessening the vices of the poorest and most miserable of his countrymen. The *Proposal for ... the Poor* is written by the hand of the accomplished lawyer and indefatigable magistrate; but the energy that accomplished so great a labour, in spite of broken health and among a thousand interruptions, sprang from the heart which had already immortalised the ragged postilion of *Joseph Andrews* and the starving highwayman of *Tom Jones*.

This last January but one of Fielding's life was not only occupied by the publication of proposals for an 'entire reconstruction of the Poor Laws.' In 1753 a London magistrate, or at least Mr Justice Fielding, was at the service of the public on Sunday no less than during the week; and on the first Sunday of the New Year the Bow Street room echoed to threats that read strangely enough when we think of the unknown petty thief, threatening sudden death to 'our immortal Fielding.' "Yesterday," says the *General Advertiser* for Monday, January 8, "John Simpson and James Ellys were commited to Newgate by Henry Fielding Esq., for shop-lifting." The charge was one of stealing five silk handkerchiefs, and when the two men "were brought before the Justice they behaved in a very impudent saucy manner, and one of them said hewished he had a Pistol about him, he would blow the Justice's Brains out; upon which a Party of the Guards was sent for who conducted them safe to Newgate." The Bow Street house, moreover, must have been full not only of prisoners and witnesses brought before the Justice, but also of victims of all manner of theft. For two comprehensive notices appear in the *Advertiser* for this month, repeating the previous invitation accorded to such sufferers in the *Covent Garden Journal*. On January 1, all persons cognizant of any burglary robbery or theft are desired to communicate immediately with Mr Brogden, clerk to Justice Fielding, "at his office at the said Justice's in Bow Street." And again, towards the end of the month, "All Persons that have been robbed on the Highway in the County of Middlesex within this three months last past, are desired to apply to Mr

Brogden, at Mr Justice Fielding's in Bow Street, Covent Garden." And here, too, came the solicitors that sought counsel's opinion on their client's behalf, with their fees; the magistrate of this period being under no disability in regard to his private practice.

It was to his reputation as an advising barrister, and perhaps a little to the kindness of heart that must have been familiar to all who knew him, that Fielding owed his connection with that extraordinary popular excitement of 1753, the mysterious case of the servant girl Elizabeth Canning. On the 29th of January 'Betty Canning' presented herself, after a month's disappearance, at the door of her mother's house in London, in a deplorable state of weakness and distress, and declared that she had been kidnapped by two men on New Year's night, taken to a house on the Hertford road, and there confined by an old gipsy woman for twenty-eight days, in a hay loft, with a pitcher of water and a few pieces of bread for sole sustenance. On the twenty ninth day, according to her own account, she escaped through a window and made her way back to her home. Her neighbours, fired with pity for her sufferings, subscribed means for a prosecution; and, says Fielding, in the pamphlet which he published two months after these events, "Mr. *Salt*, the Attorney who hath been employed in this Cause, ... upon this Occasion, as he hath done upon many others, ... fixed upon me as the Council to be advised with." Then we have the following little domestic sketch, the only picture left to us of Henry Fielding as a practising barrister: "Accordingly, upon the *6th of February*, as I was sitting in my Room, Counsellor *Maden* being then with me, my Clerk delivered me a Case, which was thus, as I remember, indorsed at the Top, The Case of Elizabeth Canning *for* Mr Fielding's *opinion*, and at the Bottom, *Salt*, Solr. Upon the Receipt of this Case, with my Fee, I bid my Clerk give my Service to Mr. *Salt* and tell him, that I would take the Case with me into the Country, whither I intended to go the next Day, and desired he would call for it the *Friday* Morning afterwards; after which, without looking into it, I delivered it to my Wife, who was then drinking Tea with us, and who laid it by."

Mr Brogden however presently returned upstairs, bringing the solicitor with him, who earnestly desired his counsel not only to read the case at once but also to undertake in his capacity of magistrate an examination of the injured girl, and of a supposed confederate of the gipsy. This task Fielding at first declined, principally on the ground that he had been "almost fatigued to death with several tedious examinations" at that time, and had intended to refresh himself with a day or two's interval in the country, where he had not been "unless on a Sunday, for a long time." The persuasions of the solicitor, curiosity as to the extrordinary nature of the case, and "a great compassion for the dreadful condition of the girl," however induced him to yield; and the next day the eighteen year old heroine of a story that was soon to set all London quarrelling, was brought in a chair to Bow Street, and then led upstairs, supported by two friends, into the presence of the Justice. An issue of warrants followed upon her examination, and a further examination of a suspected confederate of the gipsy; the gipsy herself and her chief abettor having already been arrested by another magistrate. Some days later, Fielding being then out of town, "several noble Lords" sent to his house, desiring to be present while he examined the gipsy woman; and the matter being arranged, "Lord Montfort," says Fielding, "together with several gentlemen of fashion came at the appointed time." The company being in the Justice's room, the prisoners and witnesses were brought up; and apparently some charge was afterwards brought against Fielding as to the manner of his examination, for he here takes occasion to declare, what all who knew him must have known to be the truth, "I can truly say, that my Memory doth not charge me with having ever insulted the lowest Wretch that hath been brought before me." Public opinion became hotly divided as to whether Betty Canning had indeed suffered all she declared at the hands of the gipsy, Mary Squires, or had maliciously endeavoured to perjure away the old woman's life. The Lord Mayor, Sir Crisp Gascoyne, and Fielding's old antagonist the despicable Dr Hill ardently supported the gipsy; Fielding, in the pamphlet already quoted, and which was published in March, as warmly espoused the cause of the maid servant whom he calls "a poor, honest, innocent, simple Girl, and the most unhappy and most injured of all human Beings." The excitement of the Town over this melodramatic mystery is reflected in the fact that a second edition of Fielding's pamphlet (entitled *A clear state of the Case of Elizabeth Canning*) was advertised within a few days of its first publication. [3] And, also, in the appearance of the sixpenny print, here for the first time reproduced, in which occurs the only representation of Henry Fielding known to have been drawn during his life time. This print, which bears the inscription "drawn from the life by the Right Honourable the Lady Fa—y K—w," shows Fielding's tall figure, his legs bandaged for gout, the sword of Justice in his hand and her scales hanging out of his pocket, speaking on behalf of his trembling client Elizabeth Canning; while opposed to him are my Lord Mayor, the notorious Dr Hill, and the old gipsy. The background is adorned with pictures of the newly built Mansion House, and of the College of Surgeons. [4]

But for the glimpses it affords us of Fielding as a barrister, and for his characteristic championship of what he was convinced was the cause of innocence oppressed, this once famous case might have been left undisturbed in the dust of the *State Trials*, had it not incidentally been the means of preserving two of the extremely rare letters of the novelist. These letters, [5] hitherto unpublished, are addressed by Fielding to the Duke of Newcastle, and were both written in the month following the publication of his pamphlet. The fact that both letters are dated from Ealing shows that his connection with what was then a pleasant country village was earlier than has been supposed; and the acute suggestions in the second letter seem to indicate a suspicion of some of Betty Canning's supporters, if his conviction in the girl's own innocence still remained unshaken.

"My Lord Duke

"I received an order from my Lord Chancellor immediately after the breaking up of the Council to lay before your Grace all the Affidavits I had taken since the Gipsey's Trial which related to that Affair. I then told the Messenger that I had taken none, as indeed the fact is the Affidavits of which I gave my Lord Chancellor an Abstract having been all sworn before Justices of the Peace in the Neighbourhood of Endfield, and remain I believe in the Possession of an Attorney in the City.

However in Consequence of the Commands with which your Grace was pleased to honour me yesterday, I sent my Clerk immediately to the Attorney to acquaint him with these Commands, which I doubt not he will instantly obey. This I did from my great Duty to your Grace for I have long had no Concern in this Affair, nor have I seen any of the Parties lately unless once when I was desired to send for the Girl (Canning) to my House that a great Number of Noblemen and Gentleman might see her and ask her what Questions they pleased. I am, with the highest Duty,
"My Lord,
"Your Graces most obedient
"and most humble servant
"Henry Ffielding.
"Ealing. April 14, 1753
"His Grace the
"Duke of Newcastle."

"My Lord Duke,
"I am extremely concerned to see by a Letter which I have just received from Mr Jones by Command of your Grace that the Persons concerned for the Prosecution have not yet attended your Grace with the Affidavits in Canning's Affair. I do assure you upon my Honour that I sent to them the Moment I first received your Grace's Commands and having after three Messages prevailed with them to come to me I desired them to fetch the Affidavits that I might send them to your Grace being not able to wait upon you in Person. This they said they could not do, but would go to Mr Hume Campbell their Council, and prevail with him to attend your Grace with all their Affidavits many of which, I found were sworn after the Day mentioned in the order of Council. I told them I apprehended the latter could not be admitted, but insisted in the strongest terms on their laying the others immediately before your Grace, and they at last promised me they would, nor have I ever seen them since. I have now again ordered my Clerk to go to them to inform them of the last Commands I have received, but as I have no Compulsory Power over them I can not answer for their Behaviour, which indeed I have long disliked, and have therefore long ago declined giving them any Advice, nor would I unless in Obedience to your Grace have anything to say to a set of the most obstinate Fools I ever saw; and who seem to me rather to act from a Spleen against my Lord Mayor, than from any Motive of protecting Innocence, tho' that was certainly their Motive at first.

In Truth, if I am not deceived, I Suspect they desire that the Gipsey should be pardoned, and then to convince the World that she was guilty in order to cast the greater Reflection on him who was principally instrumental in obtaining such Pardon. I conclude with assuring your Grace that I have acted in this Affair, as I shall on all Occasions with the most dutiful Regard to your Commands, and that if my Life had been at Stake, as many know, I could have done no more.
"I am, with the highest Respect,
"My Lord Duke
"Y Grace's most obedient,
"and most humble servant,
"Henry Ffielding.
"Ealing
"April 27. 1753.
"His Grace the Duke of Newcastle."

The dates of these letters show Fielding to have been at Ealing in the early spring of this year; and thus afford some confirmation of Lysons' remark in his *Environs of London*, published forty years later that "Henry Fielding had a country house at Ealing where he resided the year before his death." [6] In May a connection with Hammersmith is indicated, in the burial there of his little daughter Louisa. The entry in the Hammersmith Registers is as follows: "May 10th. Louisa, d. of Henry Fielding Esqr."

The nearer Fielding's life draws to its premature close, the greater his physical suffering, so much the more eager seems his desire to leave behind him some practical achievement. We have already seen and wondered at his gigantic scheme for poor-law reform, published in the beginning of this year of fast declining 'health and life.' Six months later came the commission in the execution of which the remains of that health and life were literally sacrificed in the effort to win some provision for his family, in the event of his own death. Early in August the distinguished Court surgeon John Ranby had persuaded him to go immediately to Bath. And he tells us, in that *Journal of a Voyage to Lisbon*, [7] from which we have, from his own lips, the details of these last months, "I accordingly writ that very night to Mrs Bowden, who, by the next post, informed me she had taken me a lodging for a month certain." At this moment, when preparing for his journey, and while "almost fatigued to death with several long examinations, relating to five different murders, all committed within the space of a week, by different gangs of street robbers," Fielding received what might indeed be called a fatal summons to wait on the Duke of Newcastle, at his house in Lincoln's Inn Fields, to consult on a means for "putting an immediate end to those murders and robberies which were every day committed in the streets." This visit cost him a severe cold; but, notwithstanding, he produced, in about four days, a scheme for the destruction of the "then reigning gangs" of robbers and cut-throats, and for the future protection of the public, which was promptly accepted, and the execution of which was confided into Fielding's hands. "I had delayed my Bath-journey for some time," he proceeds, "contrary to the repeated advice of my physical acquaintance, and to the ardent desire of my warmest friends, tho' my distemper was now turned to a deep jaundice; in which case the Bath-waters are generally reputed to be almost infallible. But I had the most eager desire of demolishing this gang of villains and cut-throats." After some weeks the requisite funds were placed at Fielding's disposal; and so successful were his methods, that within a few days, the whole gang was dispersed, some in custody, others in flight. His health was by this time "reduced to the last extremity"; but still, he tells us, he continued to act "with the utmost vigour against these villains." And, amid all his 'fatigues and distresses,' the satisfaction he so ardently desired came to him. During the "remaining part of the month of November and in all December," those darkest of months, not only was there no such thing as a murder, but not one street robbery was committed. When we recall the amazing condition of London at this time, when street robberies and murders were of almost daily occurrence, we realise the magnitude of this achievement on the part of a dying man. "Having thus fully accomplished my undertaking," Fielding continues, "I went into the country in a very weak and deplorable condition, with no fewer or less diseases than a jaundice, a dropsy, and an asthma, altogether uniting their forces in the destruction of a body so entirely emaciated, that it had lost all its muscular flesh." It was now too late to apply the Bath treatment; and even had it been desirable it was no longer possible, for the sick man's strength was so reduced that a ride of six miles fatigued him intolerably. The Bath lodgings, which Fielding, surely with his old invincible hopefulness, had hitherto kept were accordingly relinquished; and even his sanguine nature realised the desperate condition of his case. At this point in his narration he breaks off with a characteristically frank disclosure of the chief motive which had inspired him to the heroic exertions of these later months of 1753. At the beginning of the winter his private affairs it seems, "had but a gloomy aspect." The aspect of his own tenure of life we know. And hence to distress of body was added that keenest of all distresses of the mind, the despair of putting his family beyond the reach of necessity. It was gladly therefore that Fielding offered up the 'poor sacrifice' of his shattered health, in the hope of securing a pension for his family, in case his own death were hastened by these last labours for the public.

If sickness was not allowed to hinder Fielding's energies for the benefit of the public, and for the future provision of his family, neither did he permit it to dull the activities of friendship. Early in December, when his illness must have been acute, he wrote the following hitherto unpublished letter to the Lord Chancellor, on behalf of his friend Mr Saunders Welch: [8]

"My Lord,
"As I hear that a new Commission of the Peace is soon to pass the Great Seal for Westm'r. give me Leave to recommend the name of Saunders Welch, as well as to the next Commission for Middx. Your Lordship will, I hope, do me the Honour of believing, I should not thus presume, unless I was well satisfied that the Merit of the Man would justifie my Presumption. For this besides a

universal Good Character and the many eminent services he hath done the Public, I appeal in particular to Master Lane; and shall only add, as I am positive the Truth is, that his Place can be filled with no other more acceptable to all the Gentlemen in the Commission, and indeed to the Public in general. I am with the highest Duty and Respect,

"My Lord,

"Your Lordship's most obedient

"and most humble servant,

"Henry Ffielding."

"Decr 6. 1753

"To the Lord High Chancellor"

[1] *Life of Henry Fielding.* Frederick Lawrence, p. 138.

[2] Saunders Welch. *A Letter on the subject of Robberies, wrote in the year 1753.*

[3] See the *Public Advertiser* 1753 March 17, 20, 24 &c.

[4] This unique contemporary print of Fielding may be seen in the British Museum, Print Room, *Social Satires*, No. 3213.

[5] Record Office. *State Papers. Domestic* G. II., 127, no. 24.

[6] Lysons. *Environs of London.* 1795. Vol. ii. p. 229.

[7] The quotations from the *Voyage to Lisbon* are from the edition recently prepared by Mr Austin Dobson, for the 'World's Classics.'

[8] This letter is now in the British Museum. The endorsement on the back is: "Dec. 6, 1753 from Mr Fielding recommending Mr. Saunders Welch to be in the Com. of ye Peace for Westmr and Middx."

CHAPTER XVII

VOYAGE TO LISBON—DEATH

"satisfied in having finished my life, as I have probably lost it in
the service of my country."
Journal of a Voyage to Lisbon.

To a man dying of a complication of disorders the terrible winter of 1753-4
brought added danger; a winter which, says Fielding, "put a lucky end, if they
had known their own interests, to such numbers of aged and infirm
valetudinarians." But this, too, his splendid constitution struggled through; and
in February 1754, he was back in town, in a condition less despaired of, he tells
us, by himself than by any of his friends.

And if he did not allow himself to despair, neither did he, even now,
relinquish all his magistrate's work. On the 26th of February cases are actually
recorded as brought before him. [1] But within a few days, apparently, of this
date treatment employed on the advice of Dr Joshua Ward, so weakened a body
already 'enervate' and emaciated, that at first the patient "was thought to be
falling into the agonies of death." On March 6, he was, he tells us, at his worst—
that "memorable day when the public lost Mr Pelham. From that day I began
slowly, as it were, to draw my feet out of the grave; till in two months time I had
again acquired some little degree of strength."

Before the expiration of these two months that 'little degree of strength' was
again being expended in the drudgery of the Bow Street court-room.
"Yesterday," states the *Public Advertiser* of April 17, "Elizabeth Smith was
committed to Newgate by Henry Fielding Esqre; being charged with stealing a
great quantity of Linnen." [2] And five days later, on April 22, a committal is
recorded in the Middlesex *Sessions Book.* [3]

Although Fielding could now leave his sickroom, when called thence to
commit a thief to Newgate, a newspaper paragraph, dated a little earlier in this
same month of April, shows that the public were apprehensive that the
protection afforded them by their indefatigable magistrate was now of a very
precarious duration. The writer refers to the complete success of Mr Fielding's
Plan for the subjugation of criminals, executed the previous winter, pointing out
that "the Public who had such Reason to suspect the contrary have suffered
fewer Outrages than have happened any Winter this Twenty years." And without
making any direct statement as to the fast failing strength of the author and
executor of that *Plan*, he continues in words that plainly indicate the abdication
of those zealous energies: "The whole Plan we are assured is communicated to
Justice John Fielding and Mr Welch who are determined to bring it to that
perfection of which it is capable." This 'assurance' of the *Advertiser* is confirmed
by Fielding's own words in the *Voyage to Lisbon.* "I therefore" he says, speaking
clearly of the winter or spring of 1753-4, "resigned the office [of principal Justice

of the Peace in Westminster] and the farther execution of my plan to my brother, who had long been my assistant."

This blind brother, who in his turn became famous as a London magistrate, was now a Justice of the Peace for Middlesex [4] as well as for Westminster; and was at this time living in the Strand, as the Resident Proprietor [5] of that enterprising *Universal Register Office* which has won incidental immortality in his brother's pages, and which combined such heterogeneous activities as those of an Estate Office, Registry for servants of good character, Lost Property Office, Curiosity Shop and General Agency.

Another announcement in the columns of the *Advertiser* links this last Spring of Fielding's life with that earlier Spring of 1743, when as a popular play-wright and a struggling barrister, absorbed in anxiety for the health of a beloved wife and with his own health already attacked, he published that masterpiece of irony *Jonathan Wild*. Now, while he was still slowly drawing his 'feet out of the grave,' after those critical first days of March, a new edition of the *History* of that "Great Man," with "considerable Corrections and Additions," was advertised; the actual date of publication being, apparently, about March 19. The new edition appeared with a prefatory note, "from the Publisher to the Reader," which although it bears no signature conveys, undoubtedly, Fielding's intention, if not his actual words. There is the familiar protest against the "scurrility of others," the odium of which had fallen on the innocent shoulders of "the author of our little book"; and there is a solemn declaration that the said little book shows no reason for supposing any 'personal application' to be meant in its pages "unless we will agree that there are without those Walls [i.e. of Newgate], some other bodies of men of worse morals than those within; and who have consequently, a right to change places with its present inhabitants." Then follows an explicit reference to a chapter in the *History* of the arch-villain Wild, which is obviously designed to satirise the condition of English politics, if not the person of any one politician. The disclaimer, seems on the whole, to partake very properly of the ironic nature of the ensuing pages; although it recalls that youthful declaration of the young dramatist, prefixed to his first comedy acted nearly thirty years before, that no private character was the target of his pen.

At the end of these two months of March and April, spent as we have seen in acquiring some little degree of strength, and in at least attempting to expend the same on the consignment of petty thieves to Newgate, Fielding again submitted his dropsy to the surgeon, the consequences of which he now bore much better. This improvement, he tells us, he attributed greatly to "a dose of laudanum prescribed by my surgeon. It first gave me the most delicious flow of spirits, and afterwards as comfortable a nap." Lady Mary Wortley Montagu has recorded how her cousin's 'happy constitution,' even when half-demolished, could enjoy, with undiminished zest "a venison pasty, or a flask of champagne." Surely none other than Henry Fielding could have recorded with like zest this 'delicious flow of spirits' and 'comfortable nap' derived from a dose of laudanum.

The month of May, with its promise of relief from the still lingering winter, had now begun. Fielding therefore resolved, he says, to visit a little country house of his "which stands at Ealing, in the county of Middlesex, in the best air, I believe, in the whole kingdom." [6] Towards the end of the month, he had resort to a long forgotten eighteenth century panacea, the tar-water discovered by Bishop Berkeley; and very soon experienced effects far beyond his "most sanguine hopes." Success beyond Fielding's most sanguine hopes must have been great indeed; and accordingly we hear how this tar-water, from the very first, lessened his illness, increased his appetite, and very slowly added to his bodily strength. By the end of the month a third application by his surgeon revealed distinctly favourable symptoms; but still both the dropsy and the asthma were becoming more serious; and the summer, which the doctors seemed to think the sick man's 'only chance of life' seemed scarce likely to visit England at all in that sunless year. "In the whole month of May the sun scarce appeared three times" we learn, from the *Voyage*. Fearing therefore the renewed assaults of winter, before he had recruited his forces so as "to be in anywise able to withstand them," Fielding resolved, with the approval of a very eminent physician, to put an already formed project into immediate execution. This was to seek further recovery in some warmer climate. At first Aix was thought of, but here the difficulties of travel in the reign of George II. for invalids of slender means, proved insuperable. The journey by land, "beside the expense of it," Fielding found to be "infinitely too long and fatiguing"; and no ship was announced as sailing within 'any reasonable time' for that part of the Mediterranean. Lisbon accordingly was decided upon; and John Fielding soon discovered a ship with excellent passenger accommodation, and which was due to sail in three days. "I eagerly embraced the offer," writes Fielding, as though he were starting on a pleasure cruise, instead of facing all the miseries of travel, when unable to make the least use of his limbs, and when his very appearance "presented a spectacle of the highest horror"; and he adds "I began to prepare my family for the voyage with the utmost expedition." Twice, however, the captain put off his sailing, and at length his passenger invited him to dinner at Ealing, a full week after the declared date of departure. Meanwhile Fielding's condition seems at least to have become no worse, for the *Public Advertiser* of June 22 has "the pleasure to assure the Publick that the Report of the Death of Henry Fielding Esquire; inserted in an Evening paper of Thursday is not true, that Gentleman's Health being better than it has been for some Month's past."

It was not till the 26th of June that, in the memorable opening words of the *Voyage*, "the most melancholy sun I had ever beheld arose, and found me awake at my house at Fordhook. By the light of this sun, I was, in my own opinion, last to behold and take leave of some of those creatures on whom I doated with a mother-like fondness, guided by nature and passion, and uncured and unhardened by all the doctrine of that philosophical school where I had learnt to bear pains and to despise death." The morning was spent with his children, the eldest of whom was then a boy of six; and "I doubt not," he writes, "whether, in that time, I did not undergo more than in all my distemper." At noon his coach was at the door, and this "was no sooner told me than I kiss'd my children round, and went into it with some little resolution." His wife, behaving "more like a heroine and philosopher, tho' at the same time the tenderest mother in the world," and his eldest daughter, followed him; and the invalid was swiftly driven the twelve miles to Rotherhithe. Here the task of embarking a man quite bereft of the use of his limbs had to be accomplished. This difficulty was overcome with the aid of Saunders Welch, the friend of whom Fielding says "I never think or speak of but with love and esteem" [7]; and, at last, the traveller was "seated in a great chair in the cabin," after fatigues, the most cruel of which he declares to have been the inhuman jests made upon his wasted and helpless condition by the rows of sailors and watermen through whom he had been compelled to pass.

From this moment we may read of the pleasures and thoughts, the experiences and meditations, but scarcely ever of the sufferings of the dying novelist, in the pages of what has been well called "one of the most unfeigned and touching little tracts in our own or any other literature" [8] Confined for six weeks in the narrow prison of an eighteenth century trading vessel; unable to move save when lifted by unskilled hands; with food often intolerable to the healthiest appetite; with no relaxation save the company of the rough old sea-dog who commanded the *Queen of Portugal*; and fully conscious that his was a mortal illness,—the inexhaustible courage, the delight in man and in nature, the genius of Henry Fielding still triumphed over every external circumstance. Throughout the voyage, fortune, moreover, seemed determined to heap on the unhappy traveller all manner of additional discomforts; and yet when we lay down this little volume "begun in pain, and finished almost at the same period with life," [9] the pictures left on the mind glow almost as brightly as those which fill the pages written in the full vigour of Fielding's manhood, and which, as Coleridge said, breathe the air of a spring morning.

First came a delay of three days off the squalid shores of Wapping and Rotherhithe, whereby opportunity was afforded of "tasting a delicious mixture of the air of both these sweet places," and of enjoying such a concord of the voices of seamen, watermen, fishwomen, oyster women and their like as Hogarth indicated "in that print of his which is enough to make a man deaf to look at." This delay, moreover, threatened to bring Fielding within need of a surgeon when none should be procurable. His friend Mr William Hunter of Covent Garden, brother of the more famous John Hunter, relieved this apprehension; but now fresh trouble occurred in the torments of toothache which befell Mrs Fielding. A servant was despatched in haste to Wapping, but the desired 'toothdrawer,' arrived after the ship had at last, on Sunday morning, the 30th of June, left her unsavoury moorings. That Sunday morning "was fair and bright," and the diarist records how, dropping down to Gravesend, "we had a passage thither I think as pleasant as can be conceiv'd." The yards of Deptford and Woolwich were 'noble sights'; the Thames with its splendid shipping excelled all the rivers of the world; and the men of war, the unrivalled Indiamen, the other traders, and even the colliers and small craft, all combined to form "a most pleasing object to the eye, as well as highly warming to the heart of an

Englishman, who has any degree of love for his country, or can recognise any effect of the patriot in his constitution." And here Fielding gives us a notable example of his own healthy taste in recreation; a taste agreeing very ill with the scurrilous popular myths concerning him, but entirely consonant with the manifest atmosphere of his genius. He deplores the general neglect of "what seems to me the highest degree of amusement: that is, the sailing ourselves in little vessels of our own"; an amusement which need not "exceed the reach of a moderate fortune, and would fall very short of the prices which are daily paid for pleasures of a far inferior rate."

Fortune, as we have said, seemed to grudge every little pleasure that could have alleviated the condition of the helpless invalid on board the *Queen of Portugal*. The relief obtained from Mr Hunter, he tells us, "the gaiety of the morning, the pleasant sailing with wind and tide, and the many agreeable objects with which I was constantly entertained during the whole way, were all suppressed and overcome by the single consideration of my wife's pain, which continued incessantly to torment her." The second despatch of a messenger, in great haste to bring the best reputed operator in Gravesend recalls Murphy's words: "Of sickness and poverty he was singularly patient and under pressure of those evils he could quietly read *Cicero de Consolatione*; but if either of them threatened his wife he was impetuous for her relief." The remedies both of the Gravesend 'surgeon of some eminence,' and of yet another practitioner, who was sent for from Deal, were ineffectual; but about eight in the evening of the following day, when the ship under contrary winds, was at anchor in the Downs, Mrs Fielding fell asleep; and to that accident we owe one of the most characteristic passages in the *Voyage*. His wife's relief from pain would, Fielding tells us, "have given me some happiness, could I have known how to employ those spirits which were raised by it: but unfortunately for me, I was left in a disposition of enjoying an agreeable hour, without the assistance of a companion, which has always appeared to me necessary to such enjoyment; my daughter and her companion were both retired sea-sick to bed; the other passengers were a rude school boy of fourteen years old, and an illiterate Portuguese friar, who understood no language but his own, in which I had not the least smattering. The captain was the only person left, in whose conversation I might indulge myself; but unluckily for me, besides his knowledge being chiefly confined to his profession, he had the misfortune of being so deaf, that to make him hear my words, I must run the risque of conveying them to the ears of my wife, who, tho' in another room (called, I think, the state-room; being indeed a most stately apartment capable of containing one human body in length, if not very tall, and three bodies in breadth) lay asleep within a yard of me. In this situation necessity and choice were one and the same thing; the captain and I sat down together to a small bowl of punch, over which we both soon fell fast asleep, and so concluded the evening." In the record of the previous day, while sketching the humours of Jacks in office, Fielding incidentally shows himself as no less careful of the respect due to his wife than he was solicitous for her comfort. A ruffianly custom-house officer had appeared in their cabin, wearing a hat adorned with broad gold lace, and 'cocked with much military fierceness.' On eliciting the information that 'the gentleman' was a riding surveyor, "I replied," says Fielding, "that he might be a riding surveyor, but could be no gentleman, for that none who had any title to that denomination, would break into the presence of a lady, without any apology or even moving his hat. He then took his covering from his head, and laid it on the table, saying he asked pardon." To this 'riding surveyor' we owe also an indication that Fielding found room in the narrow confines of a cabin for his Plato; for the rude insolence of that functionary recalls to his mind the Platonic theory of the divine original of rulers, and he proceeds to quote a long passage from the *Laws*, which even his ready scholarship could scarce have had by heart.

Contrary winds continued to baffle all Captain Veal's seamanship, and afforded his passenger opportunities for a spirited protest concerning the need of some regulation both of the charges of long-shore boatmen, and of the manners of captains in the Royal Navy. On the evening of July 8 the *Voyage* records that "we beat the sea off Sussex, in sight of Dungeness, with much more pleasure than progress; for the weather was almost a perfect calm, and the moon, which was almost at the full, scarce suffered a single cloud to veil her from our sight"; and on the 18th of the month the *Queen of Portugal* put in to Ryde, at which place she remained wind-bound for no less than eleven days.

These eleven days Fielding spent, by his wife's persuasions, on shore, at the poor village inn which, together with a little church and some thirty houses, then constituted the village of Ryde. Of the hardships and humours of that sojourn the *Voyage* affords an account worthy of a place among the pages of either of the three great novels. The landlady, an incredibly mean and heartless shrew, inflicted daily annoyances and extortions on her wind-bound victims. The squalid building, partly constructed of wreck-wood, could scarce house the party. The food supplies, other than those the visitors brought with them, were chiefly 'rusty bacon, and worse cheese,' with very bad ale to drink. And on the first afternoon, the house was found to be so damp from recent scrubbing that Mrs Fielding, who "besides discharging excellently well her own, and all the tender offices becoming the female character; who besides being a faithful friend, an amiable companion, and a tender nurse, could likewise supply the wants of a decrepit husband, and occasionally perform his part," hastily snatched the invalid from "worse perils by water than the common dangers of the sea," and ordered dinner to be laid in a dry and commodious barn. So seated, "in one of the most pleasant spots, I believe, in the kingdom," and regaled on bacon, beans, and fish, "we completed," says Fielding, "the best, the pleasantest, and the merriest meal, with more appetite, more real, solid luxury, and more festivity, than was ever seen in an entertainment at White's."

On Sunday the three ladies went to church, "attended by the captain in a most military attire, with his cockade in his hat, and his sword by his side" (Captain Veal had commanded a privateer); and Fielding, while left alone, pursued those researches into human nature of which he never wearied by conversation with the landlord, a fine example of henpecked humanity. On the following day the ladies, again attended by Captain Veal, enjoyed a four mile walk, professing themselves greatly charmed with the scenery, and with the courtesy of a lady who owned a great house on this part of the coast, and who "had slipt out of the way, that my wife and her company might refresh themselves with the flowers and fruits with which her garden abounded." Within twenty four hours this generous householder had sent a message to the inn, placing all that her garden or house afforded at the disposal of the travellers. Fielding's man-servant was despatched with proper acknowledgements, and returned "in company with the gardener, both richly laden with almost every particular which a garden at this most fruitful season of the year produces."

That evening, on a change of wind, Captain Veal came to demand his passengers' instant return. This would have been "a terrible circumstance to me, in my decayed condition," admits Fielding, "especially as very heavy showers of rain, attended with a high wind, continued to fall incessantly; the being carried thro' which two miles in the dark, in a wet and open boat, seemed little less than certain death." Happily the wind again veered till the following morning, when Fielding and the three ladies, together with their manservant and maid, were safely re-embarked, not however without much agitation over the temporary loss of their tea-chest. This calamity was first compensated by the prompt aid of the hospitable lady aforementioned, and then averted by the diligent search of William the footman who at last discovered the hiding place of the missing 'sovereign cordial,' and thus, concludes his master, "ended this scene, which begun with such appearance of distress, and ended with becoming the subject of mirth and laughter." Once more on board, Ryde and its beautiful prospect, its verdant elms, its green meadows, and shady lanes all combining in Fielding's opinion to make a most delightful habitation, faded from view. And, by seven o'clock, "we sat down" he says, "to regale ourselves with some roasted venison, which was much better drest than we imagined it would be, and an excellent cold pasty which my wife had made at Ryde, and which we had reserved uncut to eat on board our ship, whither we all cheerfully exulted in being returned from the presence of Mrs Humphreys, [the landlady] who by the exact resemblance she bore to a fury, seemed to have been with no great propriety settled in Paradise."

It is while commenting on the charm of the view from Ryde,—"I confess myself so entirely fond of a sea prospect, that I think nothing on the land can equal it,"—that Fielding incidentally utters that extraordinary reference to Sir Robert Walpole as "one of the best of men and of ministers." The only explanation of these words at all consonant with what we know of Fielding's life seems to be that here he adopts once more his familiar use of irony.

The cheerfulness of spirit with which the invalid encountered every fresh distress, and 'exulted' in every pleasant sight and trifling pleasure, during those days at Ryde, is very fully reflected in the following letter, happily preserved from the untoward fate which has apparently befallen every other intimate word from his pen. It was written to his brother John, on the first day of anchorage off Ryde.

"On board the Queen of Portugal, Richd. Veal at anchor on the Mother Bank, off Ryde, to the care of the Post Master of Portsmouth—this is my Date and y'r Direction.
"July 12 1754

"Dear Jack, After receiving that agreeable Lre from Mess'rs. Fielding & Co., we weighed on monday morning and sailed from Deal to the Westward Four Days long but inconceivably pleasant passage brought us yesterday to an Anchor on the Mother Bank, on the Back of the Isle of Wight, where we had last Night in Safety the Pleasure of hearing the Winds roar over our Heads in as violent a Tempest as I have known, and where my only Consideration were the Fears which must possess any Friend of ours (if there is happily any such), who really makes our Well being the Object of his Concern especially if such Friend should be totally inexperienced in Sea Affairs. I therefore beg that on the Day you receive this Mrs Daniel may know that we are just risen from Breakfast in Health and Spirits this twelfth Instant at 9 in the morning. Our Voyage hath proved fruitful in Adventures all which being to be written in the Book you must postpone yr. Curiosity. As the Incidents which fall under yr Cognizance will possibly be consigned to Oblivion, do give them to us as they pass. Tell yr Neighbour I am much obliged to him for recommending me to the care of a most able and experienced Seaman to whom other Captains seem to pay such Deference that they attend and watch his Motions, and think themselves only safe when they act under his Direction and Example. Our Ship in Truth seems to give Laws on the Water with as much Authority and Superiority as you Dispense Laws to the Public and Examples to yr Brethren in Commission, Please to direct yr Answer to me on Board as in the Date, if gone to be returned, and then send it by the Post and Pacquet to Lisbon to
"Y'r affec't. Brother
"H. Fielding [10]
    "To John Fielding Esq. at his House in Bow Street Cov. Garden London."

It is probable, as Mr Austin Dobson has pointed out, that the Mrs Daniel, whose anxieties Fielding here shows himself anxious to relieve, was his second wife's mother. And by this time his brother was doubtless occupying that house in Bow Street so frequently advertised to the public, when any work was on foot for their protection, as the residence of 'Henry Fielding, Esqre.'
    The almost diabolic figure of the Ryde landlady had scarcely left his pages, when Fielding found a new subject for his portraiture, in the pretentious ill-bred follies of a young officer, a nephew of the captain, who arrived on board to visit his uncle, and who serves as an excellent foil for the simple-hearted merits of the elder man. A rising wind, however, cut short the Lieutenant's stories, and two nights later blew a hurricane which Fielding declares, "would have given no small alarm to a man, who had either not learnt what it is to die, or known what it is to be miserable"; continuing, in words that need no comment, "my dear wife and child must pardon me, if what I did not conceive to be any great evil to

myself, I was not much terrified with the thoughts of happening to them: in truth, I have often thought they are both too good, and too gentle, to be trusted to the power of any man." The sea he loved so well was not to be Fielding's grave. Early the next morning the *Queen of Portugal* was at anchor in Torbay; and the whole party sat down "to a very chearful breakfast."

For a whole week the travellers were kept wind-bound off the Devon coast, now at anchor, now making vain efforts to proceed. We hear of the 'fine clouted cream,' and the delicious cyder of the county (two hogsheads of which latter Fielding purchased as presents for his friends); of the excellence of the local fish named 'john dóree,' of the scandalous need of legislation for the protection of sea-men when ashore from land-sharks, a digression which includes a pleasant interpretation of the myth of Ulysses and Circe as none other than the dilemma of a Homeric merchant skipper whose crew Circe "some good ale-wife," had made drunk "with the spirituous liquors of those days"; of the difficulty with which Fielding could persuade his wife "whom it was no easy matter for me to force from my side" to take a walk on shore; and of the captain's grievous lamentations, which "seemed to have some mixture of the Irish howl in them," [11] when his cat was accidentally suffocated. Also, to these last wind-bound days belongs that famous incident which does perhaps no less honour to the hot tempered tyrannical old skipper than to his illustrious passenger.

Fielding, having just finished dinner, was enjoying some good claret in the cabin, with his wife and her friend—a cheerful moment, when conversation 'is most agreeable,' when Tom, the captain's general factotum, burst in on them and began, without saying a 'by your leave', to bottle half a hogshead of small beer. After requests and protests, equally unavailing, this functionary found himself, says Fielding, threatened "with having one bottle to pack more than his number, which then happened to stand empty within my reach." Thereupon Tom reported his version of the matter to the captain, who came thundering down to the cabin in a rage that knew no bounds of language or civility. This behaviour from a man who had received not only liberal payment from his passenger for accommodation, but also such frequent stores of fresh provisions that Fielding's private purse had indeed gone some way in maintaining the ship's crew, that passenger justly resented, and to a hasty resolve of quitting the ship by a hoy that should carry him to Dartmouth, he added threats of legal action. The 'most distant sound of law,' however, he tells us, "frightened a man, who had often, I am convinced, heard numbers of cannon roar round him with intrepidity. Nor did he sooner see the hoy approaching the vessel, than he ran down again into the cabin, and his rage being perfectly subsided, he tumbled on his knees, and a little too abjectly implored for mercy. I did not suffer a brave man and an old man, to remain a moment in this posture; but I immediately forgave him." It is this incident that Thackeray chooses to complete his picture of the great novelist; adding that memorable comparison between the "noble spirit and unconquerable generosity" of Fielding, and the lives of many unknown heroes of the sea: "Such a brave and gentle heart, such an intrepid and courageous spirit I love to recognise in the manly the English Harry Fielding."

Within a week of this reconciliation the ship had made such progress southward that the captain 'in the redundancy of his good humour, declared he would go to church at Lisbon on Sunday next' (not the least pleasant of the pictures which Fielding gives us of the privateer is that of his summoning all hands on deck on a Sunday morning and then reading prayers 'with an audible voice'); but again the wind played him false, becalming him near Cape Finisterre. This last calm, however, brought with it sufficient compensation: "tho' our voyage was retarded, we were entertained with a scene which as no one can behold without going to sea, so no one can form an idea of anything equal to it on shore. We were seated on the deck, women and all, in the serenest evening that can be imagined. Not a single cloud presented itself to our view, and the sun himself was the only object which engrossed our whole attention. He did indeed set with a majesty which is incapable of description, with which, while the horizon was yet blazing with glory, our eyes were called off to the opposite part to survey the moon, which was then at full, and which in rising presented us with the second object that this world hath offered to our vision. Compared to these the pageantry of theatres, or splendor of courts, are sights almost below the regard of children."

Four days later, at midnight, the anchor was cast off Lisbon, after a calm and moonlit passage up the Tagus, a passage, Fielding writes, "incredibly pleasant to the women, who remained three hours enjoying it, while I was left to the cooler transports of enjoying their pleasures at second-hand; and yet, cooler as they may be, whoever is totally ignorant of such sensation, is, at the same time, void of all ideas of friendship."

On the day following, the 24th of June, he landed, and that evening enjoyed the long unknown luxury of a good supper, in a kind of coffee-house "very pleasantly situated on the brow of a hill, about a mile from the city, [which] hath a very fine prospect of the River Tajo from Lisbon to the sea." With that pleasant prospect the Voyage closes. Begun as it was to while away the enforced solitude of his cabin, a condition, which no man, he tells us, disliked more than himself and which mortal sickness rendered especially irksome, these pages, some of which "were possibly the production of the most disagreeable hours which ever haunted the author," reveal Fielding to us if not as Mr Lowell has said "with artless inadvertence" at least with perfect fullness. The undimmed gaiety of spirit, the tender affection, the constant desire to remove those evils which he found oppressing his country-men by sea not less than on land, the 'enthusiasm for righteousnes,' the humour of the first of English novelists, burn here as brightly as though the writer were but midway in his life's voyage. The hand that exposed evil in its native loathsomeness in a Blifil and a Wild has not lost its cunning in depicting Mrs Humphreys; the eye that delighted in the green fields of England saw in the southern sunset that which made human creations 'almost below the regard of children.' And to the last the patriotic energies of the author of *Pasquin* and of the *Champion*, of the whole hearted social reformer, of the tireless magistrate, knew no relaxation. Page after page of the *Voyage* justify the passage in which he tells us how "I would indeed have this work, which, if I live to finish it (a matter of no great certainty, if indeed of any great hope to me), will be probably the last I shall ever undertake, to produce some better end than the mere diversion of the reader"; and manifest his desire, here explicitly stated, to finish life "as I have probably lost it, in the service of my country."

We have no knowledge concerning the four months following the last entry in the pages of the *Voyage to Lisbon*. On October 8, 1754, the end so calmly expected came; and in the beautiful English cemetery, facing the great Basilica of the Heart of Jesus, was laid to rest all that an alien soil could claim of 'our immortal Fielding.'

[1] The *Public Advertiser*, 1754, February 26.

[2] The *Public Advertiser* 1754, April 17.

[3] Middlesex Records. *Sessions Book*. 1754.

[4] See the Middlesex Records.

[5] See the *Public Advertiser*. February, 1754.

[6] This little house was apparently replaced by a larger house; and it is probably this second building of which a sketch is inserted in a copy of Lysons' *Environs* to be seen in the Guildhall Library. It is now pulled down.

[7] Dr Johnson spoke of Saunders Welch as "one of my best and dearest friends."

[8] Austin Dobson. *Fielding*, p. 170.

[9] "Dedication" of the *Voyage*, written possibly by John Fielding.

[10] Austin Dobson. *Fielding*, p. 179. From the autograph in the possession of Mr Frederick Locker.

[11] This and the following passage occur in the second version of the *Voyage to Lisbon*.

APPENDIX A

The Hapsburg genealogy

It appears that the Hapsburg descent, formerly claimed by the Denbigh family, must now be abandoned. The arguments against this descent, published by Mr Horace Round, have been accepted by Burke. Further, Dr G. F. Warner permits me to publish his statement that "I have myself seen the documents upon which it [the claim] rests, and found them to be unmistakeable forgeries."

As regards Henry Fielding's family it is interesting to find that his grandfather the Rev. and Hon. John Fielding was not only Canon of Salisbury, and a Doctor of Divinity, but also Archdeacon of Dorsetshire. Canon John Fielding was buried at Salisbury. His son George (Henry Fielding's uncle) was Lt. Colonel of the "Royal Regiment of the Blues," and Groom of the Bedchamber to Queen Anne and to George II. He is buried in St George's Chapel, Windsor. (J. Nichols. *History and Antiquities of Leicestershire*. 1810. Vol. iv. pt. i. p. 394.)

APPENDIX B

Receipt and Assignment of "Tom Jones"

The following documents are in the possession of Alfred Huth Esq., and are now first published

June 11 1748.

Rec'd. of Mr. Andrew Millar Six hundred Pounds being in full for the sole Copy Right of a Book called the History of a Foundling in Eighteen Books. And in Consideration of the said Six Hundred Pounds I promise to asign over the said Book to the said Andrew Millar his Executors and assigns for ever when I shall be thereto demanded.

£ s d

£600, 00, 00. Hen. Ffielding

The said Work to contain Six Volumes in Duodecimo.

Know all Men by these Presents that I Henry Fielding of St. Paul's Covent Garden in the County of Middlesex Esq'r. for & in consideration of the Sum of Six hundred Pounds of lawful Money of Great Britain to me in hand paid by Andrew Millar of St. Mary le Strand in the County afores'd. Bookseller the Receipt whereof is hereby acknowledged and of which I do Acquit the s'd. Andrew Millar his Executors & Assigns, have bargained sold delivered assigned & set over all that my Title Right and Property in & to a certain Book printed in Six Volumes, known & called by the Name & Title of The History of Tom Jones, a Foundling, inv'd. written by me the s'd. Henry Fielding, with all Improvements, Additions or Alterations whatsoever which now are or hereafter shall at any time be made by me the s'd. Henry Fielding, or any one else by my authority to the s'd. Book To Have and to Hold the s'd. bargained Premises unto the s'd. Andrew Millar, his Ex'ors Adm'ors or Assigns for ever And I do hereby covenant to & with the s'd. Andrew Millar his Ex'ors Adm'ors & Assigns that I the s'd. Henry Fielding the Author of the s'd. bargained Premises have not at any time heretofore done committed or suffered any Act or thing whatsoever by means whereof the s'd bargained Premises or any part thereof is or shall be impeached or encumbered in any wise And I the s'd Henry Fielding for myself my Ex'ors Adm'ors & Assigns shall warrant & defend the s'd bargained Premises for ever against all Persons whatsoever claiming under me my Ex'ors Adm'ors or Assigns.

In Witness whereof I have hereunto set my hand & seal this twenty fifth day of March One thousand seven hundred & forty nine.

H F fielding [Illustration: Seal.]

Signed sealed & delivered
by the within named Henry
Fielding the day and year within
mentioned, in the presence of
Jos. Brogden

APPENDIX C

"Pasquin turned Drawcansir"

The *General Advertiser* for March 13, 1752, Page 3, advertises, as for Macklin's Benefit, at the Theatre Royal, Covent Garden,
"A New Dramatic Satire of Two Acts, call'd
Covent Garden Theatre; or Pasquin turned Drawcansir
Censor of Great Britain

Written on the Model of the Comedies of Aristophanes and the Pasquinades of the Italian Theatre in Paris; With Chorusses of the People after the manner of the Greek Drama. The Parts of the Pit, and Boxes, the Stage, and the Town to be performed by themselves for their Diversion; the Part of several dull disorderly Characters in and about St. James, to be performed by certain Persons for Example; and the Part of Pasquin-Drawcansir to be performed by his Censorial Highness, for his Interest.

The Satire to be introduced by an Oration, and to conclude by a Peroration: Both to be spoken from the Rostrum, in the Manner of certain Orators by Signer Pasquin."

This advertisement is also in the *Covent Garden Journal*, with the addition of "galleries" after the word *Boxes*. According to Dibdin, *History of the Stage*, Vol. V. (preface dated 1800) p. 156, this satire was *by* Macklin.

APPENDIX D

The Walpole 'anecdote'

The following reference to Fielding occurs in a letter by Horace Walpole, to George Montagu, dated May 18, 1749. It may be prefaced by the statement that Fielding's strenuous opposition to Sir Robert Walpole was not likely to be overlooked by Sir Robert's son; and by Mr Austin Dobson's comment "his [Horace Walpole's] absolute injustice, when his partisan spirit was uppermost, is everywhere patent to readers of his Letters ... the story no doubt exaggerated when it reached him, loses nothing under his transforming and malicious pen." Walpole writes: "He [Rigby] and Peter Bathurst t'other night carried a servant of the latter's, who had attempted to shoot him, before Fielding; who, to all his other vocations, has, by the grace of Mr Lyttelton, added that of Middlesex justice. He sent them word he was at supper, that they must come next morning. They did not understand that freedom, and ran up, where they found him banqueting with a blind man, a whore, and three Irishmen, on some cold mutton and a bone of ham, both in one dish, and the dirtiest cloth. He never stirred nor asked them to sit. Rigby, who had seen him so often come to beg a guinea of Sir C. Williams, and Bathurst, at whose father's he had lived for victuals, understood that dignity as little, and pulled themselves chairs; on which he civilised."

The 'blind man' was doubtless the half brother later to be knighted for his distinguished public services, Sir John Fielding; and, adds Mr Austin Dobson, "it is extremely unlikely the lady so discourteously characterised could have been any other than his wife, who Lady Stuart tells us 'had few personal charms.' There remain the 'three Irishmen' who may, or may not, have been perfectly presentable members of society. At all events, their mere nationality, so rapidly decided upon, cannot be regarded as a stigma." Bearing in mind, on the one hand, our knowledge of Fielding as he reveals himself in his own pages, and in his friendships, and on the other the character earned by Horace Walpole's pen, it seems matter for doubt whether this 'anecdote' deserves even a place in an appendix.

APPENDIX E

Fielding's Will

Fielding's will was discovered in the Prerogative Court of Canterbury, by Mr G. A. Aitken. It is undated:—

IN THE NAME OF GOD AMEN—I HENRY FIELDING of the parish of Ealing in the County of Middlesex do hereby give and bequeath unto Ralph Allen of Prior Park in the County of Somerset Esqr and to his heirs executors administrators and assigns for ever to the use of the said Ralph his heirs &c all my Estate real and personal wheresoever and whatsoever and do appoint him sole EXECUTOR of this my last Will—Beseeching him that the whole (except my shares in the Register Office) may be sold and forthwith converted into Money and Annuities purchased thereout for the lives of my dear Wife Mary and my daughters Harriet and Sophia and what proportions my said Executor shall please to reserve to my sons William and Allen shall be paid them severally as they shall attain the age of twenty and three And as for my Shares in the Register or Universal Register Office I give ten thereof to my aforesaid Wife seven to my Daughter Harriet and three to my daughter Sophia my Wife to be put in immediate possession of her shares and my Daughters of theirs as they shall severally arrive at the Age of 21 the immediate Profits to be then likewise paid to my two Daughters by my Executor who is desired to retain the same in his Hands until that time—Witness my Hand—HENRY FIELDING—Signed and acknowledged as his last Will and Testament by the within named Testator in the presence of—MARGARET COLLIER—RICHD BOOR—ISABELLA ASH—

Proved 14th November 1754.

Extracted from the Principal Registry of the Probate Divorce and Admiralty Division of the High Court of Justice

In the Prerogative Court of Canterbury

November 1754

HENRY FIELDING Esquire—On the fourteenth day Administration (with the Will annexed) of the Goods Chattels and Credits of Henry Fielding late of Ealing in the County of Middlesex but at Lisbon in the Kingdom of Portugal Esquire deceased was granted to John Fielding Esquire the Uncle and Curator or Guardian lawfully assigned to Harriet Fielding Spinster a Minor and Sophia Fielding an Infant the natural and lawfull Daughters of the said Deceased and two of the Residuary Legatees named in the said Will for the use and benefit of the said Minor and Infant and until one of them shall attain the age of twenty one years for that Ralph Allen Esquire the sole Executor and Residuary Legatee in Trust named in the said Will hath renounced as well the Execution thereof as Letters of Administration (with the said Will annexed) of the Goods Chattels and Credits of the said deceased and Mary Fielding Widow the Relict of the said deceased and the other Residuary Legatee named in the said Will hath also renounced Letters of Administration (with the said Will annexed) of the Goods Chattels and Credits of the said deceased—the said John Fielding having been first sworn duly to administer.

In addition to the property mentioned here, Fielding possessed a library, as Mr Austin Dobson discovered, [1] which when sold six months after his death, "for the Benefit of his Wife and Family," realised £364, 7s. 1d. or "about £100 more than the public gave in 1785 for the books of Johnson." [2] Also according to the *Recollections of the Late John Adolphus*, by Henderson, Fielding purchased a 90 years' lease of a house near Canterbury, for one of his daughters.

Of the children mentioned in this will, William became, a contemporary writer tells us, "an eminent barrister at law and inherits the integrity of his father and a large share of his brilliant talents." [3] Mr Austin Dobson refers to William Fielding as being like his father "a strenuous advocate of the poor and unfortunate," and adds that the obituary notice in the *Gentleman's Magazine* records his worth and piety. [4] Harriet Fielding is said to have been of "a sweet temper and great understanding." [5] Allen Fielding became Vicar of S6. Stephens Canterbury, and was "greatly beloved by all, especially the little children," writes a descendant. Allen Fielding's four sons all took Orders, and of the second, Charles, it was written on his death, that "he had not only a heart that could feel for others, but a heart that lived in giving." [6] The noble qualities of Henry Fielding found their echo in his descendants.

[1] Austin Dobson. *Fielding*. Appendix IV. p. 212-13; *and Eighteenth Century Vignettes*, 1896, pp. 164-178.

[2] Austin Dobson. *Fielding*. Appendix IV. p. 212-13; *and Eighteenth Century Vignettes*, 1896, pp. 164-178.

[3] J. Nichols. *History and Antiquities of Leicestershire*. 1810. Vol. iv. Pt. I. p. 594.

[4] Austin Dobson. *Fielding*, p. 192.

[5] T. Whitehead. *Original Anecdotes of the late Duke of Kingston*, 1795. p. 95.

[6] *Some Hapsburghs, Fieldings, Denbighs and Desmonds*, by J. E. M. F.

APPENDIX F

Fielding's Tomb and Epitaph

Fielding's present tomb, in the beautiful English cemetery at Lisbon, was erected in 1830. On one side is inscribed:

LUGET BRITANNIA GREMIO NON DARI
FOVERE NATUM

On the other side are the following lines:

Henrici Fielding
A Somersetensibus apud Glastoniam oriundi
Viri summo ingenio
en quae restant:
Stylo quo non alius unquam
Intima qui potuit cordis reserare mores hominum excolendos
suscepit
Virtuti decorum, vitio foeditatem asseruit, suum cuique tribuens;
Non quin ipse subinde irritaretur evitandis
Ardensin amicitia, in miseria sublevanda effusus
Hilaris urbanus et conjux et pater adamantus.
Aliis non sibi vixit
Vixit sed mortem victricem vincit dum natura durat dum saecula
currunt
Naturae prolem scriptis prae se ferens
Suam et sua genlis extendet famam. [1]

[1] *Somerset and Dorset Notes and Queries.* Vol. viii. p. 353.

APPENDIX G

Fielding's posthumous play "The Fathers"

Fielding's play *The Fathers* or *The Good-natured Man* seems to have been lost (apparently after being submitted to Sir Charles Hanbury Williams) till twenty years after Fielding's death. It was discovered by M'r Johnes, M.P. for Cardigan, in 1775, or 1776, who sent it to Garrick. Garrick recognised it as "Harry Fielding's Comedy"; and, after revision, it was produced at Drury Lane on November 30, 1778. Garrick not only appeared in the cast, but also wrote both prologue and epilogue. A note, in the Morrison Manuscripts, from Garrick to D'r John Hoadley, dated January 3, 1776, concludes thus "We have found the lost sheep, Henry Fielding's Good Natured Man which was mislaid near twenty years." [1] In the following pleasant letter Sir John Fielding commends Mrs Fielding's Benefit night to Dr Hunter.

"Sir John Fielding presents his compliments to Dr. Hunter, and acquaints him that the Comedy of 'The Good-natured Man' written by the late Mr. Henry Fielding will be performed at Drury Lane next Monday being the Author's Widow's night.

"He was your old and sincere friend. There are no other of his Works left unpublished. This is the last opportunity you will have of shewing any respect to his Memory as a Genius, so that I hope you will send all your Pupils, all your Patients, all your Friends, & everybody else to the Play that Night, by which Means you will indulge your benevolent feelings and your Sentiments of Friendship. [2]

"Bow Street, Dec'r 4, 1778."

[1] Morrison Manuscripts. Catalogue.

[2] *The Athenaeum.* February 1. 1890.

APPENDIX H

Undated Accounts of Fielding at Salisbury and at Barnes

Research has so far failed to identify the period of Fielding's traditional residence in Salisbury. According to the following passage in *Old and New Sarum or Salisbury*, by R. Benson and H. Hatcher, 1843, he occupied three houses in or near Salisbury. "It is well known that Fielding the Novelist married a lady of Salisbury named Craddock [sic] and was for a time resident in our City. From tradition we learn that he first occupied the house in the Close at the south side of St Anne's Gate. He afterwards removed to that in St Anne's Street next to the Friary; and finally established himself in the Mansion at the foot of Milford Hill, where he wrote a considerable portion of his *Tom Jones*." [1]

Fielding's residence in Barnes is no less illusive. The following passage occurs in the edition of 1795 of *Lyson's Environs of London*: "Henry Fielding, the celebrated Novelist, resided at Barnes, in the house which is now the property of Mr Partington." [2] In the edition of 1811 the house is described as "now the property of Mrs Stanton, widow of the late Admiral Stanton." [3] In Manning and Bray's *Surrey* the name of the house is given: "On Barnes Green is a very old house called Milbourne House.... It was once the residence of Henry Fielding the celebrated novel writer. The widow of Admiral Stanton is the present owner of this house." [4] The Barnes Rate-books appear to throw no light on the date of Fielding's residence at Milbourne House. It is noteworthy that both the Barnes and Salisbury statements indicate a man of some means, living as befitted a Fielding.

[1] *History of Wiltshire*. Sir R. C. Hoare; volume entitled "Old and New Sarum or Salisbury," by R. Benson and H. Hatcher, 1843. p 602.

[2] Lysons. *Environs of London*, edition of 1795. Vol. i. part iii. p. 544.

[3] *Ibid*. Edition 1811. Vol. i. p. 10.

[4] Manning and Bray. *History of Surrey*, 1814, vol. iii. p. 316.

APPENDIX I

An undated letter of Fieldings to Lady Mary Wortley Montagu

The following undated letter is printed in *The Letters and Works of Lady Mary Wortley Montagu* edited by Lord Wharncliffe and W. M. Thomas. Lord Wharncliffe includes it with the letters from originals among the Wortley papers. [1]

Wednesday evening

Madam,—I have presumed to send your ladyship a copy of the play which you did me the honour of reading three acts of last spring, and hope it may meet as light a censure from your ladyship's judgment as then; for while your goodness permits me (what I esteem the greatest, and indeed only happiness of my life) to offer my unworthy performances to your perusal, it will be entirely from your sentence that they will be regarded, or disesteemed by me. I shall do myself the honour of calling at your ladyship's door to-morrow at eleven, which, if it be an improper hour, I beg to know from your servant what other time will be more convenient. I am with the greatest respect and gratitude, madam,

Your ladyship's most obedient, most devoted humble servant.

[1] Letters and Works of Lady Mary Wortley Montagu, edited by Lord Wharncliffe and W. M. Thomas. Vol. ii. p. 3, note I, and p. 22.

APPENDIX J

FIELDING'S *Tom Thumb*

This play appears to have carried some political significance in Fielding's day; if it was not, indeed, written with a political intention. This may be gathered from an article in the *Daily Post* of March 29, 1742, apropos of a performance of the *Tragedy of Tragedies*, that night, at Drury Lane. The article attributes, in detail, political intentions to the *Tragedy*—"a Piece at first calculated to ridicule some particular Persons and Affairs in Europe (at the Time it was writ) but more especially in this Island."

Printed in the United Kingdom
by Lightning Source UK Ltd.
127220UK00001B/357/A